Economic Survival Strategies of Turkish Migrants in London

Economic Survival Strategies of Turkish Migrants in London

Olgu KARAN

TRANSNATIONAL PRESS LONDON
2017

Economic Survival Strategies of Turkish Migrants in London

By Olgu KARAN

First Published in 2017 by TRANSNATIONAL PRESS LONDON in the United Kingdom, 12 Ridgeway Gardens, London, N6 5XR, UK.
www.tplondon.com

Transnational Press London® and the logo and its affiliated brands are registered trademarks.

Paperback [US Edition]

ISBN: 978-1-910781-48-7

Cover Design: Gizem Çakır

www.tplondon.com

Contents

Acknowledgements

Book writing is a journey; a very special type of journey because when you start, you do not know when journey will be over. This book is a result of not only my own efforts but also the support provided by various people involved in the process. I would like to thank first Leroi Henry and Allan Williams for guidance in writing this book. Their support, encouragement and motivation throughout this challenging period have been enormous.

I would also like to acknowledge Hülya and Cevat Taşıran for their support along this long journey.

Although I cannot disclose their names, particular thanks goes to the hard working Kurdish and Turkish migrants in North London. Without their contribution, this book could not have been written.

It is impossible to list all the friends who provided support in writing this book. However, I extend my special thanks to Kübra Ceviz, Erhan Kurtarır, and Gözde İnal.

Last but not least, my warmest thanks go to my parents, Sengül and Kaya Karan. They have encouraged me emotionally, and financially supported me through all stages of this long journey.

This is book is based on my doctoral research carried out at London Metropolitan University between 2009 and 2015.

About the Author

Dr Olgu Karan is Assistant Professor in Sociology at Başkent University, Ankara, Turkey. He obtained his PhD at London Metropolitan University's Working Lives Research Institute where he conducted the research titled "Collective Resource Mobilisation for Economic Survival within the Turkish Speaking Communities in London" supervised by Dr Leroi Henry and Professor Allan Williams. Dr Karan received his BA degree in Political Science from Bilkent University and MA degree in Political Sociology from the Dalarna University in Falun. His research interests include social exclusion, social movements, and development.

Foreword

Steve Jefferys[1]

Olgu Karan's research offers original insights for anyone interested in how and why particular parts of London are now strongly identified with migrants from particular regions of the world.

North London's Green Lanes, a street stretching from Hackney to Haringey, or in local vernacular, from Stoke Newington to Wood Green, has undergone huge transformations over the past 50 years.

Turkish Cypriot migrants first came in significant numbers to North London after the 1974 war that displaced hundreds of thousands of both Greek and Turkish Cypriots. They and later Turkish-speaking migrants mainly got jobs in London's textile manufacturing industry. Those industries largely disappeared in the 1990s.

In the 2010s Green Lanes now has several hundred Kurdish and Turkish restaurants and shops. These employ thousands of first, second and third generation Turkey-originating self-employed or family helpers.

Karan's research explains how this massive shift from employed status to self-employed took place. He records the economic devastation brought about by the rapid collapse of the textile industry, arguing this created the struggle for survival that forced thousands into self-employment.

Insightfully, Karan also explores the economic basis of this shift. As textile workers, few Turkey-originating migrants had been able to save all the capital they needed to set-up take-away cafes, restaurants or off-licences and general food stores.

The book traces the creation of ethnic partnerships and a willingness to provide loans to Imece/Zibare. These are the Turkish and Kurdish names given to village-scale collaborations for harvesting, constructing a water pipeline, providing security for village's grazing borders with neighbouring villages.

This tradition of collective action within Turkish and Kurdish villages became a key element in the cooperation that led to the pooling of savings, effort and knowledge. From the late 1990s partnerships were set up, usually between four and five people pooling their savings and sharing the risks. Among the

---

[1] Steve Jefferys is Emeritus Professor, European Employment Relations, London Metropolitan University, United Kingdom.

majority of Turkish and Kurdish migrants who came from rural areas, this enabled the rapid spread of a business dynamic where none had existed before.

Initially businesses were set up in London, and then, as new migration took place, outside London too. In the 2010s it is now rare to find a town or sizeable village without a kebab shop. Jobs became available for tens of thousands of Kurdish and Turkish migrants who spoke little or no English.

Karan shows how this collectively created social capital gradually acquired cultural capital, as the migrants' children became familiar with the English language, and as the experience of running businesses in London was shared among the migrants. Alongside these processes, he sees the emergence of a new form of ethnic identification to 'our people' – the *Türkiyeli* – based on the sharing of common experiences. And this identification, he finds, is shared by both Kurdish and Turkish communities as well as by those with religious and non-religious beliefs.

The book provides detailed insights into these migrant experiences, while also considering the theoretical explanations. It is a really welcome contribution for everyone concerned with the problems and challenges of integration and of identify today.

Chapter One
Introduction

This study seeks to explore the neglected area of research on the small business start-up and maintenance activities of Kurds and Turks in North London. In so doing, I focus on: firstly, the reasons for setting up catering and retail businesses; secondly, on the processes involved in the setting up and operating of the businesses; and finally the opportunity structure that facilitates or constrains the setting-up and maintenance of businesses.

There is very little, if any, research that has addressed the question of why and how individuals in the UK have become self-employed (Dawson et al., 2009, p.2). Particularly, scholarly studies have paid little attention to the growth of KT ethnic economy, comprising one of the highest proportions of self-employment (Dedeoğlu, 2014, pp.52-53). There have been publications on the business start-up experiences of Turkish Cypriots in the British context (e.g. Basu and Altınay, 2001 and 2002; Gabriel, 1988; Ladbury, 1984) but, these studies have failed to examine Turkish and Kurdish communities. However, there are some notable reports, for example (e.g. Dedeoğlu, 2014; Enneli et al., 2005; Erdemir and Vasta, 2007; and Strüder, 2003). This prompted the focus of this study to include both the start-up and maintenance activities of Turkish and Kurdish business owners. The current research seeks to understand the complexity, and deepen our understanding of the start-up and maintenance processes of Turkish and Kurdish owned businesses.

The study aims to make two significant research contributions. The first is to focus on the under-researched area of Turkish and Kurdish entrepreneurship, adding to the emerging literature on the relatively more recent migrant groups in the UK. To a certain extent this is because mainland Turks and Kurds are recent migrants to the UK. However, these two communities are considered to be relatively invisible in studies of ethnic diversity (GLA, 2009).

Another significance of this book is that it proposes a fresh theoretical approach to the study of ethnic entrepreneurship, namely, collective resource mobilisation influenced by Tilly's (1977) seminal work entitled "From Mobilisation to Revolution" concerning collective action. I identify eleven main problems (see the section on collective resource mobilisation) in relation to founding and operating ethnic businesses and provide a systematic analysis of each of these by utilising collective resource mobilisation theory.

The various theories utilised in previous studies on ethnic entrepreneurship take either an agency centred approach (e.g. Altinay, 2008; Altinay & Altinay,

2006; Basu & Altinay, 2002; Basu, 1998; McEvoy & Hafeez, 2009; Srinivasan, 1995; Werbner, 1984, 1990), or a structure centred approach (Bonacich, 1973). While interaction (Waldinger et al., 1990) and mixed embeddedness (Kloosterman et al. 1999, 2001) theories attempt to bring agency and structure together, these theories pay insufficient attention to the macro structural factors, such as globalisation which affect opportunities for migrant employability (Collins, 2000). Thus, interaction and the mixed embeddedness approach are unable to grasp the processes of socio-economic restructuring which have their origins in global economic shifts. The possibility of entrepreneurial praxis is thus clearly and historically conditioned. Consequently, I propose a more composite new theoretical approach which could not only produce agency and structural approaches, but also links globalisation to ethnic entrepreneurship.

The basic premise of Tilly`s book is to develop an understanding of collective action which aims to create various forms of social change. Tilly (1978) defined collective action as a rational, deliberate and organised action, which animates from the "application of pooled resources on behalf of the population as a whole" (p.212). The actual use of resources generated by networks is collective action. It entails all the ways in which people combine their efforts in the pursuit of common ends (ibid). In this study, I propose that the application of collective action to the study of ethnic entrepreneurship enables us to analyse the reasons for and the ways in which resources are mobilised as a rational collective act.

Charles Tilly's theory of collective action is basically examined in order to understand Kurdish and Turkish small business ownership that accommodates social change. An example of this is segments of the Kurdish and Turkish (KT) communities in London acting collectively to change their economic position within society. The central argument of the book is that they collectively act to set-up and maintain businesses as an economic interest group.

Various shared interests, particularly economic ones have activated networks of solidarity and instrumental ethnic ties. Economic interests and networks of solidarity mutually enforce each other. Ethnic ties are instrumental in fostering ethnic businesses. Thus, emerging interests in the host society may foster the development of instrumental ethnic attachments which do not exist in the home country. Ethnic, religious and political attachments, which may manifest themselves in hostile attitudes towards each other in the home country, could lead to cooperation with each other in the host country. In their new context, hostility between groups in the home country becomes a relatively minor issue. New forms of ethnic attachments are formed in association with the development of the survival strategies of ethnic groups. These new forms of identities could be viewed as instrumental in that they could be utilised for ethnic business development.

In addition, the power of the theory of collective action lies in its focus on the reasons for network mobilisation. It could explain why in certain parts of the world; networks are mobilised for ethnic entrepreneurship. Unlike most of the existing theories and analytical models in this field (see chapter 2), the theory of collective action has greater potential for explaining the reasons for and the emergence of interests towards business ownership.

In accordance with his definition of collective action, Tilly (1973, p.212) asks one of "sociology's grandest and oldest questions: Among all kinds of social groups, what determines the degree of collective action in any particular period and place?" According to Tilly, the level of the collective action in any context is determined by four components: interests, organisation in terms of formal and informal networks, mobilisation and opportunity structure. In a similar vein, the theoretical approach influenced by Tilly's model in this study has three main components. In this study, the second and the third component of collective action, namely organisation and mobilisation are combined into the mobilisation of networks. The term mobilisation of networks implies the generation of resources needed for entrepreneurial action. Would-be business owners need information about various issues, financial capital, skills, labour force, safety in their neighbourhood, favourable small business regulations and finally internal mechanisms to sustain solidarity within the ethnic community.

Each component of collective action is understood to be a set of processes. Each component can vary and the degree of mobilisation and collective action are dependent on the processes and interactions between the three components. According to Tilly (1978), in its simplest possible form, the capacity to act collectively is likely to work as follows: In this elementary model, shared interests promote networks, the intensity of networks facilitates increased mobilisation, and collective action is a function of all three components.

Each of these components also has a counterpart process: the change in the extent and or character of shared interests; the quality and volume of networks; and finally the mobilisation or demobilisation of networks in setting-up and operating businesses.

As Dulce et al. (2009) mention, there is a lack of agreement on the determinants, implications and outcomes of ethnic entrepreneurship. However, the major significance of collective resource mobilisation theory, in the context of ethnic small businesses is that it is as illuminating about the absence of collectivism as it is on the presence thereof. The theory would argue that, in the first instance, a sense of common interests or interest alignment in setting-up businesses is required among co-ethnics. This relates to the first research question of the book, particularly, why has the practice of becoming business owners arisen within the Turkish and Kurdish communities in London? According to the collective resource mobilisation theory, this is based upon the optimistic conviction that unemployment could be prevented and their situation could be redressed by business ownership. Secondly, the mobilisation of networks to generate resources in order to set up and maintain businesses is essential for the collective resource mobilisation theory. Hence, the mobilisation of networks is a function of interest alignment. Networks should be mobilised in order to gather entrepreneurial resources to set up businesses. Finally, the opportunity structure where businesses operate is the final component of collective resource mobilisation. These three factors in the explanation of ethnic entrepreneurship should be understood as processes which are in various degrees dependent on the ethnic group in question. I should note that this research constitutes the first application of Tilly's collective resource mobilisation model in understanding ethnic entrepreneurialism.

One of the components of the theory of collective action, namely mobilisation of networks, also allows us to incorporate theories of social capital. The second research question of this book, *how Kurds and Turks acquire and utilise economic, cultural, and social capital in setting-up and operating businesses in North London* can be examined by the operationalisation of the theories on social, cultural and economic capital.

The theory of collective action has evolved since Tilly's formulation. Criticisms of the theory have contributed to its development. For instance, framing has largely replaced interests. Framing could be considered an expansion of Tilly's model, which corresponds to the micro-mobilisation of tasks and processes in formulating the "shared meanings and definitions that people bring to their situation" (McAdam et al., 2008, p.281). Without the framing process, acting collectively would be impossible as it mediates between networks mobilised for common ends and the opportunity structure. In order to act collectively, as a minimum, people have to both aggregate around certain interests in their lives and feel optimistic about the fact that acting collectively could actually redress their situation. In other words, the absence of this cognitive process which brings and binds people together around certain interests would make the mobilisation process very difficult and probably impossible. As Jenkins (2008, p.127) mentions, "collective interests are assumed to be relatively unproblematic and to exist prior to mobilisation, instead of being socially constructed and created by the mobilisation process". That is to say, social problems in fact do not exist per se, but to a certain extent, certain situations are considered as such. Their emergence requires an autonomous public sphere where certain phenomena are framed in processes with unpredictable results.

Accordingly, another significant aspect of the book is that it opposes both *primordialist* and *instrumentalist* conceptualisations of ethnic identity and culture in ethnic entrepreneurship literature and engages with the constructivist approach which brings central ideas of primordialism and instrumentalism together. In particular, primordialism is a concept that contends "identities or attachments are 'given', a priori, un-derived, prior to all experience or interaction – in fact, all interaction is carried out within the primordial realities" (Eller and Coughlan, 1996, p.45). According to instrumentalists, contextual factors, circumstances may promote ethnic and racial identities. Ethnicity is socially constructed and "individuals are capable to 'cut and mix' from a variety of ethnic heritages and cultures to forge their own individual or group identities" (Hutchinson and Smith, 1996, p.9) based on shared experiences and interests embedded in the host society. Likewise, Edna Bonacich and John Modell (1980, pp.3-4) argue that "ethnic groups often act as economic interest groups, and when they cease to do so, they tend to dissolve". Ethnic attachments are all socially created phenomena and open to dissolution. According to instrumentalists, the ethnic ties and groups are socially constructed in order to acquire individual and collective goals. Ethnic groups can redefine their attachments in terms of whom they incorporate.

This study promotes the central ideas of 'constructivism' which sytheisises some of the ideas of instrumentalism and primordialism (see chapter 5). While the constructivist approach retains the central ideas and validity of the instrumentalist approach, it acknowledges the requirement of some sort of real or imagined primordial base such as skin colour, ancestry, place of origin, cultural practices, certain behaviours (Cornell and Hartmann, 2007) for ethnic attachment. This is called constructed primordialism. For instance, as Bonacich and Modell (1980) state, several groups that migrated from Europe to the United States, for example the Italians had little or no sense of national identity until their arrival. Thus, the place of origin and common cultural practices played a role in the construction of an ethnic identity.

Ethnic identities are instrumental in protecting and attaining power. It is an adaptation of the rational choice approach acting on the individual preferences whereby ethnic identities are built for the sake of protecting individuals' interests (Eller and Coughlan, 1996).

In addition, the processes in collective action mentioned above are also linked to the instrumentalist view of ethnic identity. According to Tilly (1977), shared interests facilitate unities. Interests promote "common identity and unifying structure" (p.54). So, the change in the extent and or character of shared interests will also affect the common identity. It provides a dynamic, shifting approach to ethnic attachment. However, the existing literature on ethnic entrepreneurship ignores the dynamics in ethnic identity formation and dissolution. Rather, they consider ethnic identity as self-evident and pre-existing. For instance, according to Waldinger (1990, p.3), ethnic entrepreneurship is "based on a set of connections and regular patterns of interaction among people sharing common national background or migration experiences". The quotation ignores the fact that interaction among people does not necessarily originate from shared national background or migration experience. Rather, shared experiences in the occupational structure and shared interests within different ethnic groups whose migration experiences corresponds to different time periods could result in new alliances and/or ethnic attachments that facilitate networks utilised for entrepreneurship. Waldinger's assertion ignores the dynamics in ethnic attachment formation or dissolution. There is no pre-existing necessity for those with common national backgrounds to contact each other and to interact.

Proponents of cultural explanations have pointed out the impact of culture on entrepreneurship (Altinay, 2008; Altinay & Altinay, 2006; Basu & Altinay, 2002; Basu, 1998; McEvoy & Hafeez, 2009; Srinivasan, 1995; Werbner, 1984, 1990) in a way those proponents of the theory focus on the cultural features of a specific ethnic community to explain the success or failure in entrepreneurship. The culturalist view, similarly to primordialism, asserts that ethnic groups are separated from each other according to their mind-sets and each ethnic community has a fixed nature and code of behaviour. They further argue and assert that certain ethnic groups are culturally better endowed for entrepreneurship than others, and cultural differences lead to divergence in entrepreneurial performance. Initially, this posed the question of whether there were significant differences between Kurdish and Turkish migrants. The cultural practices are considered as fixed and unchanging, and they largely ignore the fact that they adapt to changing circumstances. Thus, another significance of the book is that the re-enactment and persistence of ethnic collective identity and practises are dependent upon structural changes characterizing British cities and the structure of the groups. The reproduction of Turkish village-scale collaboration, practices and values to deal with adverse circumstances appears in a post-industrial London after de-industrialisation. One of the most crucial traditions that has been re-enacted after immigration was *imece* in Turkish and *zibare* in Kurdish culture.

Imece/Zibare is a Turkish and Kurdish "tradition", which is village-scale collaboration based on the need for human power or economic capital. Collaboration could be for harvesting, constructing a water pipeline, providing security for village grazing borders with neighbouring villages. It denotes the collective action of the villagers (Erginkaya, 2012).

The salience of this cultural practice is re-activated for the realisation of interest in entrepreneurship and is discussed in chapter 5.

Moreover, patriarchal relationships attached to the mode of production have initially been dissolved and reproduced according to the changes in the British economy. Initially, the shift towards waged labour in factories, where all men and women had to perform the same tasks for equal wages, led to the changes in village-scale practices such as patron-client relationships and women's gendered roles performed for the reproduction of the family. It is asserted that the woman's role and position within the family is affected when they find employment as a waged labourer. This also increases their individual power and self-confidence (Karaoglan & Ökten, 2012). The closure of factories in turn has pushed Kurdish and Turkish communities to set up small shops, to a large extent based on family labour where women's labour is unpaid and consumed within the family. The low level of women entrepreneurship in retail and catering businesses could be explained by a gender division of labour. Women started to work in coffee-shops, restaurants, and off-licences mainly helping their husbands (Tasiran, 2008). Small family businesses, which require intensive working hours with low profit margins in the retail and catering sectors, to a large extent are owned and run by men in London. Women labourers in the catering and retail businesses tend to be hidden, either working in the kitchen or supporting their husbands in running his business. (Holgate et al., 2012; Inal, 2007; Phizacklea, 1988; Strüder, 2001).

The book presents a picture of Kurdish and Turkish migrants, facing similar problems, who have socially constructed an ethnic attachment, namely *Türkiyeli* (People from Turkey) in Britain. The term *Türkiyeli* has been used since the 1980s by some left-wing academics in Turkey to overcome the nationalistic discourse that identifies people of Turkey regardless of their religion and ethnic identity as Turkish. It proposes an umbrella identity that can encompass all ethnic and religious groups and move away from Turkish centred identity and nationalistic ideology. However, while the term 'Türkiyeli' does not have any uptake among both KT communities in Turkey, the majority of KT nationals whom I encountered in London preferred to use the term 'Türkiyeli' to identify their communities. As Erdemir and Vasta (2007, p.7) also observed in their fieldwork with members of KT communities, their respondents' self-identification was the Turkish neologism 'Türkiyeli'. The salience of "Türkiyeli" identification does not mean that sub-ethnic and religious affiliations such as Alevi, Sunni, Kurdish and Turkish are eroded. However, the usage of the term "Türkiyeli" by Kurdish and Turkish shop keepers alike shows that ethnic attachments are open to changes and reformulations.

The term 'Türkiyeli' defines an ethnic attachment constructed in the UK. As circumstances change, attachments change. Grievances related to survival and adaptation to the host country play an important role in the conservation, dissolution and emergence of a newly articulated ethnic attachment. For instance, tensions and conflicts even that warfare related in the home country between Kurds and Turks do not cause enmity between Kurds and Turks in London, while daily problems and practices related to their new context strengthened ties amongst Kurdish and Turkish groups.

Initially, I intended to include Turkish Cypriots in this study. But, during the preliminary fieldwork I recognized that this aim should be abandoned due to the Turkish Cypriots' longer history in the UK, so that, they have largely moved out of the sectors which are in focus for this study. I excluded Turkish Cypriots as a target group since they are not heavily concentrated in the catering and retail sectors. Today, Turkish Cypriots mostly hold professional jobs (Atay, 2010). They have tended to become "teachers, civil servants, pharmacists, doctors, dentists, accountants, lawyers, insurers and entrepreneurs" (ibid).

Nevertheless, as I mentioned above, collective resource mobilisation is illuminating in explaining the Turkish Cypriot absence in ethnic small businesses ownership. One of the components of collective resource mobilisation, the degree of interest alignment in small business ownership can be utilized to explain their absence from the specific form of ethnic small business ownership which is the focus of this book.

In sum, the advantage of collective resource mobilisation in the context of small business ownership lies in its dynamic and shifting approach enabling us, first, to discuss how changes in the global political economy affect migrant labour markets. Collective resource mobilisation theory brings in the discussion on changes in global political economy affecting immigrants' interests and employability, particularly ethnic entrepreneurship. The theory of collective resource mobilisation emphasises the importance of macro-structural factors, i.e., shifts in the global political economy influencing ethnic entrepreneurship. Without bringing in this discussion into this book, it would have been impossible to explain the first research question of the book, i.e. *why the practice of becoming business owners has arisen within the Kurdish and Turkish communities in London*

Second, in contrast to the other theories and analytical models in explaining migrant entrepreneurship discussed in chapter two, collective resource mobilisation does not consider immigrant identity and cultural practices fixed and unchanging in space and time, rather identification of shared interests and interest alignment constructed in their new context promotes the construction of new ethnic attachments, and transposition and/or dissolution of cultural practices brought from the home country, which may be helpful in the setting up and maintenance processes of their small businesses. Thus, the theory of collective resource mobilisation entails a dynamic and shifting approach in identity construction and articulation of cultural practices in setting up and maintaining ethnic small businesses. Moreover, collective resource mobilisation theory focuses on the cognitive processes for interest alignment in start-up decisions of KT communities. The literature on ethnic minority entrepreneurship (see Light, 1972; Kloosterman & Rath, 2003; Waldinger et al., 1990) assumes the tendency towards, and interest in setting up businesses to be relatively unproblematic and to have existed prior to mobilisation rather than having been socially constructed and created by the mobilisation process. Collective resource mobilisation theory argues that in order to act collectively for setting up businesses, as a minimum, people have to both aggregate around certain interests in their lives and feel optimistic about the fact that acting collectively could actually redress their situation. In other words, the absence of this cognitive process which brings and binds people together around certain interests would make the mobilisation process very difficult and probably impossible. Without taking account such dynamics, it would have been impossible to answer the second question of the book, i.e., ***how Kurds and Turks acquire and utilise economic, cultural and social capital in setting up and operating businesses in North London***.

However, one of the major difficulties of adapting the theory of collective action to the research field in ethnic entrepreneurship is in the area of social products. Collective action in social movements obviously includes a great variety of behaviour. For instance, Charles Tilly (1978) lists petitioning, starting revolutions, praying together, demonstrating, setting market prices, resisting tax collectors, and battling royal troops as social products of collective action. While it is easier and more obvious to identify collective action in social movements, identifying some of the collective action in ethnic entrepreneurship is more challenging and requires in-depth qualitative research. The social product of collective action in ethnic entrepreneurship could be broadly defined as the actual use of resources generated by networks. Specific examples include: sharing information, the generation of economic capital through networks, dispute resolution via assemblies, petitioning against big chain stores, protection of businesses and neighbourhoods from attacks and much more.

The field studies draw on 65 interviews, consisting of 25 interviews in the preliminary fieldwork and 40 interviews in the main fieldwork phases. I chose the pilot interviewees from KT entrepreneurs from various sectors such as florists, restaurant owners, music school owners, hair dressers, and cab company owners, supermarket owners, and they were all conducted in Turkish. The reason for the unusual large number of pilot interviews is explained in the methodology chapter. The main fieldwork mainly focused on catering and retailing businesses such as restaurants, off-licences, kebab-shops, coffee-shops, supermarkets, wholesalers and various community organisations. The book draws on qualitative research methods that enable the participants' business start-up and maintenance experiences to be analysed in the context of the existing literature, and allows for the generation of a new theoretical approach to emerge based on their explanations. In addition, I analysed the role of the promotion of social solidarity by various community organisations, including social, faith based, and cultural organisations in generating resources to set up and maintain businesses since from the early years of settlement by the KT communities.

Outline of the book

Chapter one, the introductory chapter, discusses the contribution of this book to existing knowledge of ethnic entrepreneurship, and sets out the rationale, aim, and research questions of the book. I demonstrate the proposed theoretical approach to the study of ethnic businesses. In light of the proposed theoretical framework, I point out the gaps in the existing literature and clarify the contribution of the book.

Chapter two outlines and analyses several theories and analytical approaches that have been utilised to understand and explain the dynamics, reasons and the way that minority entrepreneurs set up businesses. I critically engage with these theories and analytical approaches. I critique the existing literature on several grounds: first, the existing literature considers ethnic identity as self-evident, pre-given and homogenous; secondly, and connected to the first point, the existing literature assumes that the interest in setting-up a shop, and the motivation for setting-up small businesses is pre-given, and pre-existing. The existing literature demonstrates those phenomena to be frozen objects, rather than processes that are consciously formed by the efforts of ethnic communities. I set out the weaknesses as well as the strengths of the theories operationalised to explain ethnic business formation and maintenance. Thus, I discuss why there is a need for a composite theory to study ethnic businesses. Finally, I conclude with the advantages of the proposed theory of collective resource mobilisation. I argue that the theory of collective resource mobilisation provides a composite and systemic theory for analysing ethnic small businesses.

Chapter three outlines the contextual background of Kurdish, Turkish and Turkish Cypriot entrepreneurship on three levels. First, the macro scale focuses on the global political economy of migrant entrepreneurship. I set out the link between global capitalism and small ethnic business formation and maintenance in advanced capitalist economies. Second, the meso scale outlines the changes that have taken place in the British economy since the second half of the 20th century. Third, the micro scale section aims to provide a detailed account of the CTK presence in the UK by taking into account the historically specific socio-economic conditions they face after their arrival in the UK.

Chapter four provides an account of the methodological approach adapted, and explains the research process. I set the methodological approach that is operationalised in the book, the means of collecting data and the specific research method utilised in both gathering and analysing data. Finally, I discuss the limitations of the adapted methodological approach and research method.

Chapters five, six, and seven discuss the findings of the main field work based on forty interviews, supplemented by other data sources. Each empirical chapter corresponds to a component of collective resource mobilisation theory.

More particularly, chapter five discusses the interest alignment towards business ownership in KT communities. I focus on the rationale behind business start-ups and the conditions in the KT communities that paved the way for acquiring a sense of common interest directed towards small business ownership. In this chapter of the book the main aim is to try to explain why KT people moved into and are largely concentrated in the catering and retail sectors. I argue that KT communities were aligned in their interest of setting-up small businesses. The alignment was a process that entails increasing communication and intensification of networks within the community via interpersonal networks, ethnic newspapers, telephone and mail.

The second aim of the chapter is to examine the ways in which shared interests and experiences within the Turkish and Kurdish communities instrumentally paved the way for the construction of an ethnic attachment called "Türkiyeli". I argue that identities brought from the home country are not fixed, but that ethnic identities are socially constructed and open to redefinitions.

Chapter six discusses the ways in which Kurds and Turks acquire and utilise economic, cultural, and social capital in setting-up and operating businesses in North London. The chapter aims to assess the broad research question of how members of Kurdish and Turkish minorities have become entrepreneurs and maintain their businesses as a livelihood in London. The specific objective of this broad research question is to assess the role of kinship, ethnic and institutional networks in resolving various business problems in the formation and maintenance of ethnic minority businesses. I argue that the problems related to capital, information, security, labour, skills, dispute resolution and claim making are resolved by the mobilisation of various kinds of capital such as social, cultural and economic capital. The various problems in the maintenance of small businesses include, providing security for the business premises, finding trustworthy workers if they can hire any, dispute resolution with partners and other businesses, claim making to governmental bodies to sustain better business regulations, and finally acquiring the information and skills for running their small businesses.

In addition, I suggest that the re-enactment and persistence of ethnic collective identity and practises are dependent upon the relationship between structural changes characterizing British cities and ethnic groups. The reproduction of Turkish village-scale collaboration, particularly *imece* occurs in the post-industrial city of London to deal with adverse circumstances. I argue that one of the most crucial traditions that has been re-enacted after immigration was *imece*.

Chapter seven discusses the wider institutional and economic context into which KT communities are embedded. In other words, I focus on how institutional, economic setting and regulatory structures influence and interact with business owners' agency. I focus on the wider institutional and economic context into which KT communities are inevitably inserted. While the previous chapters main focus was the micro level analysis of KT communities, such as their social capital and the processes in which networks are utilized for the purpose of setting up and maintaining businesses, this section's main concern is how institutional and economic contexts, regulatory structures influence and interacts with business owners' agency. Accordingly, I have identified several issues that could enable or restrict business start-ups and their maintenance. These are the legal regulatory framework, protection from attacks and competition.

The concluding chapter discusses the major findings, limitations of the book and recommendations for further research.

Chapter Two:

Analytical Tools and Theoretical Models in Understanding Ethnic Entrepreneurship

Ethnic entrepreneurship has constituted a growing research topic in the academic agenda, especially since the urban make-up of advanced economies changed dramatically in the closing decades of the twentieth century. There is a huge existing body of research on this topic.

One example is the analytical model of 'middleman minorities' which focuses on the buffer role of ethnic business owners between producers and masses (Bonacich and Modell, 1980). They are not producers, but rather distribute goods. Another approach is 'enclave economies', which puts emphasis on a certain location where the ethnic community is considered to be self-sufficient (Wilson and Portes, 1980; Portes and Bach, 1985). The culturalist perspective supports the opinion that some ethnic groups are culturally better endowed than others for ethnic entrepreneurship (Srinivasan, 1995; Werbner, 1984, 1990). The interactive model stresses the interplay between "ethno-cultural and socio-cultural factors (agency) with politico-economic factors (structure)" (Rath, 2007, p.4). Finally, the theory of mixed embeddedness focuses on the "interplay between ethnic minority businesses and the institutional, political and socio-economic background" (Kloosterman et al., 1999, 2001).

In this book, however, I analyse minority entrepreneurship through the lens of collective resource mobilisation. Collective resource mobilisation as an action strategy to become an entrepreneur has three main components, namely, interests, mobilisation of networks and opportunity.

Ethnic communities circulate knowledge, information, ideas, and mobilise resources with the development of "space-time compressing technologies" (Harvey, 1989) more effectively than previously in order to achieve the opportunities pursued. Access of this shared information about opportunities through networks creates effects and manipulates co-ethnics about the opportunity structures available in the advanced capitalist societies. Developing and utilising the approach of collective resource mobilisation on the one hand will bring local, and global levels of analysis together, and on the other hand, it will explain why and how members of Kurdish and Turkish communities become small business owners in London.

Accordingly, I am going to inquire into the research question as to why and how ethnic communities engage in entrepreneurship as a practice or action strategy. I argue that the why and how questions of minority business formation cannot be separated from each other because of the need for interrelated levels of analysis.

Consequently, I will first characterise the related literature in relation to their weaknesses and strengths, and then will try to show that minority business entrepreneurship in advanced economies encompasses the local, national and transnational levels as articulated fields of collective resource mobilisation. The assertion of the review is that the collective resource mobilisation perspective on the transnational, national and local embedded contexts provide a more composite ground for the theorisation of minority ethnic entrepreneurship in advanced capitalist economies than other approaches such as agency centred approaches, which utilise culturalism, theories of social and cultural capital, transnationalism, sojourning and ethnic enclave economy. That is to say, the analytical tools and theories I discuss below let us grasp some facets of minority entrepreneurship. They may be useful to grasp ethnic groups' structure, the role of values and traits of an ethnic community in entrepreneurship, the characteristics of social relations utilised by minority entrepreneurship, as well as the role of the distribution of social and cultural capital to measure discrepancies in ethnic entrepreneurship. However, they do not sufficiently engage one of the research questions of this book, more specifically, why ethnic communities in one part of the world become business owners as a practice. The structural factors in which ethnic communities are embedded constitute the characteristics of ethnic group mobilisation and group solidarity. For instance, the reason why so many members of the KT communities in London mobilised entrepreneurial resources in a very short period of time to start up business in London cannot be examined by the agency theories. Agency theories do not explain the reasons for starting businesses, but those theories focusing on agency can be operationalised to analyse how ethnic community members become entrepreneurs and what role they play.

Even though, there were attempts to bring structure and agency levels of analysis together for example in interactionist theory, mixed embeddedness and the theory of middleman minorities, I argue that they fail to explain the structural factors leading towards business ownership. For instance, these theories pay insufficient attention to the macro structural factors, such as how globalization influences opportunities for migrant employability (Collins, 2000). They fail to give an account of the possibility of entrepreneurial praxis that is historically conditioned. Thus, interaction and mixed embeddedness approaches are unable to grasp the processes of socio-economic restructuring which has its origins in global economic shifts. I will discuss the global economic shift will in detail in the next chapter.

In conclusion, in this chapter I first discuss the existing theories and analytical models for understanding ethnic minority businesses. The discussion is going to concern their strengths and weaknesses. This will be followed by the reasons for proposing the theory of collective action. In so doing, I will defend the proposition that the questions, aims and objectives of this study can be examined by the utilisation of collective resource mobilisation theory.

Analytical tools

The analytical tools utilised are typological models, which are applied to evaluate the convergence or divergence of a phenomenon to the typology.

Middleman minorities

One long-standing analytical model of ethnic minority business in the United States and developing countries is the 'middleman minority' theory of Edna Bonacich (1973). According to McEvoy and Hafeez (2009), the middleman approach looks at particular ethnic communities as suppliers of services to the mass population. The concept of middleman minorities provides an analysis of ethnic business owners in terms of their occupied position between masses and elites.

According to Bonacich and Modell (1980), middleman minorities play a buffer role between the ruling classes and the mass population. The term has been derived from colonial economies where elite sections of the colonised people undertake a buffer role between the colonised and the colonisers, and the term has been applied to ethnic entrepreneurship to describe the buffer role of petite bourgeoisie (i.e. minority elites) minorities between minority customer communities and the dominant native host society. As Pyong Gap Min (2008, p.69) states, "middleman minorities concentrate in trading and usually distribute merchandise produced by members of the dominant group to minority customers". They are not primary producers, but act between elites and masses. In the classic version, they tend to be viewed as the middle class between the capitalist class and the working class. Middle minorities in urban societies distribute the products of elites in poor neighbourhoods where means of survival are scarce, police protection is scant, income levels are low and local services provided by municipal authorities are weak. Big chain stores do not prefer to invest in such areas due to the low levels of income and high rates of crime, such as arson and theft. In such circumstances, middleman minority stores become an easy target for poor people who are in need of the products they sell (Gold, 2010). According to Bonacich (1987, p.461), a middleman is "the person who fronts for the big oppressors and does their bidding". Like in colonial economies, middleman is the white man's face in an urban environment. As Min (2008, p.70) looks at Korean owned retail businesses in minority neighbourhoods of New York and Los Angeles, which depend on white suppliers, and notes numerous conflicts with both white suppliers and black customers. As Min further argues (ibid) the middleman minorities are viewed as marginal; they are regarded with "considerable hostility" by both the elite and the masses, and are described as very dependent on their sponsors (i.e. the native elites).

I should note that middleman minorities do not overlap with ethnic minorities as a whole group. In other words, the reason for individuals from ethnic minorities to be middleman minorities is to serve as agents in an intermediary role for big merchandise production companies who distribute the products across national boundaries and ethnic groups within a country.

One recent utilisation of the term middleman minorities by Terjesen & Elam (2009, p.1114) concerns "transnational entrepreneurs who can be found outside ethnic enclaves, and serve as bridges across communities of great geographic, cultural, and psychological distance".

Middleman minorities are also fluent in both minority and host country languages. According to Drori et al. (2008) "middleman minorities are those entrepreneurs who take advantage of ethnic resources such as language, networks, and skills to trade between their host and origin societies". They utilize their cultural capital to trade across ethnic boundaries.

Middleman minorities could be useful for analysing intergroup relations such as conflicts between ethnic communities (e.g. Min, 2008). It is an analytical tool for looking at the role played by ethnic business owners. But, one of the main arguments for not utilizing middleman minority theory in this book is that it cannot explain why they play the middleman role. It focuses on ethnic group characteristics (e.g. Bonacich, 1980) and their function in a society. It concentrates on the question of what ethnic minority entrepreneurs do in a capitalist society rather than focusing on the research questions of the study. More particularly, middleman minorities cannot be utilised for answering the questions firstly, why the practice of becoming business owners has arisen within the Turkish and Kurdish communities in London. Secondly, how Kurds and Turks acquire and utilise economic, cultural, and social capital in setting-up and operating businesses in North London.

Furthermore, there are significant reservations as to whether it is possible to apply the concept of middleman minorities to businesses owned by Kurds and Turks in multicultural neighbourhoods in London where their sponsors are from numerous ethnic origins. Even though it is true that members of Kurdish and Turkish communities are concentrated in particular trades such as catering and retail, they do not depend on heavily non-ethnic suppliers and they do not solely serve non-ethnic customers either. The target groups of this book are Turkish and Kurdish owned off-licences, restaurants, supermarkets, kebab shops, coffee shops and wholesalers. The suppliers of Kurdish and Turkish businesses are mainly co-ethnic groups, Cypriots and Indians, due to the fact that, apart from off-licences, the products they sell are related to ethnic cuisine. For instance, kebab shops across the UK are supplied by co-ethnic or minority manufacturers. Likewise, some of the produce in supermarkets and the entire produce in restaurants are supplied by ethnic manufacturers. Off-licences on the other hand mainly distribute non-ethnic products. Even in their case, distributers of the produce are not native British wholesalers; Cypriot and Indian companies tend to provide the produce. Cypriots and Indians are early arrivals to the UK. Cypriots mainly provide food produce to the ethnic supermarkets and Indians supply off-licence items such as alcoholic drinks, and tobacco. Furthermore, Turkish companies can also import produce from Germany as it is cheaper than obtaining them from Turkey.

Finally, the positioning of ethnic shop owners above the working class is not without problems. First, the question arises of criteria applied to measure social position. For instance, most of the Turkish and Kurdish small businesses work fourteen hours a day, seven days a week, which leads to a serious risk of health problems. Most of them cannot reserve time for either recreational activities, or even spending time with their children. On the other hand, a waged labourer could have a better quality of life in comparison to a shop owner. Thus, ethnic business owners are not necessarily positioned above the waged labourers on the occupational ladder.

Enclave economies

Another major analytical model of ethnic minority business in the United States is the 'ethnic enclave' approach of Alejandro Portes and his colleagues (Wilson and Portes, 1980; Portes and Bach, 1985). According to Portes (1981), enclave economies have two characteristics: First, they are concentrated in ethnic residential areas, and second, residential areas are almost always populated by co-ethnic groups (Drori and Lerner, 2002). These ethnic economies include "any ethnic or immigrant groups' self-employed, its employers, their co-ethnic employees, and their unpaid family workers" (Light & Gold, 2000, p.9). According to Portes and Manning (1986, p.330), locational cluster is the defining characteristic of ethnic enclave economies:

Once an enclave has fully developed, it is possible for a newcomer to live his life entirely within the confines of the community. Work, education, and access to a variety of services can be found without leaving the bounds of the ethnic economy. This institutional completeness is what enables new immigrants to move ahead economically.

These entrepreneurs are dependent almost entirely on the available local resources provided by co-ethnics such as information, capital, social networks and employees (e.g., Drori and Lerner, 2002; Light & Bonacich, 1988; Light & Gold, 2000; Waldinger et al., 1990). According to Light and Gold (2000, p.15), an ethnic enclave is a special case with few real life examples fit to its requirements since locational clustering, employees and economic interdependency as in Miami's little Havana are not features of all ethnic economies.

In comparison to middleman theory, the ethnic enclave approach focuses on residential areas, places populated by co-ethnics. While the middleman minority moves between places, and communities, the ethnic enclave directs attention to the minority ethnic groups bounded by a locational cluster (McEvoy and Hafeez, 2009, p.5). According to the proponents of the ethnic enclave economy, the ethnic groups' need for cultural products such as food, books, music and clothes is the main basis for such economies, which could be served by minority ethnic business owners. Acquisition of the knowledge for such products enables minority ethnic business owners to provide the cultural products to the minority community. Thus, according to Strüder (2003, p.7) ethnic enclave economies contain "deep horizontal and vertical integration of business activities in co-ethnic communities".

Portes and his colleagues (ibid) argued that ethnic communities obtained better financial gains in such ethnic clusters than they did in the mainstream economy. In the general case, the ethnic enclave approach demonstrates that the locational concentration of the group is likely to support various businesses that sustain the ethnic group in various economic sectors (Zhou, 2004).

Furthermore, ethnic enclaves may dissolve over time. For instance, demographic change is one of the ways that ethnic enclaves fade away. New migrants often move and set up shops in the locations of ethnic enclaves, hence, the area becomes diversified in terms of people and businesses. In most cases, the follow-up migrant group displaces the former group (Terzano, 2010).

According to Light and Gold (2010), the main objection that could be raised against enclave economy is its dependence on locational clustering; the importance and role of social networks and transnational ties in generating resources for the minority entrepreneurship do not fit this model. For instance, cultural enterprises that provide artefacts related to cultural industry rely on daily contacts with the home country in order to exploit the immigrant's desire to acquire and consume cultural goods such as compact discs, concerts, books, local cuisine, festivals, videos and the latest musical hits. Consequently, it is not only the exploitation of local resources that emphasises spatiality where minorities are concentrated in certain places, but entrepreneurs relying on networks that go beyond locality as well. There is a certain degree of transnational social capital which is an integral part of enclave economies. That is to say, solidarity networks go beyond local boundaries. For instance, an entrepreneur aiming to target the tastes of co-ethnics needs a good chef with good knowledge of ethnic cuisine. If the host society does not provide schools to educate chefs with the knowledge of ethnic cuisine, then the entrepreneur has to employ a chef from the home country. Such examples question the concept "enclave economies" in terms of to what extent they are an enclave. Similarly, firms in the retail market depend on a steady supply of imported goods from the home country, such as foodstuffs and clothing. Furthermore, entrepreneurs need cultural capital, i.e., knowledge of local markets, to determine the produce they can distribute in the host country.

Secondly, in order to define an ethnic economy under the category of ethnic enclave economy, there needs to be vertical and horizontal integration of businesses. The ethnic community should be self-sufficient in producing the services that are necessary for the survival of the community. As in the argument above, ethnic businesses have to have co-ethnic suppliers.

Sojourning

Sojourner mentality has been widely utilised to emphasise the migrant's hard working life attitude in the host society. One of the major characteristics of a sojourner is that she or he "spends many years of his lifetime in a foreign country without being assimilated by it. In terms of psychology, a sojourner is not willing to organise herself or himself as a permanent resident in the host country. The sojourner stays on abroad but never loses the homeland tie" (Siu, 1952, p.34). Sojourners are, in a way, economic migrants. According to the sojourning narrative, they envisage suffering for a while in the host country whilst looking forward to returning to the country of origin with better living conditions. For this reason, the narrative relates that sojourners can stand long working hours. They send remittances to their home and do not consume much (Bonacich, 1973).

The argument further states that this sojourning mentality contrasts with that of settled migrants and natives. While natives and settled migrants generally do not demonstrate thrift behaviour, the temporary migrants work long hours in order to ensure future good days in the home country. Temporary migrants are eager to accumulate capital as quickly as possible to be used in the home country. Therefore, "they postpone the reward for their efforts to their return to the home country" (Pécoud, 2004, p.20).

In a slightly different way, Piore (1979) has asserted that the reason for migrants to accept unattractive jobs is the temporary nature of their presence in a country. On the other hand, the native population fills the high status jobs while migrants "are not affected by the bad image and low prestige associated with these jobs" (Pécoud, 2004, p.20).

However, as Waldinger (1989) points out, working conditions in ethnic enterprises tend toward high levels of competition, marginal returns, high shop-closure rates, and long working hours for their owners, and employees. In addition, health risks, including physical and psychological problems, are one of the consequences of working long hours at shop-keeping. Hence, it is common to observe the same mentality at work for both temporary and permanent minorities, such as working long hours, thrift, sending their savings to their home country and reserving little time or money for consumption.

The observation made by Waldinger is important since it mentions variables other than the sojourning mentality to explain migrants' working lives. For instance, intense competition and marginal returns lead to employees being sacked and longer hours to prevent failures. In a competitive context with marginal returns for consumption, working long hours becomes a necessity. It is not the duration of stay and intention to return to the home country that determines the willingness to suffer, but the context within which they are embedded. Thus, it is possible to say that the sojourner mentality focuses on the mental factors of migrants rather than on structural factors as Waldinger mentions.

In conclusion, middleman minorities and the enclave economy are applied to specific contexts. The concepts were derived from, for instance, middleman minorities with respect to Jews in Europe, Armenians in Turkey, the Chinese in Southeast Asia, the Indians in East Africa, the Arabs in West Africa and Koreans in the United States (Bonacich and Model, 1980; Min, 2008). While they occupy a position in trading between producers and consumers, they face hostility from both sides. Likewise, the concept of enclave economy has been operationalised to describe the Cuban economy of Miami (Light and Gold, 2000) indicating self-sufficiency in local clusters. There are few other examples fitting this model, i.e. the enclave economy. A broader, inclusive term utilised by Light and Gold (ibid), is that of an ethnic economy which "consists of co-ethnic self-employed and employers and their co-ethnic employees". Middleman minorities and enclaves are ethnic economies; however, not all ethnic economies are middleman minorities and enclave economies as discussed above. The Kurdish and Turkish ethnic economy in London is neither a middleman minority nor an ethnic enclave economy. While the solidarity between middleman minorities is explained by the hostility they face in the host society, the reasons behind collective mobilisation for ethnic businesses in the KT communities are the shared experiences and conditions such as economic restructuring.

Theoretical models

In this section, I examine the theoretical models on ethnic small business ownership that have been utilised to understand and explain the dynamics, reasons and the way that minority entrepreneurs set up businesses. The section critically engages with the theories. It sets out the weaknesses as well as the strengths of the theories operationalised to explain ethnic business formation and maintenance. Thus, I discuss why there is a need for a composite theory to study ethnic businesses. Finally, I conclude with the advantages of the proposed theory of collective resource mobilisation. I argue that the theory of collective resource mobilisation provides a composite and systemic theory for analysing ethnic small businesses.

Cultural explanations

Proponents of cultural explanations have pointed out the impact of culture on entrepreneurship (Altinay, 2008; Altinay & Altinay, 2006; Basu & Altinay, 2002; Basu, 1998; McEvoy & Hafeez, 2009; Srinivasan, 1995; Werbner, 1984, 1990). They focus on the impact of supposed values of a specific ethnic community on the success and failure of entrepreneurship. Similarly, the focus on culture is utilised to measure why some people are more entrepreneurial than others (Basu & Altinay, 2002). They believe that some cultures contain economically useful practices. The assertion is that certain ethnic groups are culturally better endowed for entrepreneurship than others. The cultural practices are considered to be fixed and unchanging, and they ignore the fact that they adapt to changing circumstances. They emphasise the impact of the cultural attributes of an ethnic minority in advanced economies on setting up and running a business. They argue that cultural differences lead to divergence in entrepreneurial performance.

In this account, group characteristics brought from the home country are shown as cultural capital which allows the minority entrepreneur to set up on his/her own by relying on the ethnic community (Cassarino, 1997, p.3). Their cultural capital was facilitated and transposed into their host country context to extract economic capital from it.

However, there are several objections against cultural explanations from different positions. They mainly argue that entrepreneurship cannot solely be explained by the personal attributes and characteristics of enterprise owners (Waldinger et al., 1990). The key critiques of this model support the idea that the usage of culture has entered into the research field as if each minority group has shared values, beliefs, norms and traditions that distinguish the groups from each other (see Vermeersch, 2011). This view maintains that, minorities bring home country cultural values to the host country. Each minority group is considered as a homogeneous group that has a "collective programming of mind" (Hofstede, 1991). They highlight the significance of values like thrift, close knit family circles, community networks, trust and self-sacrifice which provide the means for some ethnic communities to compete successfully in business (Altinay, 2008; Altinay & Altinay, 2006; Basu & Altinay, 2002; Basu, 1998; McEvoy & Hafeez, 2009; Srinivasan, 1995; Werbner, 1984, 1990). Like the sojourner mentality, the determinants of success in ethnic business ownership are viewed as an aspect of the innate qualities of ethnic groups.

That is to say, minority groups are put into compartments that have or lack a business culture for successful entrepreneurship. Entrepreneurship can then be stimulated by the favourable features of immigrants' culture. Werbner's (1984, p.169) study of Pakistani business owners in Britain, for instance states "self-sacrifice, self-denial and an emphasis on hard work and savings (in brief, a "Protestant ethic") … characterise the Pakistani 'ethos'." In a similar vein, working on "factors influencing business growth: the rise of Turkish entrepreneurship in the UK", Altinay (2008, p.33) states "in the case of Turkish ethnic minority entrepreneurship… small business owners managed to break out of the ethnic enclave and move away from traditional Turkish culture with Islamic dominance." Thus, the analysis emphasises the positive correlation between "moving away from traditional Turkish culture with Islamic dominance" (ibid) and business success. In other words, he considers Islamic values to be incompatible with modern capitalism.

Similarly to the primordialist view of ethnicity, the culturalist view of ethnic businesses fails to recognise the role of agency fully. By ignoring the role of agency, culturalist approaches cannot account sufficiently for the fact that individuals are capable of mixing and articulating various cultural heritages and ethnic identities (Vermeersch, 2011).

Furthermore, business culture goes hand in hand with the criminalisation of the cultural features of minority groups. They bring in 'cultural repertoires' associated with corruption and immorality. This highly essentialist analysis, for example, associates African 'cultural repertoires' with an absence of public morality such as that evident fraud and crime (Bayart et al., 1999).

Overall, the culturalist view of minority entrepreneurship distinguishes between favourable and unfavourable cultures for the capitalist economy. Some 'good' minority cultures enable enterprises to flourish whilst some 'bad' ones provide an obstacle to minority entrepreneurship.

Similarly, the culturally determined social networks perspective has "become trapped in a "social capitalist" paradigm that conceptualises networks as 'social capital' to the extent that they promote economic efficiency and accumulation" (Meagher, 2005, p.219). Thus, the distinction between cultures and their hierarchy has been created by defining some geographically located people as if they are incapable of forming adequate social ties for economic efficiency and accumulation (Meagher, 2005, p.223). Arguably, the distinction and the hierarchy constructed in the culturalist paradigm operate as a tool for capitalism. It ascribes certain behaviours and role models compatible with capitalism.

Critiques of cultural explanations stress the fact that such explanations lead to cultural stereotyping (Collins, 2000; Pécoud, 2004), it is even suggested that if these 'cultural traits' are deemed to be inherent, then such theories verge on racist explanations (Westwood & Bhachu, 1988, p.26). While "non-immigrant business people are usually approached as individuals displaying a strong entrepreneurial spirit" (Pécoud, 2004, p.20), migrants' otherness, having collective cultural attributes imported to the country of destination, was under consideration for measuring the successful determinants of entrepreneurship. They ignore the existence of different cultural groups and heterogeneity within the migrants' home country. Thus, it is solely the fixed cultural attributes culturalist theorists presume minorities possess that culturalises minorities in a way that explains and determines their position, status, and economic well-being in a society. For the culturalist theories, the inequality between minorities and the majority in society is the result of the migrants' otherness, and the theory is constructed to measure divergence and convergence from and with the established norm. The success or failure of a particular group in business is viewed according to the deviated or compatible cultural attributes of minorities. In so doing, cultural explanations of minority entrepreneurship create an epistemological and ontological distinction between Western capitalist societies and the rest. The rest has been designated and mapped as an "otherness".

On the contrary, I argue ontologically that as a survival strategy within a very competitive environment in advanced capitalism, minority businesses have to develop patron - client relationships with their co-ethnics and pursue close co-ethnic family ties. Patronage implies an inequality of status and a flow of favours from the superior partner which cannot be matched by the weaker client, who in exchange provides cheap labour to his or her patron. The relationship may be regarded as socially necessary by both parties. While the veteran ethnic business owner becomes a safety net for the newly arrived co-ethnic, who is a potential source of exploitation, the client may be provided with information about the host country, shelter and pocket money by her or his co-ethnic patron. Moreover, it provides a framework within which a man or a woman, who has needs that cannot be met within his or her kinship network, can ask and obtain favours of co-ethnics without losing his or her own self-respect. A relationship of patronage tends to be established with the act of migration rather than being a previous condition for this act. Patrons in Britain have generally started to work 'at the bottom' as clients, and have gradually set up for themselves a small business. They have brought over, first of all, their closest kin; they then employ from a wider circle of relatives and co-villagers. They may also recruit from the families of friends in Britain, or from families of employees to whom they stand in a relationship of patronage (Westwood & Bhachu, 1988).

In other words, the maintenance of a cultural tradition and/or re-production of patron – client relations in immigrant groups are a response to the need to organise to survive in an advanced capitalist society. That is to say, the production relations that are attached to feudalism or 'backwardness' appear in a capitalist economy. The characteristics of social relations attached to the home country, and cultural practices related to those relations, transposed to the production relations of the country of destination. Cultural practices transposed or created in the host country help migrants to exploit small business opportunities. The existence of many cultural practices and their transposition to a new context after immigration does not emerge automatically. In some conjunctures they may dissolve, and then be reinvented, but they usually result from structural conditions and "they are, in this sense, an emergent product" (Portes and Sensenbrenner, 1993, p.1330). Problems related to survival and adaptation to the host country play an important role in the conservation, dissolution and re-emergence of cultural practices.

The debate revolves around the respective importance of these two sets of factors, such as structure versus cultural determinants of immigrant entrepreneurialism. On the one side of the debate, it is argued that immigrants have the right mentality and culture (Basu, 1998). On the other side, it is argued that structural conditions are the determining factor for immigrant entrepreneurialism. For instance, the success of South Asian entrepreneurs has been vigorously argued to be an expression of 'cultural' features (Basu, 1998). However, on the other side of the debate, according to Ram (1992), Asian drive into small business ownership is better explained by a survivalist strategy during a period of de-industrialisation and huge unemployment. Members of ethnic communities tend to be affected more severely than native workers as the mainstream labour market has been characterised by discrimination.

However, both sides of the debate ignore the interplay between culture and structure. While cultures are not static and they respond to socioeconomic changes as stated above, at the same time the responses to the changes also shapes structures.

For instance, authors of a Marxist leaning have asserted that the minority groups' cultural attributes could be evaluated "as a reaction to structural factors such as high unemployment and discrimination" (Pécoud, 2004, p.20).

Thus, in order to survive economically, immigrants are pushed to develop such cultural features (see Chan and Ong, 1995). Such a view brings the wider environment into the analysis where minorities are embedded, rather than focusing on the cultural attributes of minorities as an explanatory theory.

In the next section, I focus on a theory that brings the wider environment into the analysis of minority entrepreneurship.

Structuralism

One alternative theory to the culturalist approach stresses that, individuals from ethnic groups act within the context of the changing political, cultural, social and economic structures. In other words, unlike culturalist theories, it stresses that individuals and groups act within a historical changing political economic context, not in a vacuum where changes in political economy are ignored. Minority businesses are not the result of isolated initiatives by agents whose cultural attributes of the country of origin contributed to the creation of their small business enterprises. In this respect, structuralism investigates the opportunity structure faced by the minority group.

The structure side indicates the aspects external to the ethnic minority group (Pécoud, 2002b).The structural opportunities and constraints available for immigrants are the focus of an explanation for ethnic entrepreneurship.

In contrast to the cultural explanation, the structural interpretation takes into account the structure of the economy, government policies, racial discrimination, violence and harassment as the determinants of minority entrepreneurship. It focuses on the factors external to ethnic communities that push them into self-employment (Volery, 2007).

Even though there are attempts by culturalist theories to incorporate the structure of the wider environment into analyses of minority entrepreneurship rather than just focusing on the cultural attributes of minorities, they largely focus on the characteristics of minorities. For example, Altinay (2008), working on factors influencing business growth in Turkish entrepreneurship researches how cultural attributes affect business entrepreneurship. The performances of minority business firms were measured in terms of the effect of the minorities' religion, education, cultural skills, co-ethnic labour, capital, co-ethnic information and co-ethnic markets on Turkish entrepreneurship. The application of opportunity structures in the host society to the cultural attributes again only concerns the small business owner's cultural background (Altinay, 2008).

On the other hand, the structure sets the context for where new immigrant arrivals find opportunities and restrictions. Changing economic circumstances and economic re-structuring resulted in a fundamental transformation of the labour market in Britain. It has led to general shifts away from large scale production to flexible production and "from employment in large firms to self-employment in small ones" (Volery, 2007, p.30), which provided the basis for outsourcing, and informalisation (Fielding, 1993). This shift has affected certain immigrant groups more severely than native populations. For example, until the midst of the 1990s, the KT minorities used to be employed in textile factories in London, UK. The KT minorities found themselves unemployed when textile businesses collapsed and the factories moved to China, East Europe and Turkey (Inal & Ozkan, 2009, p.506). As Strüder (2003) argues, during the 1970s and 1980s the textile factories employed over 90 percent of the KT communities. The textile sector collapsed towards the middle of the 1990s, and various other trades have been taken up such as retail and catering businesses in Britain. Rath (1998) observes that Turkish businesses in Amsterdam started to mushroom in the early 1980s when the formal sector ceased to produce new jobs for unskilled workers; that is, when the supply of jobs dried up, immigrants turned to self-employment. Simon (1993, p.130) makes the same point about immigrant-owned businesses in France during that period. However, the literature on ethnic economies does not provide a theoretical model to explain this global trend towards ethnic business ownership. There is a lack of focus on the link between globalisation and ethnic businesses.

Accordingly, from a structuralist viewpoint, the legal, institutional settings, labour market policies and the existence of a potential market are crucial factors in determining the opportunities and constraints for minority business participation in the host society (Rath, 2000). For a business to be set up there needs to be a demand for the products and services that immigrant businesses offer (Aldrich and Waldinger, 1990).

In addition, the role played by historically contingent circumstances in shaping the prospects for minority entrepreneurship could be the level of (de-)commodification in a sector. Esping-Andersen (1990, 1999) shows how different national institutional contexts, experiencing a structural change in the form of a post-industrial transition, can have a different post-industrial employment path. To paraphrase Esping-Andersen, it is possible to say that differences in institutional structures and regulatory frameworks also lead to divergent post-industrial self-employment trajectories. Divergent trajectories result in various opportunity structures for ethnic immigrants (Kloosterman & Rath, 2003). For instance, the national institutional setting determines the division between markets, public and familial provision. As Kloosterman and Rath (ibid) further argue,

> *If the public sector takes care of a whole range of low-wage activities or if the familial domain is relatively large, the scope for small businesses is*

accordingly smaller than in the case where market is the main provider for all kinds of household services (e.g. childcare, housecleaning, etc.) or municipal services (e.g. maintenance of public gardens, catering, etc.).

Government provision of such services could well undermine the development of businesses in those sectors (Anderson, 1990). Government policies, economic institutional contexts, legal systems and regulatory structures play a major role in a migrant's decision to set up shop (Kloosterman, 2000). Alternatively, migrants' embeddedness in the regulatory structures of the national context may or may not enable their entry to business activities (Pecoud, 2002a).

In addition, job loss and racial discrimination push disadvantaged ethnic communities into business ownership (Light and Gold, 2000; Wahlbeck, 2007). Here, entrepreneurship constitutes an escape route for many ethnic communities from the manual jobs to which they are confined by racism and racial discrimination. Due to exclusion from the general labour market, many immigrants tend to look for business opportunities in sectors in which there is over competition and with high failure rates or marginal profit rates given self-reliance. Setting up a business emerges as a potential path for redressing their situation and lack of activity in the labour market, "including their socio-economic disadvantage and what is perceived as their failed "integration" (Pécoud, 2002a).

Of equal importance, according to Sheila et al. (1981), to any would-be entrepreneur is the possibility of finding and securing a suitable site to pursue business activities. The discriminatory attitude of estate agents towards minority groups, and restrictions in allocating newly constructed development areas in the city, could become obstacles for small minority business development. Consequently, a property owned by fellow-countrymen may be easier to rent. This can also be a contributing factor for minority owned businesses concentrating in certain regions.

During the 1980s, entrepreneurship became a necessity for many shaken out of the labour-intensive manufacturing industries in which they were located, whose residential concentration in the decaying inner cities had further reduced the alternatives for those made redundant (Phizacklea, 1988, p.21). According to the proponents of the structuralist view, economic de-regulation and re-structuring leave migrants with no other option but setting up businesses. The problems associated with the mainstream labour market are seen as the cause of immigrants' self-employment (ibid).

As an externality to the minorities' self-mobilisation of resources, government assistance for minority entrepreneurship gained a new momentum after the civil disorders in both the U.K and the US. The encouragement of small business has been viewed as a propagation of Thatcher's government policy after the Brixton riots. As Westwood and Bhachu (1988, p.18) state, "backed up by Lord Scarman (1981) arguing, in the wake of the Brixton disturbances in 1981, that black people had to secure a real 'stake in their community' through business enterprises".

According to Ram and Jones (2008, p.66), "specialist agencies or programmes directed explicitly at ethnic minority business clients – emerged in response to the Scarman Report on the 1981 urban riots, which recommended enterprise promotion as an antidote to what is now termed 'social exclusion". Thus, the Scarman report constitutes a turning point for governmental discourse which has shifted its role from being a social welfare state that promotes social inclusion through its policies, to one of self-help and self-reliance of excluded minorities.

Within this conjuncture, minority business enterprise development is propagated as a security measure. It is interesting to note that, so far, minority business research in advanced capitalist countries has not interlinked human security and development studies as a social policy oriented research. As Duffield (2005, p.1) notes, "human security is commonly understood as prioritising the security of people, especially their welfare, safety, and well-being, rather than that of states". Similarly, government assistance programmes directed towards minority businesses in the US started after the 1960s. Minority groups started to receive provisions and special minority enterprise support programs were created (Waldinger et al., 1990, p.39).

Accordingly, changing opportunity structures — policy measures to combat civil unrest, booms and recessions, changing government industry policies, new technologies are all determining the possibility for ethnic communities to become business owners (Collins, 2000).

In this respect, the opportunities embedded in a particular locality are tied to the circumstances of the global economy. The environment in which the minorities are embedded creates certain production relations. This also strongly indicates the way in which the shifts in the global political economy have an impact on the opportunity structures for new immigrants. As Waldinger et al, (1990, p.21) mention, "groups can work only with the resources made available to them by their environments, and the structure of opportunities is constantly changing in modern industrial societies". That is to say, opportunities and constraints for immigrant entrepreneurship are context dependent.

Interaction Theory
In contrast to culturalist, and structuralist theories, proponents of interaction theory advocate that determinants of business ownership cannot be assessed

solely according to the personal characteristics of owners or in line with the structuralist account that ignores agency (Aldrich & Waldinger et al., 1990). According to the interaction model, social structural and cultural analysis focuses one side of the determining factors for ethnic entrepreneurship. Thus, Waldinger and his associates (1990) asserted a comprehensive theory that brought the opportunity structure and agency related views together, "based on the principle that entrepreneurship is the product of the interaction between group characteristics and the opportunity structure" (Collins, 2003, p.16).

Waldinger (1983, p.59), in his structuralist conception, deliberately seeks to go beyond the cultural framework by contending that "the ethnic affinities that underlie the immigrant-owned firm are neither ascribed constants nor temporally persistent bonds, but rather products of structural conditions linked to the organization of the markets and the technology of production". Family, kinship, close co-ethnic networks, and labour become extremely important for setting-up and running businesses. Community networks which may offer advice and information for potential entrepreneurs are collective resources for minority businesses. In addition, as Aldrich and Waldinger (1990, p.130) state "ethnic labour force is largely unpaid and kin and co-ethnics work for long hours in the service of their families". Moreover, "self-exploitation is a strategy that small immigrant store owners can successfully pursue" (Waldinger et al., 1990, p. 26). While co-ethnics provide cheap labour to be exploited, the employers provide co-ethnics with a safety, risk reducing net in the wider society. Employees also have the chance to learn the business for their future plans. Thus, being a client to the patron is, in other words, a step towards business ownership and patronage in the future. New co-ethnic arrivals in the host society often have no other choice than to work in ethnic niches for survival. The blocked social mobility faced by members of ethnic communities force them to set up businesses as the only means of economic survival. The reciprocal and mutually dependent relationship between co-ethnics and employers is a conditional solidarity which ends when the employee has enough resources to set up a business of his or her own.

The theoretical contribution of interaction theory enabled researchers to combine minority attributes with the wider structural attributes of society. As Waldinger et al., (1990, p.112) state "framework is based on ethnic groups' access to opportunities, group characteristics, and emergent strategies which are embedded in changing historical conditions. The opportunity structures entail market conditions (particularly access to ethnic/non-ethnic consumer markets), and access to ownership (in the form of business vacancies, competition for vacancies)". Furthermore, in the interactionist model, there are two main aspects of the opportunity structure used to evaluate the dynamics of labour market cooperation and social mobility of ethnic business owners (Lassalle, 2008). The first aspect deals with accessibility: Markets should not apply restriction to new migrants setting up a business. The second aspect focuses on the growth potential of the markets where ethnic minorities start new businesses (ibid). Thus, strategies for ethnic would-be entrepreneurs emerge from the "interaction of opportunities and group characteristics" (Waldinger et al., 1990, p.114). This interactive approach has been acknowledged as a development towards a more composite theoretical model (Rath, 2006). However, the interactionist model can be utilised to explain how ethnic communities moved into self-employment rather than why they become small business owners.

Accordingly, interactionism is a model that explicitly points out the interplay between agency and market structure. As Strüder (2003, p.10) asserts the "focus here is on how the interaction of agency, culture and structure leads to the emergence of ethnic entrepreneurship. Particular emphasis is put on the fit between offers of the agency side, so-called "ethnic resources" and the structures, particularly "opportunity structures," which differs in different locations".

According to Waldinger et al. (1990, p.3), ethnic entrepreneurship is based on "a set of connections and regular patterns of interaction among people sharing common national background or migration experiences". However, the quotation ignores the fact that interaction among people does not necessarily originate from a shared national background or migration experience. Rather, shared experiences in the occupational structure and shared interests within different ethnic groups whose migration experiences correspond to different time periods could result in new alliances and identity constructions that facilitate networks utilised for entrepreneurship. Waldinger's assertion ignores the dynamics in ethnic attachment formation or dissolution. There is no pre-existing necessity for common national backgrounds to contact each other and interact. In other words, according to my best knowledge, the existing literature treats ethnic identity and interests with respect to business formation as pre-existing.

Moreover, interactionism as an attempt to bring agency and structure does not focus on the regulatory context of the institutional setting and the governmental policies that enable or constrain certain business set-ups. That is to say, interactionist theory does not take into account that the "entry to markets for newcomers may be blocked directly by rules and regulations" (Kloosterman and Rath, 2001, p.2).

In the next section, I focus on a more sophisticated theory for explaining ethnic businesses.

Mixed embeddedness

Criticism of the interactionist model has been raised by more recent contributions by continental European researchers (Kloosterman, Van der Leun & Rath, 1999; Kloosterman & Rath, 2001, 2003; Rath, 2002; Pang and Rath, 2006). Their main criticism ofthe interactionist model discussed above was that it mainly focuses onthe supply side of entrepreneurship, while ignoring the context where entrepreneurialism has been regulated and differentiated (Pang and Rath, 2006). Hence, interactionist theory has paid no attention to the array of regulatory context – institutional settings, governmental policies, and laws - that constrains and facilitates certain economic activities (Rath, 2002, p.12). For instance, "while virtually anyone can establish a private business in the United States, in Germany and even more so in Austria individuals must apply for special licenses even to sell flowers in restaurants and bars, and they need the approval of a particular organization to engage in most forms of production or service" (Rath, 2007, p.5).

Some scholars (Kloosterman, Van Der Leun & Rath 1999; Kloosterman & Rath, 2001, 2003; Rath, 2002) proposed a more nuanced mixed embeddedness approach to immigrant entrepreneurship that recognises the regulatory structures and market dynamics. The advantage of this multi-level mixed embeddedness approach lies in its focus on interplay between ethnic social networks and political, economic structures. As Rath (2002, p.13) states, "it acknowledges the significance of immigrants' concrete embeddedness in social networks, and conceives that their relations and transactions are embedded in wider economic and politico-institutional structures".

Even though the mixed embeddedness model stresses the importance of immigrant's agency, it fails to explore the agency dimension empirically (Tatli et. al., 2014; Trupp, 2014). Economic actions of ethnic entrepreneurs are viewed as responses to larger structures beyond their influence without taking into account the entrepreneur's own sense of these structures, meanings, and definitions that people bring to their situation in the confrontation and negotiation between themselves and structures (Tatli et al., 2014, p.59). In a similar vein, Anthias and Cederberg (2006, p.4) argue that the push pull model, based on neo-liberal economic theory and Marxist approaches fall short in explaining "...the ways in which knowledge and communication channels and opportunities for work are mediated by social actors in specific social locations". In other words, the existing literature assumes that the interest in setting-up a shop, and the motivation for setting-up small businesses is pre-given, and pre-existing, rather than processes that are consciously formed by the efforts of ethnic community members' agency.

According to Kloosterman et al.'s (1999) theory of mixed embeddedness, factors determining ethnic business success are not only dependent on ethnic social networks, but also on the wider economic structure. As they further contend, outcomes will be strongly determined "by the wider economic and institutional context into which immigrants are inevitably also inserted" (ibid, p.257).

The mixed-embeddedness (Kloosterman et al. 1999; Kloosterman & Rath, 2001) model is a more refined theory than the interactionist model for explaining the dynamics in ethnic businesses. It focuses on the interplay between ethnic minority businesses and the regulatory context as well as the political, institutional and socio-economic background (Strüder, 2003).

The dominant interactionist model paid no attention to the political institutional setting of ethnic businesses, but rather limited itself to "concentrating principally on the structure of economic opportunities and constraints created by market forces" (Ram & Jones, 2008, p.63). By ignoring the State, the interactionist model does not have the power to explain the differences between country specific ethnic business performances, and in fact assumes a world where opportunities and constraints are equal for each country. For example, Kloosterman and Rath (2003, p.9) talk about typologies of opportunity structures as such:

> *In corporatist countries with a thick institutional context (a plethora of rules and regulations, both formal and informal), obstacles may arise in the form of the requirement of permits to start a particular line of business or even any business as in Germany, or in the form of exclusionary rules that protect insiders by allowing, for example only a limited number of bakeries. In addition, institutions that determine or even foster the accessibility to, for instance, financial resources or the availability of commercial properties with regard to newcomers can also be crucial in shaping the opportunity structure for immigrant entrepreneurs. Regulation, to be sure, is not just a matter of repression and constraining, but also enabling.*

At the same time, rising immigration with no other employment opportunities for some migrant groups have fuelled labour intensive opportunities such as ethnic business ownership. Like I said earlier, while theories like culturalist and interactionist models focus on the supply side of ethnic business ownership by exploring the different levels of entrepreneurship between ethnic groups. On the other hand, according to Kloosterman and Rath (2001, p.2), the mixed embeddedness approach also looks "at the embeddedness of the immigrant entrepreneurs in social networks, but it does this by explicitly relating it to the opportunity structure in which these entrepreneurs have to find possibilities to start a business, and subsequently maintain, or expand that business".

In addition, the national institutional setting determines the extent of private business activities as Kloosterman and Rath (2003, pp.8-9) put it:

If the public sector takes care of a whole range of low-wage activities, or if the familial domain is relatively large, the scope for small businesses is accordingly smaller than in the case where market is the main provider for all kinds of household services (e.g. childcare, housecleaning, etc.) or municipal services (e.g. maintenance of public gardens, catering, etc.). This division is partly related to the role of a legal minimum wage. If a relatively high legal minimum wage exists (especially in conjunction with a strongly developed welfare system), the profitability of the market provision of labour-intensive, low-value added services is seriously undermined. In this case, the public sector, the family or informal provision will take place or services will not be provided at all. A relatively high legal minimum wage may also impede those types of low-value added manufacturing –such as the garment industry- that have a strong inclination to be in close proximity to large consumer markets. These 'background institutions' that diverge from country to country determine to a significant extent the shape of the opportunity structure for small businesses and, accordingly, the set openings that aspiring immigrant entrepreneurs face in a particular context.

To summarise, mixed-embeddedness is a theoretical contribution to the literature on ethnic businesses. The approach is intended to bring agency and structure together with a focus on the supply of ethnic entrepreneurship, the shape of market structure and the institutional setting.

However, mixed embeddedness ignores the macro-structural factors. According to Rath (2002, p.4), the model "acknowledges the significance of immigrants' virtual embeddedness in social ties and their relations and transactions that are embedded in a more abstract way in external economic and politico-institutional context". However, the embeddedness of ethnic business owners or would-be entrepreneurs is restricted in national settings. This in fact leads to insufficient attention to changing economic structures in the global political economy. It does not emphasise or pay sufficient attention to the relationship between globalisation and opportunity structures for immigrants, particularly with respect to the new paths to entrepreneurship. This is also important in explaining changing immigration patterns. The proposed theory of collective resource mobilisation is an attempt to fill that gap.

Transnationalism

According to Basch et al. (1994, p.6), transnationalism could be defined as:

> *multi-stranded social, economic, and political relations that link together migrants' societies of origin and settlement, and through which they create transnational social fields that cross national borders. Transnationalism broadly relates to the development and maintenance of ties and interactions that link people, communities across the borders of nation states.*

Similarly according to Portes (2001, p. 186), while international, multinational refer to the activities conducted by states, other nationally-based institutions, and institutions that transcend the border of a single nation-state, transnational activities would be those initiated and carried out by non-institutional actors, be they organized groups or networks of individuals across national borders. The activities that take place on their own behalf are informal and out of state regulation and control.

The concept of transnational social networks points out the opportunities that develop from social interaction (Portes, 1995). The ability to energize these social relations, and hence to mobilise resources, is seen as 'social capital' (Bourdieu, 1986). It is an agency centred approach emphasising the role of "space-time compressing technologies" (Harvey, 1989) that widens, deepens, and speeds up worldwide interconnectedness (Held et al.1999; Landolt, 2001). Portes et al. (2002), "provide a very general definition of transnational entrepreneurs as individuals who travel abroad at least twice a year for business and whose success depends on regular contact with foreign countries" (cited in Terjesen & Elam, 2009, p.1096). They tend to be viewed as modern day middleman minorities (ibid). Knowledge of at least two countries is essential for transnational entrepreneurs. In this sense, "transnational entrepreneurs are individuals with unique perspectives and resources who are especially well equipped to navigate multiple institutional environments in the interests of transacting international business" (ibid).

Migrant transnationalism has first been defined as: "the process by which trans-migrants, through their daily life activities forge and sustain multi-stranded social, economic, and political relations that link together their societies of origin and settlement, and through which they create transnational social fields that cross national boundaries" (Basch et al., 1994, p.7; as cited in Landolt, 2001). While the diffusion of "space-time compressing technologies" (Harvey, 1989), such as mobile phones, fax and e-mail as well as low cost transcontinental jet travel enable transnational exchanges and facilitate the consolidation of trans-border activities of individuals within an immigrant community, it does not explain why they do so. As Waldinger (1999, p.228) states, "network theory represents at once the most distinctively sociological and the most successful sociological contribution to international migration. Admittedly, network theory does not explain the activation of migration streams". In other words, it gives emphasis to the agency side of entrepreneurship without focusing on the wider environment where migrants are embedded and factors lead to entrepreneurship. It is noteworthy to state that, similar to the cultural theories, transnationalism's "emphasis on social capital, ethnic networks in explaining qualitative and quantitative differences in the entrepreneurial activity in different minority groups are predominantly explained by attributes and resources of minority groups" (Engelen, 2001, p.203). As a consequence of this, it disregards the institutional dimension as if entrepreneurs "operate in an institutional vacuum" (ibid). Thus, the relevance of the 'institutionalist' account and structural forces - booms and recessions – such as in the early 70s 'oil crises, which provided an impetus to the shaping of the global economy in terms of capital investment in developing countries is downplayed in the literature so far. The dynamics that are shaping the world economy have crucial impacts in determining the activation of migration streams and their characteristics. To put it differently, rather than merely describing networks, there is a need to answer a much deeper question of where and why strong bonds of kinship emerge in one country or region, rather than another (Petras, 2006). In sum, there appears to be a need for a more composite theory not only to bring agency and structure of entrepreneurship together, but also to bring together micro, meso and macro scales. The next section provides the basis for such an approach.

Collective resource mobilisation

As I state in the introduction, this project advocates the value of applying Charles Tilly's (1977; 1978) theory of collective action to ethnic entrepreneurship literature. So, this section discusses the proposed theory of collective action. According to Tilly (1977, p.3-4), the theory of collective action has four components, which are;

> **Interests**: *the shared advantages or disadvantages likely to accrue to the population in question as a consequence of various possible interactions with other populations.*

> **Organization**: *the extent of common identity and unifying structure among the individuals in the population; as a process, an increase in common identity and/or unifying structure (we can call a decline in common identity and/or unifying structure disorganization).*

Mobilization: the extent of resources under the collective control of the contender; as a process, an increase in the resources or in the degree of collective control (we can call n decline in either one demobilization).

Opportunity describes the relationship between the population's interests and the current state of the world around it.

As I discussed in chapter one, the advantages of collective resource mobilisation in the context of small business ownership lie in its dynamic and shifting approach enabling one, first, to discuss how changes in the global political economy affect migrant employability. This dynamic and shifting approach provided by collective resource mobilisation theory is also fruitful in explaining why some communities are heavily concentrated in small business ownership, while some others moved out or never interested in small business ownership.

Second, with the exception of the collective resource mobilisation theory, the other theories and analytical models in explaining migrant entrepreneurship discussed above consider immigrant identity and cultural practices fixed and unchanging in space and time. On the other hand, collective resource mobilisation theory emphasises the identification of shared interests and interest alignment constructed in their new context. The shared interests and interest alignment promotes utilisation of new ethnic attachments that does not exist and/or used in the home country, new definitions of themselves and transposition and/or dissolution of cultural practices brought from the home country, which may be helpful in the setting up and maintenance processes of their small businesses.

The first component of collective resource mobilisation has faced serious objections (Snow et al., 2008). The problem with collective interests is that they are considered to be pre-existing and self-evident to prior mobilisation (Jenkins, 2008). However, for many ethnic groups articulation of shared interest does not happen, they do not define their "real shared interests" or they are ill-informed and not conscious of their interests. Consequently, critics of Tilly's work focused on micro-mobilisations aiming to frame the interests of groups. It entails a process of social construction which handles the "shared meanings and definitions that people bring to their situation" (McAdam, 2008, p.281).

In this book, I interpret the components of collective action in relation to the context of ethnic businesses. I thought that KT individuals act collectively to accomplish common ends. The second component of collective resource mobilisation, organisation, includes both formal and informal organisations based on networks. Instead of organisation, I use the word "networks" in this study. Actually, collective action derives from solidarity networks, informal as well as formal. Indeed, Charles Tilly's model dissents from the formal organisational model which states that the force of social change is primarily through the social movement organisations (McAdam et al., 2004). While Tilly (1977) coined the term organisation in his study on social movements, he did not use it exclusively to denote formal networks. For instance, he has documented the crucial role played by various network based settings, such as work and neighbourhood, in particular in facilitating and structuring collective action. Influenced by Tilly's work, several scholars (McAdam, 1982; Evans, 1980) have applied his insights to other social movements, such as the role of local black churches and colleges in the emergence of the American civil rights movement and informal friendship networks in the women's liberation movement. In this regard, one of the advantages of applying collective action theory is that it provides an account of the role of formal as well as informal networks in ethnic entrepreneurship. The formal networks in the case of ethnic entrepreneurship are community, cultural, business organisations, and informal networks including friendship, kinship, hometown networks and co-ethnics.

Interests entail the "gains and losses resulting from a group's" (Tilly, 1977, p.1-10) action. Interest identification is a process for forming a unifying identity. I combine the second and third component of the theory of collective mobilisation, specifically, organisation and mobilisation as mobilisation of networks. Mobilisation of networks denotes the process of activation of networks for ethnic businesses. In other words, the issue here is not a passive ethnic network, but rather an active network focusing on a purposeful act. Mobilisation of networks relates to the group's internal structure and its capacity to act in its own interest and mobilise the resources needed for action. It is the volume of resources under collective control (Tilly, 1977). The fourth component "opportunity concerns the relationship between a group and the world around it" (Tilly, 1977, p.1-11).

Entrepreneurs need resources to set up and operate their businesses. One of the crucial tasks of this book is to identify and classify the resources needed for entrepreneurial activity. There are seven problems identified by Waldinger et al; (1990, p.46) in founding and maintaining businesses.

(1) Acquiring the information needed for the establishment and survival of their firms,

(2) Obtaining the capital needed to establish or to expand their business,

(3) Acquiring the training and skills needed to run a small business,

(4) Recruiting and managing efficient, honest, and cheap workers,

(5) Managing relations with customers and suppliers,

(6) Surviving business competition,

(7) Protecting themselves from political attacks.

All these problems listed by Waldinger et al. (ibid) are related to an ethnic group's internal capacity to act in its own interests and could be resolved by the mobilization of networks. The strength and quality of network mobilisation determines the capacity to act in their own interests.

In addition to the list above, I identified four more problems. These include:

(8) is identifying the perceived interest by an ethnic community in business formation, which could be defined as an interest alignment viewed as a common-sense tendency by an ethnic community to set-up shops to find a solution to their unemployment. This primary condition, interest alignment constitutes the first step towards business ownership. It entails the cognitive micro-mobilisation of the shared interests of an ethnic community and has the power to explain why some communities are more involved in ethnic business ownership. The process of interest alignment is a pre-condition for ethnic entrepreneurship.

(9) is the changing opportunity structures focusing on the changes in global political economy.

(10) concerns bridging networks to mainstream strategic elites and members of civil society organisations so that business owners can voice their demands to acquire favourable working conditions.

(11) concerns the political-institutional setting, i.e., regulatory structures which might enable or constrain business start-ups and operation.

In sum, there are eleven main problems identified when founding and operating their businesses and they are thoroughly examined through the lens of collective action in this study. I classify the problems into two separate categories. In the first classification, the focus is on the internal capacity of the entrepreneurial ethnic group, while the second includes the wider structures and the interplay with them and the ethnic group.

The advantage of collective resource mobilisation theory in the context of ethnic small businesses is that it is as illuminating about the absence of collectivism as it is on the presence of collectivism. It allows researchers to systematically analyse why an ethnic minority group is over represented or absent in self-employment. Resource mobilisation "consists of people's acting together in pursuit of common interests" (Tilly, 1977, p.1-11), which is a result of interaction between those three components.

It encompasses micro, meso, and macro levels. The macro level is the changes in the global political economy; the meso level focuses on the sectors, regions and national level; and finally, the micro level points out the mobilisation of networks within the KT communities to achieve common goals.

At the macro level, changes in the global political economy have an impact on migrants' employability in advanced capitalist economies. Certain production in advanced capitalist economies could be transferred to lower wage zones so that workers, including migrants, in the advanced economies could face unemployment, which could also be a push factor triggering self-employment. Consequently, changes in the global political economy could be the reason for starting a new business for many migrants as their previous life pattern is shattered by the forces of capitalist globalisation. The displaced labour from the less developed world and unemployed surplus population in advanced economies collectively mobilise resources via networks to establish meaningful livelihoods in the embedded opportunities of the host country.

At the meso level, the focus is on the role that regulators – like national planning guides and local government – and market forces play in shaping the competitive environment. More specifically it contains the constraints and opportunities for ethnic entrepreneurship.

Finally, at the micro level, the focal point is the seven issues I identified and classified earlier, more particularly, the ways in which those issues are addressed by the ethnic community. It is asserted that the ability to open and operate ethnic small businesses is dependent on the collective mobilisation of forms of capital. The following section will focus on processes in the mobilisation of capitals for KT businesses. Particularly, Bourdieu's (1986) forms of capital such as economic, social and cultural capital will utilised to analyse not only the ways in which those problems are handled but also, how inequalities in the distribution of each type of capital in a particular moment in time lead to different entrepreneurial strategies within the KT communities.

Forms of capital

Pierre Bourdieu's (1986) work on forms of capital emphasises the conflicts and power relations in stratified societies where capitals are not distributed equally. Unequal distribution of capital is one way of maintaining a position in the hierarchy of the social ladder. According to Bourdieu (1986, p.47), capital manifests itself in three different forms, specifically;

as economic capital, which is immediately and directly convertible into money and maybe institutionalized in the forms of property rights; as cultural capital, which is convertible, on certain conditions, into economic capital and maybe institutionalized in the forms of educational qualifications; and as social capital, made up of social obligations ("connections"), which is convertible, in certain conditions, into economic capital and maybe institutionalized in the forms of a title of nobility.

Using Bourdieu's conceptualisation of differences in the control of capitals may explain why some entrepreneurs can set up their businesses easily, whilst it takes much longer time for other co-ethnics. Similarly, it could explain why some ethnic entrepreneurs had to activate different degrees of cultural and social capital to set up their shops while others did not have to activate social networks to set up theirs.

Yet, Bourdieu's theory of forms of capital presents a highly complex description as it engages with the interaction and convertibility of different forms of capital such as social, cultural and economic. More specifically;

Economic capital refers to the resources that can be immediately and directly transposable into money (Bourdieu, 1986). The various forms of economic capital are finance capital, trade shares and factories.

While it is important to make a distinction between economic, cultural, and social capital for analytical purposes, the boundaries between the capitals are fluid as envisaged by Bourdieu (1986). In modern differentiated societies, access to sources of income in the labour market builds upon class based resources such as cultural capital and social capital in the form of networks (Swartz, 1997).

Cultural capital, according to Bourdieu (1986, p.47) exists in three subtype states, namely embodied, institutionalised and objectified. The embodied form of cultural capital refers to the "long standing dispositions of mind and body" such as someone's dialect or accent, while the objectified state addresses goods such as books, machines, dictionaries and paintings. Finally, in its institutionalised form, educational credentials such as certificates and diplomas are sources of cultural capital. However, cultural capital also includes informal skills, and features transmitted through family, peer groups and associations.

Accordingly, Bourdieu's notion of various forms of capital enables us to analyse how one form of capital can be transposed into another form. They are subject to cycles, generating returns. One form of capital can be transposed into another. As Bourdieu (1987, p.4) comments:

Thus agents are distributed in the overall social space, in the first dimension according to the global volume of capital they possess, in the second dimension according to the composition of their capital, that is, according to the relative weight in their overall capital of the various forms of capital, especially economic and cultural, and in the third dimension according to the evolution in the time of the volume and composition of their capital, that is according to their trajectory in the social space.

Moreover, cultural capital has a dynamic character in migration (Erel, 2010, p.654). For instance, institutionalised cultural capital, such as university diplomas acquired in the home country, may be subjected to non-recognition in the host country. The validation of cultural capital has a dynamic character as it is open to ups and downs, creating new cultural resources.

As I noted earlier, forms of capital, according to Bourdieu's conceptualisation are not acquired equally either in every ethnic migrant community or at the individual level. As Raghuram et al (2010, p.626) mention, "for Bourdieu, the purpose of theorizing forms of capital was, in large part, to trace the ways in which privilege (especially that of class position) is sustained and often enclosed amongst those within particular social strata". To consider an ethnic migrant community as a homogeneous entity neglects the fact that there are intra-group hierarchical distinctions and exclusions within the ethnic migrant community (ibid). These distinctions and exclusions are based on different degrees of forms of capital attainment.

Social capital like the other two capitals, according to Bourdieu's notion, focuses on the factors that constitute social inequality (Anthias & Cederberg, 2009). In comparison to Robert Putnam's (1993) affirmative conceptualisation, Bourdieu uses social capital as a critical concept. The amount and quality of resources possessed by their associates also determines the level of the inequalities originating from a person's access to social capital. More specifically, social capital places emphasis on social interactions that raise the ability of an actor to act on behalf of her/his interests. Membership of civic groups and activity in social networks can be mobilised in efforts to improve the social positions of co-ethnics.

Bourdieu's work (1986) on forms of capital has been fruitful in examining the role of economic capital, social relations and cultural capital in the study of social classes. While Robert Putnam's theorising of social capital has been more influential than Bourdieu's work (Erel, 2010). His definition of social capital is "those features of social organisations, such as networks, norms and trust, which facilitate coordination and cooperation for mutual benefit" (1993, pp.35-36). In contrast to affirmative conceptions of social capital, according to Bourdieu,

> *Social capital is the aggregate of the actual or potential resources which are linked to possession of a durable network of more or less institutionalized relationships of mutual acquaintance and recognition – or in other words, to membership in a group – which provides each of its members with the backing of the collectively-owned capital, a 'credential' which entitles them to credit, in various senses of the world (Bourdieu, 1986, p. 51).*

Social capital in economic life is a resource for the attainment of scarce means such as economic capital, labour force, skills and information. According to Vasta (2004, p.9), "a simple definition of a social network is that it refers to links made through personal relationships including kinship, friendship and community ties and relationships". In a similar vein, Massey et al. (1987, p. 396) assert that social networks are "sets of interpersonal ties that link migrants, former migrants, non-migrants in origin and destination areas through the bonds of kinship, friendship, and shared community origin". Furthermore, according to Bourdieu (1986, p.248), "relationships may exist not only in the practical state by providing material and symbolic exchanges, but they may also be socially instituted and guaranteed in the name of a family, a class, or a tribe or of a school, a party, etc.". Similarly, Portes and Sensenbrener (1993) define social capital as "those expectations for action within a collective that affect the economic goals and goal-seeking behaviour of its members, even if these expectations are not oriented toward economic sphere". On the other hand, Putnam (2007, p.137) focuses on the integrative functions of the social capital which involve "social networks and the associated norms of reciprocity and trustworthiness", which allow cooperation and coordination free from conflicts of interest.

According to Putman, social capital is an affirmative concept in the sense that the level of social capital involved in the networks or broader social structures is essential in determining "the quality and quantity of a society's social interactions" (World Bank, 2000). Thus, Putnam's acknowledgement of the concept is nothing more than a diagnosis of the problems of an establishment that requires glue or cement feature for their solution. The lack of social capital results in problems which are free of interests and class.

In addition, in Bourdieu's conceptualisation, differences in the control of capital may explain why some entrepreneurs could easily set up their shops while it took so much time for other co-ethnics. Similarly, it could explain why some ethnic entrepreneurs had to activate different degrees of cultural and social capital to set up their shops while some others did not need to activate social networks to set up their businesses.

In this regard, Putnam's distinction between social capital based on bonding capital and bridging capital is worthwhile for explaining the low validation of KT business owners' networks in broad society. According to Putnam (1993), bonding social capital occurs among homogeneous populations, within a community. The relationships and trust formed within the close proximity of KT shops and neighbourhoods which could be defined as bonding capital may not result in mobilisation for voicing demands to resolve a neighbourhood problem. Strong bonding capital does not automatically lead to bridging capital. Bonding capital, however, is a preceding requirement for the development of bridging social capital (Ryan et al, 2008). Bridging social capital refers to cross-cutting ties where members of one group connect with members of another group to pursue support or access information (Larsen et al, 2004). As Larsen further argues, "examples of bridging social capital include calling a city department to voice a complaint about public services or forming a neighbourhood group to conduct a protest" (Larsen et al, 2004, p.66).

Collective resource mobilisation not only has the ability to answer the why and how questions of entrepreneurship, but is also capable of explaining the interplay between agency and structure. I stress the question of why members of KT communities set up businesses by the components of collective resource mobilisation theory, particularly by the empirical chapters on interests and opportunities. I focus on the question of how KT communities' members become entrepreneurs by the third component of the collective resource mobilisation theory, namely mobilisation of networks, which also brings the micro, meso, and macro levels together in respect of strategies for founding and operating businesses.

In the following sections, I discuss the three components of collective action. The proposed theory of collective action has three components: interests, mobilisation of networks and opportunity structure. In the following section, I discuss the first component, namely interests, which determines the reason for setting- up businesses.

Interests

Interests could be defined as the cause of human behaviour, including social behaviour. Interests supply the impulse that drives social behaviour, which could take various forms, such as competition, collaboration, subordination, opposition and so on (Swedberg, 2005). According to Tilly (1977, pp.1-10), interests are the possible gains and losses of the population in question resulting from interaction with other groups. Diverse forms of interest arise from various interactions. As Georg Simmel (1971, p.23), one of the founders of the discipline of sociology states, "interaction always arises on the basis of certain drives or for the sake of certain purposes". It is possible to speak of an interest group or group interest when many people come together and proceed jointly along a path towards a common end (Swedberg, 2005). According to Simmel, interests drive human behaviour and his principal formulation in "The Problem of Sociology" is:

> *Sociation is the form (realized in innumerably different ways) in which individuals grow together into a unity and within which their interests are realised. And, it is on the basis of their interests – sensuous or ideal, momentary or lasting, conscious or unconscious, causal or teleological – that individuals form such unities.*

In a similar vein, according to Tilly (1977), shared interests facilitate unities. Interests promote "common identity and unifying structure among the individuals in the population" (p.3-4). Interests are a precondition for the mobilisation of networks for common ends. One of the crucial points regarding interests is the ways in which members of an ethnic community conceive and formulate them (Tilly, 1978, p.56). The theory of collective action argues that, in the first instance, a sense of common interests or interest alignment in setting-up businesses is required among co-ethnics. It deals with the framing of interest in a particular space and time. In this regard, it is necessary to elaborate on *interest alignment* processes empirically. The term interest alignment is interpreted and derived from Snow et al.'s (1986) *frame alignment*. According to Snow et al. (1986, p.464), "by *frame alignment,* we refer to the linkage of individual and SMO interpretive orientations, such that some set of individual interests, values and beliefs and SMO activities, goals, and ideology are congruent and complementary". The term frame alignment could be considered to be an expansion of Tilly's model as I mentioned earlier in the introduction. It denotes the socially constructed and renegotiated nature of interests in movement participation. More particularly, it focuses on the "grievance interpretation ... processual and dynamic nature of participation, and overgeneralization of participation-related processes ..." (Snow et al., 2008, p.261).

Influenced by social movements theory (Snow et al., 2008, p.464), interest alignment in ethnic entrepreneurship refers to the link between ethnic group and entrepreneurial orientations, such that ethnic group "interests, values and beliefs" and entrepreneurial orientations, "goals and ideology are congruent and complementary".

For instance, Light (1972) mentions that explanations for the low level of self-employment of Black African British and Caribbean communities in the

United States tend to ignore the historical dimension, particularly colonial legacy. The values associated with certain jobs in the service industry prevent Black African and Caribbean communities to step into self-employment in core industrial countries. While those communities "have low rates of business ownership, they contribute importantly to the life of those societies in which they live by, among other things, creating new forms of culture that fuel the culture industry" (Pécoud, 2004, p.21)

In other words, in the case of Black African and Caribbean communities in the United States, interests, values and beliefs as well as entrepreneurial orientations, goals, and ideology do not overlap with small business ownership serving mainstream society. Thus, the ethnic groups' interpretation of prospects for a livelihood in small business ownership is dependent on how they "locate, perceive, identify, and label occurrences within their life space and the world at large" (Snow et al., 2008, p.464).

The interest alignment process in small business ownership entails increasing communication within the ethnic group via interpersonal networks, ethnic newspapers, telephone and mail. The process involves defining social reality and occurrences within their life space, and feasible alternatives for a livelihood. Consequently, interest alignment not only shapes social reality, but also provides an action strategy for possible means of survival.

Framing could be considered as an expansion of Tilly's model, which corresponds to the social constructivist view of the micro-mobilisation of tasks and processes in formulating "shared meanings and definitions that people bring to their situation" (McAdam et al., 2008, p.281). Without the framing process, acting collectively would be impossible as it mediates between networks mobilised for common ends and opportunity structures. The framing process could be viewed as the generation and diffusion of interests directed towards mobilising and/or counter-mobilising ideas and meanings, which is enabled or constrained by the cultural and social context (Benford and Snow, 2000). The term 'framing' provides an opportunity to examine the ways in which an ethnic identity is constructed and how experiences and grievances are interpreted in their social context. The concept of frame as utilised by various disciplines in social science is derived from the work of Goffman (1974). For Goffman, frames refer to "schemata of interpretation" which focus on people's cognition of situations and occurrences. The process of interpretation of grievances, events and experiences is a necessary condition for interest alignment within the community. Frames provide interpretations of events, occurrences and experiences with respect to people's lives. They answer the question, "what is going on here?" (p.46). Frames denote how a particular event is perceived and contextualised and how meanings related to them are produced.

According to social movements scholars Benford and Snow (2000, p.614),

> *Framing denotes an active, processual phenomenon that implies agency and contention at the level of reality construction. It is active in the sense that something is being done, and processual in the sense of a dynamic, evolving process. It entails agency in the sense that what is evolving...*

KT communities in London act collectively to redress their economic situation and achieve social change. In order to act collectively, people at least have to both aggregate around certain interests in their lives and feel optimistic that acting collectively could actually improve their situation (McAdam et al., 1996, p.5):

> *At a minimum people need to feel both aggrieved about some aspect of their lives and optimistic that, acting collectively, they can redress the problem. Lacking either one or both of these perceptions, it is highly unlikely that people will mobilize even when afforded the opportunity to do so.*

In order to act collectively, at the minimum, people have to both aggregate around certain interests in their lives and feeling optimistic about acting collectively could actually redress their situation. There has to be a perception that the risk and uncertainty associated with the businesses are manageable and the benefits are far greater than the costs. In other words, the absence of this cognitive process which brings and binds people together around certain interests would make the mobilisation process impossible. This is based upon the optimistic conviction that unemployment could be prevented and their situation could be redressed by this.

There are several sources which have shown that there is a greater proclivity for ethnic minority groups to be self-employed rather than be employed as waged or salaried workers (Auster & Aldrich, 1984; Bates, 1989; Light & Bonacich, 1988; Sanders and Nee, 1996). In addition, the percentage of immigrants in self-employment is higher than that for natives.

First, it has been argued that due to discrimination in the labour market, immigrants are more likely to enter self-employment as a means to overcome economic survival barriers in the labour market (Bates, 1997; Light, 1972). A second argument claims that immigrants' prior employment in the home country in self-employment provides a form of cultural capital, skills, which motivate the transition into self-employment (Yuengert, 1995). A third theory is that the concentration of the ethnic minority population in ethnic enclaves results in demand for ethnic products. Co-ethnic business owners are in a better position due to their cultural capital to exploit the desire for ethnic products (Aldrich et al., 1985; Light, 1972; Light and Rosenstein, 1995). A fourth argument is related to immigrants' sojourning attitudes as discussed in the previous chapter. Such a sojourning mentality motivates entry into self-employment (Portes and Sensebrenner, 1993; Sowell, 1995).

However, there is a lack of emphasis on macro structures such as changes in the global political economy, i.e. they do not pay sufficient attention to the "important links between the processes of *globalisation* and racialisation and the opportunity structures for immigrants" (Collins, 2003, p.13).

Furthermore, the motivating interests for self-employment may be different for the second generation (Masurel et al., 2003). The second generation refers to "persons who were born in the host country or immigrant to the host country at an age younger than six" (Baycan et al., 2005, p.13). While the interest formation for the first generation of migrants exhibits more push factors, that for the second generation of migrants involves more pull factors (ibid). The interests in entrepreneurship for the first generation originate from unemployment, discrimination and obstacles to the recognition of qualifications such as validating their diplomas. However, the second generation might choose self-employment due to better earnings, flexible working hours and autonomy. That is to say, as Baycan et al. (ibid) further argue, "while first-generation immigrants could be called more frequently 'forced entrepreneurs', second-generation immigrants may act more frequently as 'voluntary entrepreneurs'". In addition, second and third generations of migrants are expected to be less likely to become self-employed as they possess skills such as language fluency and host-nation educational credentials, which may lead to paid employment (Dhaliwal and Kangis, 2006).

However, less attention has been paid to the crucial role of the gender dimension in ethnic self-employment (Baycan et al., 2006; Inal and Yasin, 2010). This is explained by the fact that when researchers conducted their work, they mainly focused on the status of women as either unpaid or underpaid family members in ethnic businesses. Women's engagement in ethnic minority businesses is often viewed as an extension of domestic labour in the household as a way of helping the family (OECD, 2010). Women's unpaid labour is consumed within the family businesses. As Baycan and Nijkamp (ibid) further argue, there is a belief, on one hand, that the number of women labour migrants is relatively small, and on the other hand, as with Turkish labour migration (Sonmez & Mcdonald, 2008) to Western Europe, it is primarily men aged between 20 and 35 without families who left Turkey in the first place. It is family unification that led to the increase in the Turkish women's population in Western Europe (ibid; Unat, 1995). It is possible to state that after the Second World War, until the oil crises in the mid-1970s, women followed their husbands in migration, and when they worked, they found employment "alongside their husbands, filling the same labour market functions" (Kossoudji and Ranney, 1984 as cited in OECD, 2010). However, the lack of attention to the gender dynamics of self-employment has changed in the last decade. The increase in the number of women ethnic entrepreneurs has been reflected in the research conducted on ethnic women business owners (Baycan-Levent et al. 2003).

In this regard, given the fact that a large proportion of the KT communities are self-employed, it is empirically necessary to elaborate on the reasons for being self-employed. That is to say, the question as to why the KT communities to a large extent moved into self-employment needs to be elaborated empirically by focusing on historical conditions and agency of the entrepreneurs, and more particularly the common-sense tendency to set up a shop as a solution to unemployment during the 1990s. The investigation focuses on the framing processes to find a solution to unemployment in the KT communities. The common-sense tendency is for a framing process generated by the KT communities is a framing process I refer to as the *interest alignment* process. As mentioned before, interest alignment indicates the linkage of ethnic group and entrepreneurial orientations in such a way that ethnic group interests, values and beliefs and entrepreneurial orientations, goals and ideology are congruent and complementary. Interest alignment is a necessary condition for the micro-mobilisation of resources for entrepreneurship. Micro-mobilisation indicates simply the various interactive and communicative processes that shape interest alignment and is a process "referring to largely verbal efforts to restore or assure meaningful interaction" (Snow et al., 2008, p.464) within any ethnic community to accomplish common ends. It focuses on the organisational and collective processes to produce certain understandings of social reality. Interest alignment is constituted primarily by information diffusion through interpersonal or intergroup networks, the notice boards of ethnic organisations, the ethnic newspapers, the telephone and direct mail.

Moreover, this actually corresponds to the ideas of the instrumentalist view of ethnic identity formation. It points out the socially constructed nature of ethnic ties within which their interests are realised. In contrast to the culturalist and primordialist conceptualisations of ethnicity, Tilly's collective resource mobilisation theory does not treat ethnic group identity as a pre-existing fact. It distinguishes itself from essentialist views. As Craig Calhoun (1997, p.18) asserts;

Essentialism refers to a reduction of the diversity in a population to some single criterion held to constitute its defining "essence" and most crucial character. This is often coupled with the claim that the essence is unavoidable or given by nature. It is common to assume that these cultural categories address really existing and discretely identifiable collections of people.

In sharp contrast to the essentialist ideas of culturalism and primordialism, the theory of collective resource mobilisation is inspired by the instrumentalist critique of primordialism and culturalism. Instrumentalists hold the view that the constitution of ethnic identity is a process open to reformulation. Instrumentalists disagree with the assumptions of primordialists, who take the view that diversity in a population could be reduced to a single defining cultural essence. On the other hand, as Vermeersch (2011, p.6) argues, "instrumentalism has directed attention toward ethnicity as a calculation of social, economic, and political profits…" The calculation is carried out through cognitive processes for people sharing a distinct position in the workplace, experiencing the same kind of discrimination, suffering from the same kind of problems in daily life (Vermeersch, 2011). Yet, as Sun- Ki Chai (1996, p.281) asserts, "some sort of ascriptive commonality is after all necessary for a group to be ethnic in any meaningful sense, but the salience and level of inclusiveness of different ascriptive characteristics in determining ethnic boundaries varies according to differences in circumstance". In a similar vein, Daniel Bell (1975, p.171) states that, "ethnicity … is best understood not as a primordial phenomenon in which deeply held identities have to re-emerge, but as a strategic choice by individuals who, in other circumstances, would choose other group memberships as a means of gaining some power and privilege".

There are several questions that need to be answered in explaining this tendency. Under what conditions will an ethnic community come to acquire a sense of common interests, mobilise networks and resources towards small business ownership? To what extent do they believe ethnic minority groups' interests to be identical to each other? A valid theory of collective resource mobilisation in ethnic entrepreneurship must explain why some ethnic minority communities do not engage with entrepreneurship. Part of the problem lies in the networks, but part of it clearly lies in the fact that ethnic groups have diverse interests and/or do not have a sense of common interest.

In this book, the term, frame *alignment*, will be used to understand the ways in which KT communities produce a certain interpretation of reality. I argue that frame alignment is a cognitive process for discussing the remedies for overcoming the difficulties faced by the ethnic community. More particularly, unemployment as a problematic condition or a feature of ethnic minority life is no longer seen as a misfortune and immutable. Therefore, the process of interest alignment is concerned with the rational calculation that prospective entrepreneurs weigh the anticipated costs of action or inaction *vis-à-vis* the benefits. The interest in setting-up a shop should not . be treated mechanistically and non-processual. The relative deprivation and unemployment faced by a community does not automatically result in motivation for setting-up businesses. First, it is necessary to look empirically at the actual micro-mobilisation structures facilitating processes of *interest alignment* through which certain patterns of action towards self-employment are demarcated as more or less risky, feasible, and morally essential.

Thus, this book defends the idea that the concept of interest alignment offers a useful contribution to the study of ethnic entrepreneurship. With regard to interests for starting-up businesses, it can be said that they are created through framing. Interests do not exist a priori. Rather, they are defined and constituted through framing, namely via processes in *interest alignment*.

The *interest alignment* process in small business ownership entails increasing communication within the ethnic group via interpersonal networks, ethnic newspapers, telephone, and online. The process involves defining social reality, and occurrences within their life space, and feasible alternatives for a livelihood. Consequently, *interest alignment* not only shapes social reality, but also provides an action strategy for possible means of survival.

In Marxian terms, the usage of "class for itself" involves proletarians whose consciousness of a common fate led to solidarity bonds and collective action. The solidarity bonds are indeed workers' social capital (Portes, 1988). Likewise, the actual experiences of KT communities reflect the intersection of class and ethnicity. The KT communities have experienced a common fate as people were thrown into a similar situation, which enabled them to develop a collective consciousness of their social reality. In turn, this also led to solidarity bonds and the mobilisation of resources for survival in small business ownership.

Accordingly, the KT communities have developed common scripts in response to the features of the social reality they confront. Commonalities in entrepreneurial orientations are responses to the social reality they are trying to change, i.e. unemployment. They have common interests as they share a common situation. Resources tend to be collectively mobilised when many individuals' interests overlap.

As Abadan-Unat (1995, p. 279) states in her analysis of Turkish Migration to Europe, since the late 1950s Turkish migration to, and settlement in countries has occurred in six major phases. Each phase represents a distinct interest for migration and occupational opportunities. The phases are listed as follows:

- between 1956-61: recruitment through intermediaries;
- between 1961-72: migration on the basis of bilateral agreements;
- between 1972-75: recession and the employment of foreign workers and the legitimation of illegal migrants;
- between 1975-78: family reunification
- between 1978-85: introduction of visas, the increase in asylum requests

- 1986 onwards spread of ethnic business.

While the above analysis marks the changing interests in migration, it also provides an account of changing opportunities in employment. The labour force invited to Britain to re-build the country after the Second World War is no longer welcomed by the state. The opportunities for a livelihood have shifted away from waged labour and towards self-employment.

Accordingly, tighter migration controls are clearly promoted by the current coalition government in the UK. The Conservative-Liberal coalition in the UK has pledged to cut net migration to tens of thousands by 2015. As the home secretary Theresa May expressed in the Guardian Weekly: "We will have to take action across all routes to entry – work visas, student visas, family visas – and break the link between temporary routes and permanent settlement" (December 2010, p.13). The tightening up migration into the advanced capitalist economies is a common trend which is also a reflection of the changes in global political economy.

A change in the migration policy is a reflection of the changing opportunities in employment. Migrants are no longer invited to work in manufacturing jobs. In the case of the KT communities in the UK, individual members of the community who would have previously found employment in textile industry were suddenly unemployed in the mid-1990s. Unemployment has been experienced within the whole community. During this period, community members exchanged information and discussed feasible alternatives for means of survival.

Given the fact that companies have moved manufacturing jobs to lower wage zones and have imposed greater selectivity and specificity on the movement of labour across their borders, the new spatial mobility of labour towards higher wage zones takes place through networks of minority businesses. In contrast to previous decades, people from less-developed countries are not invited to the UK to fill labour shortages, other than in areas of specific, usually, high-level skills. Arguably, economic restructuring is the driving force behind the KT people's entrepreneurialism.

Consistently, the formation of networks of minority businesses in advanced capitalist economies is a strategy of people from third w regions for obtaining higher wages and relatively better living conditions. Because of the changes in the global political economy, being a wage-labourer is no longer of interest for securing better living conditions in the advanced economies. Rather, rational strategic endeavours by ethnic minority people to construct shared contexts for the advanced economies and themselves are that which legitimate and motivate entrepreneurship. Thus, interests focus on the group sense of empowerment prior to involvement. At a minimum, a group needs to define their grievances and diagnostic frame, and present a feasible solution, the prognostic frame. The diagnostic and prognostic framing of interests requires micro-mobilisation. As mentioned before, micro-mobilisation connotes the various interactive and communicative processes that shape interest alignment.

The following section discusses the second component of collective action, namely mobilisation of networks, which is a function of interests.

Mobilisation of networks

Mobilisation of networks involves the "process by which a group acquires collective control over the resources needed for" (Tilly, 1978, p.3-26) entrepreneurial action facilitated by networks, co-ethnics and kinship. As Tilly (ibid) states, the word *mobilisation* "...identifies the process by which a group goes from being a passive collection of individuals to an active participant in public life". It entails the collective control over capitals that, this book contends, facilitates ethnic business ownership and the strategic activation of forms of capital that ethnic business owners commonly confront. More specifically, what I mean by the collective control over resources is the consumption of strategic information promoting ethnic businesses, economic capital, reliable and cheap labour, reconstruction of cultural practices, and protection of business premises by the ethnic communities. It denotes the utilisation of strategically formed ethnic attachments to invoke economic interests. As I discussed in the previous section, it can acknowledge the collective determination of interests for survival.

According to Tilly's (1977, p. 3-45) mobilisation model, the broad general "factors within a population affecting its degree of mobilisation are the extent of its shared interest in interactions with other populations and the extent to which it forms a distinct category and a dense network", i.e. its interest and its organization. As Tilly (ibid) further argues, the external conditions determine the degree of a population's power to act on its own interests. They could either be enabling or constraining to act on their own interests. The opportunity structure determines the incentives and obstacles affecting the group's ability to act in its own interests. However, I am going to discuss this in the next section.

Ethnic strategies arise from the interaction of processes in interest alignment and opportunity structures, as entrepreneurs mobilise resources to meet market conditions, adapting to, or creating solutions to problems.

Entrepreneurs need to mobilise scarce and therefore valued resources, so that activating strong ties to kin and co-ethnics is usually important for setting up and maintaining ethnic minority firms.

Family, kin, close co-ethnic networks and labour become extremely important for setting–up and running businesses. Information about the host society (accurate or misleading) portrayed by the migrant activates other home town co-ethnics to take their chances abroad. Information is transmitted through communication or personal interaction between migrants and their home communities. As Moch (1992, p.17) states, "migration networks function as "personal information fields", which means that the newcomers always possess incomplete information about the options open to them". Social capital is utilised to derive cultural capital. Ethnic business is labour intensive; availability of family or community members as employees at low rates is an essential advantage for many entrepreneurs (Mars and Ward, 1984, p.18). Community networks, which may offer advice and information for potential entrepreneurs are collective resources for minority businesses. Family, kin and co-ethnic labour is generally unpaid, and they work long hours in the service of their employers without any unionisation. Self-exploitation is a strategy that small immigrant store owners can successfully pursue. Networks can efficiently activate the labour supply since employees can recruit someone who is searching for a job. As Waldinger (1997, p.8) mentions, "reliance on referrals capitalises on an already existing set of family and friendship connections". Networks that provide a low-wage, flexible labour force is crucial in this respect. It provides a competitive advantage over native firms. As he further argues, "the same connections that span immigrant communities constitute a source of "social capital", providing social structures that facilitate action, in this case the search for jobs and the acquisition of skills and other resources needed to move up the economic ladder" (Waldinger, 1997, p.2).

In terms of acquiring training and skill, apprenticeship in another co-ethnic's business is helpful. Working for a small ethnic firm allows immigrants to learn nearly all aspects of business management, a goal that entry-level workers in large native-owned firms can rarely attain. Thus co-ethnic employee participation in management is possible not only because of ethnic trust, but also because of the small firm size.

Success stories "provide a basis for almost unquestioned support within the community for the ideology of small business" (Collins et al., 1995, p.7). Successful entrepreneurs serve as potential role models, reinforcing the drive for mobility through self-employment. Actually, success stories initially provide the motivation for migration for potential entrepreneurs. Migrants to the UK present their experiences and opportunities to their co-ethnics in mainland Turkey and in the country of migration. Success stories of migrant entrepreneurs represent the path towards a better life in the country of migration. The stories and the riches of successful entrepreneurs become a magnet for their co-ethnics in their country of origin and migration. Migration with the aim of setting up businesses constitutes a viable solution to their problems in Turkey. It is the idea of following the same path as their successful co-ethnics that motivates new start-ups. Thus, information provided by co-ethnic business owners is essential for new openings.

As Waldinger (1996) mentions that "as from the standpoint of ethnic workers, the opportunity to acquire managerial skills through a stint of employment in ethnic immigrant firms both compensates for low pay and provides a motivation to learn a variety of different jobs". Small businesses provide an opportunity for learning all aspects of the business for future entrepreneurs. For employers who hire co-ethnics, the short term consideration is lower-priced labour. Immigrants from low income countries will accept these low-wage jobs; unemployed native workers will not (Light, 2004) and as Waldinger (1985) states, "over the long term, the immigrant owner can act on the assumption that the newcomer will stay long enough to learn the relevant business skills".

In terms of capital, distant relatives can be an important source. For instance, during the early settlement phase of the Turkish community in Berlin, a distant friend or relative was often brought in as a business partner. Such partnership is rare today: capital is now usually provided and guaranteed through a network of close relations (Ülker, 2004).

In terms of labour, ethnic entrepreneurs rely heavily upon family and co-ethnics "for the cheap, loyal labour essential for their survival and success" (Light & Gold, 2000, p.141). In immigrant firms, "ethnicity provides a common ground on which the rules of the workplace are negotiated" (Waldinger et al., 1990, p.38). Furthermore, "authority can be secured on the basis of personal loyalties and ethnic allegiance" (ibid), also from referrals, rather than on the basis of harsh discipline, forcefulness and direct-control techniques (Waldinger, 1986). In other words, the dark side of the social capital has a disciplinary function, which situates immigrant workers in an exploitable and vulnerable position as well.

According to Boissevain and his colleagues (1990, 142) "family labour is largely unpaid, and relatives and co-ethnics, while not always paid excessively low wages, are prepared to work longer hours, and at times that outsiders find unacceptable". Whereas indigenous employers are confronted by a shortage of indigenous workers, immigrant employers usually have no such problems. They recruit an attached labour force by mobilising "direct connections to the ethnic community from which they emigrated" (Waldinger et al., 1990, p.38). Unpaid family members are one of the options for acquiring labour force.

In terms of competition, intensive internal competition usually occurs when large numbers of immigrants open similar types of businesses. Immigrants are often followed into the same ethnic niche by others with similar skills and plans for mobility. According to Waldinger et al. (1990), the strategies for coping with competition for minority entrepreneurs are as follows: (1) self-exploitation: work longer hours, pay oneself lower salary, (2) horizontal or vertical expansion: move forward and/or backward in the chain of production, and/or open more shops of the same type, (3) create/join formal trading associations; and finally, (4) use of marriage to join formerly competing families

In terms of provision of information and advice, which are essential for entrepreneurs, public gathering places like mosques, cultural festivals, shops, home town associations and tools related media such as newspapers and the internet are sources. Before setting-up their businesses, would-be business owners need information about markets, the ethnic composition of the area and laws and regulations regarding small business ownership. Once established, they need information about supplies, prices, warnings of market fluctuations, successful products, industrial trends and so forth. Those sources are also essential for newcomers. Newcomers turn to settlers for help in finding jobs and may first "seek employment in an immigrant firm where they can work in a familiar environment with others who know their language". Newcomers' dependence on their bosses/patrons makes them likely to accept conditions that may fall below standard; it is also the case that owners will be more likely to place trust in workers who depend on them.

The resources that could be mobilized as an action strategy of entrepreneurship are available to individual entrepreneurs on the basis of the degree of acquired forms of capital. In other words, the volume and the quality of acquired capital determine the discrepancies in ethnic minority business ownership. Individual entrepreneurs independently adopt different strategies due to different levels of capital owned by would-be business owners. The mobilisation of resources via networks could take place through the re-enactment of rural tradition. Rural cultural practices based on "collective work" are based on voluntary tacit consent for village-scale collaboration, mutual aid and solidarity. They concern reciprocity in the free undertaking of tasks. Such cultural practices transposed to the urban settings are positive factors in the mobilisation of resources directed towards business ownership.

The level of resources controlled by the community is a crucial factor affecting new business start-ups and operation. Resources such as financial capital, access to networks, cultural capital for setting up and maintaining business and information enable ethnic communities to make strategic decisions for the purpose of entrepreneurial action.

Opportunity

According to Tilly (1977), interests, mobilisation and organisation of a group constitute one side of the mobilisation model. It mainly deals with the internal structure of the group. This side of the model is incomplete as it only deals with the capacity to act. The other side of the model focuses on the immediate incentives or opportunity to act (ibid). As Tilly (1978, p.3-5) further argues, "opportunity describes the relationship between population's interests and the current state of the world around it". Opportunity involves the external factors which enable or constrain KT business start-ups and maintenance. It takes into account external actors to the group and their interplay with the internal processes of the group.

Like the structuralist viewpoint I discussed earlier, the opportunity component of the mobilisation model focuses on external factors such as the legal, institutional settings, labour market policies, changes in the global political economy and the existence of potential markets. These factors are crucial in determining the opportunities and constraints for minority business participation in the host society (Rath, 2000). For instance, in order to maintain and set-up ethnic businesses, there should be a potential market for the services provided by the ethnic businesses (Waldinger et. al., 1990). In other words, the opportunity side of the mobilisation model takes into account the structure of the economy, government policies, racial discrimination, violence and harassment as the determinants of minority entrepreneurship.

In addition, I assert that there are several issues associated with opportunity structures which might enable or constrain business start-ups and maintenance: 1) surviving business competition; 2) bridging networks to mainstream strategic elites and members of civil society organisations so that ethnic business owners can voice their demands to acquire favourable working conditions; 3) protecting themselves from political attacks; 4) political – institutional setting, i.e. regulatory structures which might enable or constrain business start-ups and operating.

The structural processes influence the opportunities for a livelihood in profound ways. They change the opportunity structures for ethnic groups. Forms of inclusion and exclusion have been defined and redefined by the changes in structures (Castells 1989; Fainstein et al., 1992; Sassen, 1991). This social division in the urban fabric prevents socio-economic development and weakens the quality of urban life. Those who lack educational competence and are excluded from information economy in urban areas, yet remain living with close proximity to the upper classes, constitute a serious political and social issue (Rath, 2006). In these circumstances, supporting ethnic minority businesses and the new opportunities it facilitates in various sectors may become government policy as discussed in previous sections.

As Rath (2006, p.2) asserts,

Unqualified people find it harder to benefit from the knowledge economy. They are faced with relatively high levels of unemployment, even in times of economic development, and low levels of upward occupational mobility. This is particularly the case for immigrants from the Third World countries. If they are active in the labour market, they tend to populate sectors with a high demand for manual or unskilled workers and with low entry barriers, such as cleaning or catering (Engelen 2001; Rath 2002b). This indicates that there is a growing, and ethnically specific, divide between the highly educated, well paid knowledge workers in Western societies and the workers concentrated in the lower tiers of the labour market or even more seriously marginalised. These developments are also gender specific, as the changing opportunity structure produces different outcomes for men and women.

Throughout Western Europe, unemployment rates for foreign residents had reached alarming proportions by the mid-1980s due to the restructuring of the economy. Though many ethnic groups have faced structural unemployment, governments are far more reluctant than in the past to undertake either macro-economic or training and employment policies to tackle this situation. In this context, a business development policy is an attractive option for governments trying to encourage job creation in ethnic and minority communities. For example, as Blanchflower and Oswald (1991) state that, research on the "labour market processes in the 1980's for the UK has shown that rising self-employment corresponded to phases of increasing unemployment". Furthermore, according to Strüder (2003, p.4), "in recent years, fostering self-employment has become one of the top priorities for economic policy throughout the world, particularly in the industrialised western countries". The enterprise culture as envisaged by Thatcher during the 1980's is seen as a remedy to the structural economic crisis (Scase, 2000; Rainnie, 1991). Consequently, it is possible to state that, the opportunity component of the mobilisation model focuses on factors external to ethnic communities that push them into self-employment (Volery, 2007).

Conclusion

The various theories utilised in previous studies on ethnic entrepreneurship either assume an agency centred approach (e.g. Altinay, 2008; Altinay & Altinay, 2006; Basu & Altinay, 2002; Basu, 1998; McEvoy & Hafeez, 2009; Srinivasan, 1995; Werbner, 1984, 1990), or a structure centred approach (Bonacich, 1973). While interaction (Waldinger et al.,1990) and mixed embeddedness (Kloosterman & Rath, 2001) theories attempt to bring agency and structure together, these theories pay insufficient attention to the macro structural factors, such as globalisation, affecting opportunities for migrant employability (Collins, 2000). Thus, the interaction and mixed embeddedness approaches are unable to grasp the processes of socio-economic restructuring, which has its origins in global economic shifts. The possibility for entrepreneurial praxis is thus clearly historically conditioned. Consequently, I propose a more composite new approach which not only utilises agency and structural approaches, but also the much neglected area of maintenance activities of ethnic entrepreneurship.

It is not possible to apply the analytical model 'middleman minorities', which focuses on the buffer role of ethnic business owners between producers and masses (Bonacich and Modell (1980) to the KT community members. The reason for this is that they do not depend on mainly non-ethnic suppliers and they do not solely serve non-ethnic customers either.

The main objection that could be raised against enclave economy in this study is its dependence on locational clustering; the importance and role of social networks and transnational ties in generating resources for minority entrepreneurship do not fit this model. For instance, cultural enterprises that provide artefacts related to cultural industry rely on daily contacts with the home country in order to exploit the immigrant's desire to acquire and consume cultural goods such as compact discs, concerts, books, local cuisine, festivals, videos and the latest musical hits.Likewise, the sojourner mentality is rejected as an explanation of migrant working life attitude in the host society on the basis of structural conditions, which are characterised by over competition and marginal returns. In a competitive context with marginal returns for consumption, working long hours becomes a necessity.

In a manner similar to the sojourner mentality, cultural theories focus on the values and attributes of a specific ethnic community to measure the success and failure of entrepreneurship. This view maintains that minorities bring home country cultural values to the host country. It ignores the fact that individuals from an immigrant background are capable of shifting their cultural heritages and ethnic identities. Sojourner mentality neglects the fluidity of ethnic identities and cultural practices. It ignores the existence of different cultural groups and heterogeneity within the migrants' home country.

One alternative theory to the culturalist approach, structuralism stresses that individuals from ethnic groups act within the context of the changing political, cultural, social and economic structures. It focuses on the structural opportunities and constraints present for immigrants, which are the focus of an explanation for ethnic entrepreneurship. According to the structuralist viewpoint, the legal and institutional settings, labour market policies and the existence of a potential market are crucial factors in determining the opportunities and constraints for minority business participation in the host society.

Interactionism as an attempt to bring agency and structure does not focus on the regulatory context of the institutional setting and the governmental policies that enable or constrain certain business set-ups. Criticism of the interactionist model has been raised in more recent contributions by continental European researchers, for example with reference to the theory of mixed-embeddedness. Their main criticism of the interactionist model discussed above was that it mainly focuses on the supply side of entrepreneurship while ignoring the context in which entrepreneurialism has been regulated and differentiated. Hence, interactionist theory has paid no attention to the array of regulatory contexts – institutional settings, governmental policies, and laws - that constrains and facilitates certain economic activities.

The theory of the mixed embeddedness approach to immigrant entrepreneurship is more nuanced in a way that recognises the regulatory structures and market dynamics. The advantage of this multi-level mixed embeddedness approach lies in its focus on the interplay between ethnic social networks and political and economic structures. However, mixed embeddedness ignores macro-structural factors. The embeddedness of ethnic business owners or would-be entrepreneurs is restricted in national settings. This in fact leads to insufficient attention being paid to changing economic structures in the global political economy. Moreover, the mixed embeddedness model fails to explore the agency dimension empirically since economic actions of ethnic entrepreneurs are viewed as responses to larger structures beyond their influence without taking into account the entrepreneur's own sense of these structures, meanings, and definitions that people bring to their situation (Tatli et al., 2014, p.59).

The analytical tools and theories discussed above let us grasp some facets of minority entrepreneurship. They do not explain one of the research questions of this book, more specifically, why members of ethnic communities in one part of the world become business owners. In order to answer the question, I propose a new approach called collective resource mobilisation, which has three components: interests, mobilisation of networks and opportunity structure. The collective resource mobilisation approach will not only bring together local, national and global levels of analysis, but it will also explain why and how minorities become entrepreneurs and which decisions are based on an entrepreneurial context.

Collective resource mobilisation theory argues that interests and mobilisation of networks of a group constitute one side of the mobilisation model. It mainly deals with the internal structure of the group. This side of the model is incomplete as it only deals with the capacity to act. The other side of the model focuses on the immediate incentives or opportunity to act. As Tilly (1978, p.3-5) argues, "opportunity describes the relationship between population's interests and the current state of the world around it".

The second component of collective resource mobilisation theory, namely mobilisation of networks involves the "process by which a group acquires collective control over the resources needed for" (Tilly, 1978, p.3-26) entrepreneurial action facilitated by networks. As Tilly (ibid) states, the word *mobilisation* "...identifies the process by which a group goes from being passive collection of individuals to an active participants in public life". It entails the collective control over social, cultural and economic capital that, this book contends, facilitates ethnic business ownership and the strategic activation of forms of capital that ethnic business owners commonly confront. More specifically, what I mean by the collective control over resources is the consumption of strategic information promoting ethnic businesses, economic capital, reliable and cheap labour, reconstruction of cultural practices, and protection of business premises by the ethnic communities. Thus, advantage of collective resource mobilisation is that, it enables us to understand various forms of collective action, for the realisation of setting up businesses, such as the acquisition of capital, information and skills, maintaining businesses, especially protecting business premises, collective bargaining with companies providing electricity and gas, voicing demands to government bodies, the employment of assemblies for dispute resolution, and campaigning against the development of chain stores. In other words, the realisation of interests also brings the social structure into the analysis of ethnic minority businesses.

The third and final component of the collective resource mobilisation is opportunity. As Tilly (1978, p.3-5) argues, "opportunity describes the relationship between population's interests and the current state of the world around it". Opportunity involves the external factors which enable or constrain KT business start-ups and maintenance. It takes into account external actors to the group.

The theory of collective resource mobilisation argues that, in the first instance, a sense of common interests or interest alignment in setting-up businesses is required among co-ethnics. It deals with the framing of interests in a particular space and time. It enables a researcher to understand the question of what makes members of Turkish and Kurdish communities in London become small business owners. In so doing, it enables the discussion on globalisation as a contributing factor to the path for ethnic minority self-employment to be incorporated.

Chapter Three:

Cypriot, Turkish, and Kurdish Entrepreneurship in the UK

In this chapter, my main aim is to focus on the dynamics of entrepreneurship in Turkish Cypriot, Turkish and Kurdish (CTK) communities in a historical context. The sources of data draw on the existing academic and policy literature and statistics. I will do this by discussing processes in the British economy in connection with the changes in the global political economy, and how it has affected the national context and CTK communities. The discussion emphasises the important links between the processes in the global political economy and the changing opportunity structures for immigrants and minorities. Thus, I aim to assess questions such as what is the context for CTK communities have moved into self-employment. I argue that the changes in the British political economy have also changed opportunity structures for CTK communities and activated entrepreneurship as a survival strategy. Structural changes adapted by governments in the political economy provide the context, and mobilisation of resources by CTK communities provides the means to cope with the current socio-economic conditions, namely, immigrants have established their own businesses as a response to the structural changes in the local economy. As processes of globalisation have already been called upon to explain the dynamics of activation of migration streams as well as the questions of where and why networks emerge for immigrants, this chapter will provide the contextual background for CTK entrepreneurship in the UK.

In the following section, I will first focus on the dynamics in the global political economy in which it has consequences for the national economies. When discussing the macro level changes in the global political economy, I am going to investigate how these changes in the global economy have called attention to the re-structuring of the British economic context. So, I will link the processes in the global political economy to the British context. Finally, within this British context, I will focus on the CTK communities and their agency in coping with the changing circumstances in employment.

Global political economy of migrant entrepreneurship: from industrial wage labour to self-employment

As I state in the last chapter, transnationalism does not explain the dynamics of the activation of migration streams and the interest underlying this collective action. The theoretical models I discuss above do not focus on the fundamental reason for migration that migrants look for opportunities in the host country. With the exception of the collective resource mobilisation theory; the theoretical models discussed above merely describe networks. However, there is a need to answer a much deeper question of where and why strong bonds of ethnicity emerge in one country or region, rather than another (Petras, 2006).

In this respect, how can we understand the current streams of migration and the interests at stake with immigrants? It is vital to look at the global re-structuring of the economy and processes in globalisation starting from the 1970s. The 1970s mark profound changes in the global economy through the introduction of new patterns of production, new labour control systems and technologies (Standing, 1999).

According to Waters (1996, p.2), "although the word 'global' is over 400 years old", the term 'globalisation' first appeared in Webster in 1961, and it is only in the first half of the 1980s that it entered into academic studies (Waters, 1996, p.2), but its hegemonic popularity in explaining current changes in the social, cultural and economic fabric goes back only to the 1990s (Waters, 1996, p.2; Fine, 2004, p.215). Rosenberg (2005, p.3) defines globalisation as the Zeitgeist of the 1990s. In other words, the term globalisation, within a very short time period, has come to be key to a new social theory which transcends the classic territorially bounded one in conceptualising the contemporary world (Giddens, 2002).

According to Rosenberg (2005, p.11), the most widely utilised definitions of globalisation are as "a geographical term denoting a process over time of spatial change – the process of becoming worldwide". As Rosenberg further argues, in these definitions, besides space and time, there is no other explanatory variable upon which the analysis can be based. In other words, there is a circular argumentation in those definitions through which the term globalisation is construed as an outcome of itself, i.e. a self-referring construct. For instance, Giddens (1990, p.64) defines globalisation "as the intensification of worldwide social relations which link distant localities in such a way that local happenings are shaped by events occurring many miles away and vice versa"; while according to Scholte (2000, p.85), globalisation entails de-territorialisation; Held and McGrew (2003, p.68) conceptualise globalisation as "a process (or set of processes)which embodies a transformation in the spatial organisation of the social relations and transaction -assessed in terms of their extensity, intensity, velocity and impact – generating transcontinental or interregional flows and networks of activity, interaction and the exercise of power"; and finally Waters (1996, p.3) presents globalisation as "a social process in which the constraints of geography on social and cultural arrangements recede, and in which people become increasingly aware they are receding". What is common in these argumentations is according to Rosenberg (2000, p.3):

> *In the logical structure of their argumentation, what presents itself as the explanandum – globalisation as the developing outcome of some historical process – is progressively transformed into the explanans: it is globalisation which now explains the changing character of the modern world – and even generates 'retrospective discoveries' about past epochs in which it must be presumed not to have existed.*

On the other hand, it is fruitful to call globalisation the neo-liberal economic logic of capital accumulation that is a product of particular historical developments. In this sense, we cannot understand the present fully without at least some understanding of the past. In other words, today's global economic map is an outcome of a long period of evolution of structures and relations.

Writing about "mass migration and economic restructuring", Anthony Fielding (1993, p.9-10) attempts to construct a three layered conceptual framework within which the relationships between economic restructuring and mass migration can be analysed and understood. According to him, the size and nature of mass migrations to, from and within Europe are determined by economic restructuring in which the economic processes could be classified under three headings: the first relates to the frequent and rapid changes in the stages of the business cycle; the second concerns the reorganisation of production; and the third includes the economic processes that serve to differentiate countries, regions and cities in fundamental ways. There is actually a link between these processes, i.e. the connection between the business cycle and restructuring. As he contends, "as the economy expands, indigenous labour becomes scarce, expensive and difficult to manage. Employers turn to foreign labour, which is recruited on short-term contracts. When the economy enters a recession, these contracts are not renewed, and the immigrant workers are forced to return home" (Fielding, 1993, p.10).While Fielding's comment applies to guest workers in Germany, this study shows that in Britain, when these contracts were not renewed, Turkish and Kurdish migrants were generally able to find employment in various sectors, such as the retailing and catering sectors. Developments in transportation and communication together with the free market economy and the ability of capital to move manufacturing jobs abroad have reconfigured the geography of the reserve army of labour. Consequently, there is no need to recruit foreign labour during times of expansion. The reconfigured geography of the reserve army of labour has enabled capital to invest significantly more freely wherever it wants according to profit maximizing strategies.

This explains the shift from national sectorial specialization to anew international division of labour. More specifically, national sectorial specialization refers to all the specialized tasks of production performed in one country for one product. However, the new international division of labour refers to a different type of production organization, namely the separated tasks of production distributed throughout the countries of the world (Fielding, 1993).

Rosa Luxemburg defines the nature of capitalism as the need of outside, non-capitalized strata to extract surplus value, which means that capitalism essentially needs to expand. In other words, in order to survive, "the capitalist system had to aim for continuous expansion" (Castles & Kosack, 1981, p.28). In Luxemburg's words,

> *The existence and development of capitalism requires an environment of non-capitalist forms of production, but not every one of these forms will serve its ends. Capitalism needs non-capitalist social strata as a market for its surplus value, as a source of supply for its means of production, and as a reservoir of labour power for its wage system. (Luxemburg [1913]2003, p.348-9)*

The use of the notion of 'outside' refers to goods, land, relations, labour power, knowledge and services that have not yet been enclosed, capitalised. Accordingly, for capitalism to operate, commodification of the 'outside' is necessary for its stabilization. Reserve labour power is needed for the reasons Castles and Kosack mention (1981, p.43):

> *If employment grows and the reserve army contracts, workers are in a better position to demand higher wages. When this happens, profits and capital accumulation diminish, investment falls and the men are thrown out of work, leading to a growth of the reserve army and a fall in wages. This is the basis of the capitalist economic cycle.*

Accordingly, it is possible to argue that capital's drive to minimize costs and maximise profits has caused changes in international migrations which are directly tied to labour organisation and movement. As Castles and Miller (1993) mention, there have been two main phases of change in the global labour market since the Second World War. The first one refers to the period between 1945 and the early 1970s. As Castles and Miller (ibid) further argue, it marks the economic strategy of large scale capital concentration, driving investment and expansion of production in the existing advanced capitalist economies countries. Hence, vast numbers of migrant workers were invited from low income countries to fill cheap labour shortages in the fast-expanding industrial areas of Western Europe, North America and Australia. As Petras

(2006) asserts, "immigration policies have served the capitalist class by creating a reserve army of cheap labour to lower wages, to undermine unionization". The global re-structuring of the economy is in one way a response to the labour movement that sustained higher wages and better working conditions in the advanced capitalist economies. The accelerating rates of labour cost resulted in capital searching for investment opportunities in the developing world, closing factories in high wage zones, and deregulation. The second phase is marked by the 1973-1974 'oil crises'. The second phase calls attention to a unitary world market, where capital flows relatively more freely across continents in response to profit maximizing strategies.

Structural adjustment programmes separating the political from the economic sphere and provided the grounds for capital moving relatively freely around the globe as an expansionist strategy (Harvey, 2007, p. 23). The separation not only involves a distancing of direct state involvement from the production process but also implies that states should be obliged to regulate labour market, juridical, regulatory, institutional and infrastructural arrangements for capitalism to operate. The development of freely functioning competitive markets enabled the advanced capitalist countries to insert its capital as a material social force inside other social formations. Thus, as Panitch and Gindin (2005) state, this had a substantial effect on social relations, property rights and labour relations, and "integrated production of multi-national corporations had an effect on restraining protectionist impulses and reinforcing pressures for free trade". As Petras (2006) mentions:

> *These conditions resulted in the lowering of protective barriers and the subsequent penetration and domination of local markets by subsidized agriculture exporters and large-scale manufacturers. It results in the destruction of millions of small peasant plots and medium size farms, which cannot compete with subsidized agricultural imports.*

Consequently, this process goes hand in hand with the creation of a dispossessed surplus population. The policies of the Turkish state that favoured the large landowners during the 1950s are discussed in the third section of this chapter. Nevertheless, neo-liberal policies have freed companies to search the world for the most skilled and dis-empowered workers. The role of structural forces such as new strategies for capital accumulation, flexibilisation, the global assembly line, and the "need to outsource services and parts of the production process in order to reduce costs" (Strüder, 2003, p.3) in metropolitan areas in advanced economies, can be the reasons for the activation of migration streams. Sassen (2001) states that in this new international division of labour, jobs in producer services, finance and top-level administration remain located in the advanced capitalist world, where they are very well-paid indeed.

Many manufacturing jobs are exported to low-income countries. The export of manufacturing jobs occurs when transnational corporations close factories in high-wage regions of Europe and North America and open new ones in newly industrialized or low-income countries. In either overseas setting, labour is much cheaper than in the developed countries.

Accordingly, prior to 1973, national governments and international organisations had claimed, generally, that labour migration was beneficial to the countries of origin, helping to stimulate their economic development. However, in January 1974, we can observe a policy shift at the Second European Regional Conference of the ILO which stated:

It was widely felt that there should be a new concept of cooperative development, giving more consideration to increasing employment in developing countries. For that reason, improving arrangements for the transfer of capital as a way of obviating emigration for reasons of economic need and demographic pressure was felt to be necessary.

Transnational capital was shifting investment and employment to the periphery. In fact, the capital was not automatically going to countries that had supplied labour. Investment and employment movement to the periphery only happened when economic and political conditions were attractive. Hence, international migration is a major consequence of the North-South gap. Labour follows the profits and escape debts. The predominant direction of migration tends to be from economically depressed areas to economically dynamic locations for the reason stated above. The national economies of depressed areas that have debts to the financial institutions try to attract foreign capital with their low wage labour regimes. As a consequence, labour can drive toward the equalisation of wages through spatial mobility. They move across national barriers to seek better working conditions and locations where labour power can be exchanged for higher earnings and well-being (Petras, 1981, p.48). In this respect, immigration policies "are directly linked to the business cycle" (ibid). Consequently, analysis of current migration policy in advanced economies is directly interlinked with the global structure of the economy (Petras, 2006).

On one hand, labour seeks options for better conditions and higher market prices for its labour power through spatial mobility; on the other hand, capital has a "perpetual need for ready and appropriate supplies of labour for its expanding process of capital accumulation" (Petras, 1981, p.48). Thus, transnational capital has an interest in sustaining low wage zones a where reservoir of labour is already under its command. As a result, advanced capitalist economies have placed increasing legal restrictions and regulations on who may cross their national boundaries. The quest for lower wages and capital's drive to extract surplus value by maximizing profits and minimising costs paved the way for corporations to move manufacturing operations abroad. Sassen (1988), for instance, has stressed how the lifting of economic barriers for foreign investment and the displacement of certain advance economies' manufacturing jobs abroad have fostered new migratory streams to advanced capitalist economies. It is possible to argue that, according to Castles and Miller (1993), "patterns of international migration and their labour market consequences are tightly bound up with the nature of capital flows, investment, international trade, direct and indirect foreign military intervention, diplomacy and cultural interaction". The uneven development of the capitalist economy is indicated by the "hierarchy of wage levels, or disparate thresholds for the remuneration of labour" (Petras, 2006), which distinguish core, semi-periphery and periphery (Wallerstein, 1974). A low rate of reward for labour in the form of real wages and general well-being prevails at the periphery.

It is asserted that the global re-structuring of the economy through structural adjustment programmes creates migratory flows of people and new surplus populations within both developing countries and advanced capitalist economies, which have been regulated and disciplined by the self-help ethos of minority entrepreneurship since the 1980s (Westwood & Bhachu, 1988, p. 6-7). The structural adjustment programmes de-regularised economies, and knowledge and information become essential assets for the 'globalised' flexible production (Harvey, 1989; Sassen, 2001; Wilpert, 1998).

The displaced labour from the less developed world and the unemployed surplus population in advanced economies collectively mobilize resources to establish meaningful livelihoods in the host country (Petras, 2006). I propose that collective resource mobilisation involves the mobilization of common resources such as knowledge, ideas, information, social relationships, and affects.

The re-structuring of the global economy in advanced capitalist economies is a consequence of the labour movement that forced capital to reorganise production. The reorganisation of production, i.e. flexible production, involves more subcontracting, more flexible labour, and greater vertical integration (Kim & Short, 2008, p.41). Moreover, it helps firms to reduce employment costs and weakens "power of organized labour as management regains more control over the deployment and pace of work" (ibid). That is to say, re-structuring is a consequence of capital's drive to maximise profit and reduce costs of labour that benefited from high wages and better working conditions during the industrial boom. Thus, this paved the way for exporting the manufacturing jobs to low wage zones. As Dicken (2010, p.494) contends:

Within the older industrialized countries, three broad geographical trends in these processes of manufacturing decline are apparent:

• Broad interregional shifts in employment opportunities, as exemplified by the relative shift of investment from 'Snowbelt' to 'Sunbelt' in the US, from north to south within the UK.

• Relative decline of the large urban-metropolitan areas as centres of manufacturing activity and the growth of new manufacturing investment in non-metropolitan and rural areas.

• Hollowing out of the inner cities of the older industrialized countries: in virtually every case, the inner urban cores have experienced massive employment loss as the focus of economic activity shifted first from central city to suburb and subsequently to less urbanized areas.

In conclusion, business cycles shaped by the profit maximising strategies of capital affect the opportunity structures for immigrants. It is important in understanding the changes in the labour market and new paths of immigrant labour market incorporation. It can be the driving force behind immigrant entrepreneurialism. People strive to make a living by running their own businesses as self-employed entrepreneurs as a response. The case of the Thatcherite era, characterised by de-regulation and de-industrialisation in the UK, was a starting point for the support for the self-help enterprise culture. It was a period that wage-labourers turned into self-employed business owners in large numbers. In he following section, I will discuss de-industrialisation and de-regulation in Britain in detail.

Meso scale: British context

In the mid-1950s the UK had been perhaps more industrialised than any other country in history, with more workers in industry than in all services; yet by 1983 there were almost two service workers for every industrial worker (Hall, 1991 as cited in Turner 1995, p.3).

It used to be a common view of the UK that it was the 'workshop of the world' (Turner, 1995). This phrase was used to indicate that the UK was the centre for manufacturing and exporting of industrial products throughout the world. Particular places within the UK were portrayed as world-class, excellent production sites for various kinds of manufacturing, such as the West Midlands for engineering products, specifically the production of motor cars and car components; Sheffield, the birthplace of stainless steel, for steel products; Clydeside and North East of England for shipbuilding; South Yorkshire, Nottinghamshire and South-Wales for coal; Lancashire and the East Midlands for textiles and clothing; Hertfordshire and the North West for defence goods and aircraft manufacture (ibid).

The whole array of manufacturing areas has witnessed de-industrialisation, and manufacturing is no longer a defining characteristic there. For instance, "the percentage of the world export of the manufacturing captured by British companies has halved in thirty years, from 16.3 per cent in 1960 to 8.4 in 1990" (Turner, 1995, p.1). Employment in the manufacturing industry has also decreased by more than 50% from 8.5 million in 1994 to 4 million in 1966 (Turner, 1995). The economic and industrial change has mostly affected the steel, motor vehicle, textile, engineering and defence industries. One effect of the economic restructuring was the creation of an unemployed surplus population from the previously employed, and the elimination of employment plans for future generations as in both the coal and steel industries. As Turner (ibid) further argues, "there was inter-generational reproduction of labour". Consequently, anxiety and uncertainty about the future work prospects of the younger generation dominated as economic security had been disrupted by economic restructuring.

In the case of the UK, the collective power of labour was diminished by attacks on organised workers from the steel and car industries as well as from the mines and dockyards and makes it harder to organise and to take industrial action. The wholesale privatisation of state owned utilities (gas, telecommunication, water), and means of transport (buses, trains, docks) transferred workers from the public to the private sector with dramatic changes in working conditions (Wills et. al.,2010, p.3).

Furthermore, as Blanchflower and Oswald (1991) state, "analysis of labour market processes in the 1980's for the UK has shown that rising self-employment corresponded to phases of increasing unemployment". It goes hand in hand with the urban riots, following which support for minority businesses was first introduced by governmental bodies. At a national level, the government signalled to the social policy of supporting small businesses after the Brixton riots. Boosting enterprise in disadvantaged areas was considered to be a policy measure against the ill-effects of restructuring. Lord Scarman (1981, p.11) on the Brixton riots contends:

Many of the young people of Brixton are born and raised in insecure social and economic conditions and in an impoverished physical environment. They share the desires and expectations which our materialist society encourages. At the same time, many of them fail to achieve educational success and on leaving school face the stark prospect of unemployment...

Without close parental support, with no job to go to, and with few recreational facilities available, the young black person makes his life on the streets and in the seedy commercially run clubs of Brixton.

In order to secure social security, the statutory bodies identified the "long term need to provide useful, gainful employment and suitable educational, recreational and leisure opportunities for young people, especially in the inner city" (ibid, p.108). The official report on the Brixton riots in South London, backed by Lord Scarman (1981) proposed that the fostering small business ownership among the black population would be a helpful in order to find solution for unemployment, criminality and welfare dependency. In other words, while one of the consequences of restructuring is mass unemployment in the old industrial cities of the developed world, promotion of self-employment could be a cure for the disturbances of restructuring.

In conclusion, the processes in political economy resulted in de-industrialisation, moving manufacturing jobs out of the UK while an increases in both high and low end service sector employment became dominant in the old industrial cities of the UK. According to Nigel Griffiths (2002), Small Firms Minister, "ethnic minority businesses are amongst the most entrepreneurial in the society. There are 250,000 ethnic minority enterprises in the UK contributing £13 billion a year to the British economy". More specifically, according to the London Development Agency, "there are 100,000 ethnic businesses in the London area employing around 800,000 people, which corresponds to almost half of the all ethnic minority businesses in the UK" (London Chamber of Commerce and Industry, 2003). Moreover, according to the London Employer Survey (1999), ethnic minorities own 17% of private sector enterprises in London.

It is within this context that we can analyse the entrepreneurial agency of the Turkish and Kurdish communities. In the next section, I focus on to the presence of Turkish Cypriot, Turkish and Kurdish communities in the UK.

Micro scale: CTK agency context

Migrations to the UK

This section aims to provide a detailed account of the CTK presence in the UK by taking into account the historically specific socio-economic conditions they face after their arrival in the UK. I make the contextualisation of CTK presence in the UK by taking into account the wider context of the labour market and migrations to the UK from other parts of the world. In order to do that, I will firstly trace phases of migration to the UK, which are strongly related to the structural conditions applicable at the time.

As Castles and Miller (1993, p.55) state, Britain was the first industrial country to fill labour shortages with immigrants. When newly created jobs could not be filled by the native population during the phase of industrialisation, Britain had to turn to its nearest colony, Ireland, to recruit Irish workers. The 1822 and 1846-47 famines in Ireland played a key role in massive Irish migrations to Britain, the USA and Australia. The number of Irish people in Britain exceeded 700,000 by 1851 (Ibid). Starting from the last quarter of the 19th century up to 1914, Britain was also a destination for 120,000 Jewish refugees from Russia (Ibid).

Britain continued to attract labour from outside of its borders after the Second World War, and between 1946 and 1959, it is estimated that 350,000 Irish moved to Britain (Castles et al., 1984, p.41). The number of European foreigners entering Britain between 1946 and 1951 reached 460,000. In addition, the British government employed 90,000 ""European Voluntary Workers" from refugee camps to take temporary jobs in the post-war boom" (Ibid). As Castles further mentions, about 100,000 Europeans with work permits entered Britain in the same period.

Another source of migration during the post-war period, especially during the 1950s was from Commonwealth countries. The needs of a booming economy and industrial growth resulted in the recruitment of workers by London Transport and the British Hotels and Restaurants Association from the West Indies, India, and Pakistan (Castles et al., 1984, p.42). Moreover, according to Kyriakides and Virdee (2003), since its foundation in 1948, the National Health Service has become one of the largest employers of racialized migrant labour in Britain. As they highlight, while migrant health workers have relevant skills for the British economy, this could not move beyond lower occupation levels (ibid).They were marked as racialized other, "un-British" and inferior.

As could be seen, the main aspects of migration to Britain were related to Britain's industrial features and labour shortages. I should mention that Britain has also been very selective in importing labour from other countries. Thus, it is possible to say that Britain has met its labour shortages firstly from its ex-colonies. While after the Second World War large numbers migrated from the Caribbean to Britain, this number is now very small. The European Community is the major source of migrants coming to Britain (Abercrombie et al., 1994). This is related to the shift from post-colonial to European relationships.

However, the migration policy shifted from encouraging immigration towards selectively controlling migration by establishing a quota system in 1962. Up to 1962, Britain had issued indefinite residency rights to immigrants from its colonies. The contemporary strategy for regulating immigration could be defined as a managed "third-way perspective. It is in between extremely restrictionist and highly expansionist immigration flows" (Crawley, 2003; as cited in Koffman et al., 2009, p.16). It is shaped by the necessities of the re-structuring, which gave weight to the "scientific, financial and managerial sectors, and to a lesser extent, health, which tends to marginalise the less skilled who, in contrast, are deemed to compete with established labour forces and pose pressures on welfare expenditure" (Ibid).

Within this national framework of UK migration policies, the next section focuses particularly on Turkish Cypriot, Turkish and Kurdish (CTK) migrations to the UK.

Cypriot, Turkish and Kurdish Migrations to the UK

Even though mainland Turkey was not colonised, the Turkish-born presence constitutes one of the largest migrant populations in Western Europe, including in the most populated country Germany, where it amounts to two million (Change Institute, 2009). On the other hand, the CTK population in Britain is unique since Turkish Cypriots have not migrated in large numbers to any other European country. Each of the CTK communities in the UK has a different migration history, social background, reasons for migrating, as well as being faced with different labour market conditions. Migrations to the UK reflected the heterogeneity in Turkey. The majority of the CTK communities in the UK migrated to and reside in London (King et al., 2008), more specifically settled in the northern boroughs of London, namely Enfield, Hackney, Haringey and Islington (Sirkeci et al., 2016).

In the title of this study, I use the term 'Turkish' as an operational construct referring three major ethnic communities, namely Turkish Cypriots, Turkish and Kurdish. The reason to classify all these three communities as 'Turkish' is that they are all coming from Turkey, including Turkish controlled part of Cyprus. Otherwise, I have no intention to imply homogeneity (For more discussion on this topic see Sirkeci et al., 2016). There are important differences within these groups. Even the term 'Turkish speaking' is problematic and has a totalising effect since the mother tongue of the Kurds is Kurdish. However, the first generation of the Kurdish community in the UK, were educated in Turkey prior to their arrival and they can speak Turkish. London's Turkish Cypriot, Turkish and Kurdish communities came from a variety of historical and social backgrounds and migrated to the UK at different periods. Nevertheless, the focus of my study is CTK communities who are either migrants from Turkey or their descendants. Thus, throughout the book I refer to all these three groups as their ethnic names, namely Turkish Cypriots, Turkish and Kurdish.

The most important social divisions and hierarchies within the migrants groups from Turkey to the UK originate from "class, rural-urban divisions, western cultural orientation, belonging to and identification with Turkish-ness or an ethnic minority identity in Turkey, of which Kurdish identity is the most salient, and gender" (Erel, 2010, p.655). According to intersectionality theorists such as Brah and Phoenix (2004, p.76), this "multiple axis of differentiation - economic, political, cultural, psychic, subjective and experiential – intersects in historically specific contexts".

Table 3.1. Resident population born in Turkey by areas and boroughs of London, 2011.

	Born in Turkey	% of Turkish born in total	% of Turkish born among foreign born	% of Turkish born among non-EU foreign born	% of foreign born in total
London	59,596	0.73	1.99	2.98	36.68
Inner London	31,717	0.98	2.32	3.61	42.21
Outer London	27,879	0.56	1.71	2.48	33.07
Top 10 London Boroughs					
Enfield	13,968	4.47	12.74	25.17	35.08
Haringey	10,096	3.96	8.88	17.92	44.60
Hackney	8,982	3.65	9.33	15.42	39.08
Islington	3,777	1.83	5.17	9.23	35.43
Waltham Forest	3,279	1.27	3.29	5.42	38.65
Barnet	1,952	0.55	1.41	2.23	38.86
Croydon	1,382	0.38	1.29	1.69	29.58
Lewisham	1,294	0.47	1.39	2.03	33.74
Southwark	1,123	0.39	0.99	1.41	39.43
Westminster	1,056	0.48	0.90	1.43	53.32

Source: Sirkeci et al., (2016)

Until 2011 census, there was a lack of official statistics of Turkish, Kurdish and Turkish Cypriot communities in the UK, because they tend to be classified under broad ethnic group categories, such as White, mixed/ multiple ethnic groups, Asian/Asian British, Black/African/Caribbean/Black British.

However, according to the 2011 census, the Turkish-born population living in England and Wales numbered 91,115 (excluding migrants who stayed or intended to stay for less than 12 months) (Sirkeci et al., 2016). This is an increase of 72.3 percent from 52,892 in 2001. This does not include the second generation of UK-born children of Turks and Turkish Kurds.

According to the 2011 census, the size of the Turkish-related population or the numbers speaking Turkish or with Turkish ethnicity seems significantly lower than often assumed. So far, estimates have ranged from 250,000 (Duvell, 2010), 300-350,000 (Costu & Turan, 2009) to 150,000 nationals and 500,000 people of Turkish origin, including 300,000 Cypriot Turks (Home Office, 2011). These figures depend greatly on the definition of the population measured. For instance, the Home Office once mentioned that the Turkish population to be 500,000 including 300,000 Turkish-Cypriots. However, the 2001 census gives a number of 77,156 Cypriots of whom around 45,000 were Turks, Robin & Aksoy in 2001 estimated that they numbered 100,000 to 120,000 and Enneli et al. (2005) state a number of 75,771 Cypriot-born people of whom only 17,915 were Muslim. Hence, the Home Office and many other figures seem hugely inflated.

Table 3.2. Population born in Turkey by countries of the United Kingdom, 2011.

	Born in Turkey	% of Turkish born in total	% of Turkish born among foreign born	% of Turkish born among non-EU foreign born	% of foreign born in total
UK Total	93,916	0.15	1.17	1.88	12.65
Great Britain	93,539	0.15	1.19	1.89	12.83
England	89,484	0.17	1.22	1.92	13.84
Wales	1,631	0.05	0.97	1.73	5.48
Scotland	2,424	0.05	0.66	1.23	6.97
N. Ireland	377	0.02	0.32	1.13	6.58

Source: Sirkeci et al., (2016)

Moreover, the 2009 report commissioned by the Greater London Authority provides statistics on the KT communities, particularly communities living in the London area. Thus, these communities have been described as 'invisible', because the focus of population studies of ethnic diversity is on classifications in broad ethnic groups such as White, Black, Irish, Asian, Chinese, and so on. The census figures are considerably lower than the estimates given by various local surveys and studies. The numbers do not show the true size of the current populations. "One estimate gave the size of the Turkish, Kurdish and Turkish Cypriot population in the UK as 230,000, with 100-140,000 living in and around the boroughs of Hackney, Haringey, Islington and Enfield" (GLA,2009), while the highest CTK number estimate is half a million (Olay, 2005; as cited in Cam, 2006, p.14)

An unpublished study by Tasiran (2013) based on the Annual Population Survey, 2011 finds also the number of KT people in the United Kingdom between 150,000 and 200,000 people. I also believe this number is the most realistic figure. The reason for this is as follows: Firstly, the estimation is based on the annual population survey conducted by the office for national statistics, while other estimations are dependent on the viewpoints of the autors. The annual population survey covers the whole UK population, while the other estimations do not depend on any evidence covering whole UK. Secondly, the figures provided by the annual population survey gathered information according to people's place of birth, while some others depend on immigrant status. Consequently, naturalised KT people did not numbered in these estimations.

A report for the London Development Agency estimated the Turkish community (including Turkish Cypriots) to number about 150,000 (as cited in GLA, 2009). As the CTK communities in London are recent migrants to the UK in comparison with the general London population, the 2001 census states that 58 per cent of Turkish Cypriots in London were born outside the UK, as were 76 per cent of Turkish people, 85.5 per cent of Kurd, and 27.1 per cent of all London residents. A comparison with 1991 figures suggests that the distribution pattern of people born in Cyprus has changed with a decrease in London and an outward movement from North London to Hertfordshire and Essex. Other places that have seen an increase are Manchester, Coventry, Lancaster and Morecombe, as well as Lincoln and Sleaford. On the other hand, the number of people born in Turkey living in Britain doubled over the same period, and two-thirds of this increase was in London.

According to the information gathered from 2011 census, a "large majority (65%) of this community lives in London. There were 59,596 Turkish-born residents, the 15th largest migrant community in the capital. Within London, the 3 boroughs with the largest Turkish-born communities are Hackney, Haringey and Enfield, which together host 55% of the Turkish-born population of the city" (D'Angelo et al., 2013, p.6).

Age structure
The age structure of the communities reflects their likely time of arrival in the UK. Turkish Cypriots have been in the UK the longest and have an age structure very similar to the overall population. The Turkish population is younger and the Kurdish population, who have mostly arrived more recently, are younger still. Similarly, the self-employment and unemployment rates reflect their likely time of arrival in the UK. The rate of self-employment was higher for Cypriots, but average for Turkish people and lower for Kurds. There was, however, a higher unemployment rate than among the general population, amounting to nearly 13 per cent for the Kurdish population and

nearly 10 per cent of the Turkish population; both are more than double the general rate of 4.7 per cent (Küçükcan, 1999).

Similarly, Mehmet Ali (2001) "suggests that the characteristics of migrants to the UK in the 1970s and 1980s were quite different. Many of the 1970s' cohort were originally from rural areas in Turkey, whereas a significant proportion of immigrants from Turkey in the 1980s were intellectuals, including students and highly-educated professionals" (as cited in Thomson, 2006, pp.19-20). According to Enneli et al. (2005), both groups acquired supports from the Turkish Cypriots based in London. Accordingly, it might be possible to state that the collapse of the welfare state together with re-structuring paved the way for the networks of successively articulated communities.

Furthermore, according to the Greater London Authority (2009), over 25 per cent of Londoners born in Turkey, and 19 per cent of those born in Cyprus were involved in the wholesale and retail trades, compared with 14 per cent of the general population. The most common employment and business activities are in the retail and catering areas, including restaurants, takeaway foods, cafés and supermarkets. The other jobs they do are minicab offices, off-licences, jewellery, finance, fashion and import-export, construction and manufacturing. Unemployment was more than twice as high for Turkish and Kurdish people than the London average.

Gender

In general there are a higher proportion of women than men in the UK. This is mostly due to the fact that women tend to live longer (GLA, 2009). The gender division in the Turkish Cypriot and Turkish populations is almost the same, whilst the Kurdish population consists of a higher proportion of males. This is a feature of more recently arrived migrants who are not yet able to bring their families, or who are not yet financially prosperous enough to start a family (GLA, 2009).

According to the 2001 census, the proportion of CTK population by gender in London was respectively as follows: 49.8 per cent of the Turkish Cypriots; 49.8 percent of the Turkish, and 45.7 per cent of the Kurdish population were female, while the percentage Turkish Cypriots and Turkish males was 50.2 that of Kurds went up to 54.3 per cent. It should also be noted that the statistics for the Kurdish population also includes Iraqis and Syrians.

As King et al. (2008, p.9) state that, "the first Turks to arrive, in the early 1970s, were single men who were joined by their wives and children later in the decade. To some extent, this model of migration replicated the much larger migration from Turkey as 'guest-workers' to Germany, the Netherlands, France, Belgium and Austria in the 1960s and 1970s". In addition, large numbers of young men coming to the UK in the 1970s originally migrated from rural parts of Turkey, "but had often migrated internally to one of Turkey's big cities prior to their international move" (Mehmet Ali, 2001).

Employment and economic status

One recent Labour Force Survey analysis of Turkish-born migrants has been conducted by the Institute for Public Policy Research (IPPR, 2007), and uses data from 2005-2006. The findings of the IPPR publication – Britain's Immigrants – show that the Turkish-born population is socio-economically far behind the UK population. For instance, "41 per cent of the working age Turkey-born population, excluding students and also Cypriot Turks, were employed compared to 78 per cent of the UK population, and the average annual income of the economically active working age Turkey-born population was £14,750 compared to the UK average of £21,250" (GLA, 2009).

According to a study by the London Development Agency, "The Turkish Forum estimates that there are as many as 10,000 Turkish enterprises in the UK. Most businesses are small local ones, and provide for community needs, such as catering, retail and textiles. Some of these businesses retain strong trading links with Turkey or Turkish Cyprus, and often operate in similar sectors, but on a much bigger scale, and can employ large numbers of people in London or elsewhere".

After this brief introduction to the current conditions of CTK communities, it is worth looking at the particular migration histories of each CTK community.

Turkish Cypriots

Although Turkish Cypriots are not a primary focus of this research, they have played an important role among Turks and Kurds in providing a social, economic and cultural environment for the new comers. The migration of Cypriots to Britain may be seen as part of the wider movement of immigration from the New Commonwealth countries to Britain that occurred during the post-war period. The roots of migration must be seen in the island's colonial past. Turkish Cypriots migrated principally for economic reasons to improve their financial prospects (Inal, 2007b).

As the Cypriot community took root in Britain, reports sent to those in Cyprus encouraged kinsfolk to look for employment prospects in London. As Oakley (1979, p.23) states, "letters and visits both ways are the important means of communication between the home country and the settlement over-seas". This continuous and rapid exchange of information between settlers in London and their networks at home provides information about their economic prospects in London. Thus, over a period of time, a whole section of villages reconstructed themselves in Britain. In addition, elderly people migrated too, taking care of their grand-children and helping their children to run the shop (Inal, 2007b).

Following the UK Migration Act of 1962, Turkish Cypriot migration slowed whilst Turkish Cypriots continued to arrive either via family reunification, or following the 1974 war in Cyprus as refugees (Change Institute, 2009). Another sector that was first initially exploited by Cypriot Turks was the direct use of traditional village skills in tailoring and dressmaking in the textile trade. They first started working as employees in firms originally owned by Asians and Jews, and later took over the businesses in the clothing and textile industry (Atay, 2010). Again, as with the catering industry, it is possible to argue that new migrant arrivals joined the businesses of already settled immigrants who provided a safety net, and, in return, the new arrivals provided cheap and reliable labour to the already-existing immigrants.

The earliest settlers to the UK, Turkish Cypriots, migrated in significant numbers between 1945 and 1955. They constitute the oldest community amongst the CTK. As Robins and Aksoy (2001, p.690) contend, "Turkish Cypriots arrived mainly with their families, intending to settle in the UK, and emphasised their affinity with the 'British way of life' as a pragmatic attempt to be accepted. They were assisted by earlier Greek-Cypriot migrants in finding housing and employment – predominantly in the textile industry and in hotels and restaurants in London". This was largely due to the fact that the older generation of Turkish Cypriots can speak both Turkish and Greek as they used to live side by side with the Greek Cypriots until the partition of Cyprus in 1974. "Over time, the Turkish Cypriots have become more self-sufficient as a group by establishing their own businesses such as textile factories, retail and wholesale shops" (Thomson, 2006, p.19).

Turkish Cypriot employment in the UK

Although Turkish Cypriots are not a primary focus of this research, it is setting their context for the migration, settlement and employment. The dispersed nature of Turkish Cypriot settlement in London is evidence of their access to both the mainstream economy in the city and the migrant enclaves which house dispersed nature of their settlement is partly a consequence of labour market demand for migrant labour in mainstream spheres during the industrial boom. Prior to the Second World War, early settlers worked in the service industries, such as hotel and restaurant trades, usually in premises owned by Italians. However, following the declaration of war between Italy and Britain, most Italians went back to Italy (Enneli et al., 2005), and Greek Cypriots and later Turkish Cypriots filled their places in this trade. Turkish Cypriots are late arrivals compared to the Greek-Cypriots, and were initially dependent on the Greek community for assistance in housing and employment

(Change Institute, 2009). Actually, there has been a general pattern among new arrivals to work in the premises owned by previous immigrants to the UK. In other words, the involvement of Turkish Cypriots in the catering sector was not related to their work experiences in their home country, but was rather a response to the opportunities at that time (Inal & Özkan, 2009, p.492).

Turks

After the Turkish Cypriots, Turks from the mainland Turkey were the second group to arrive to the UK. Like Turkish Cypriots and Kurds, they are largely concentrated in London (King et al., 2008). Turkish migration from mainland Turkey to the UK started in the late 1960s. This was largely a consequence of the policies of the ruling party which came to power in 1950. The increased mechanization of farming production and the introduction of more rational techniques reduced the need for labour intensive farming. In 1948 there were about 2,000 tractors, which increased to 40,000 by 1954 (Gitmez, 1979). The explosive development of farming made small farmers and landless farm workers vulnerable. Planting patterns had changed radically. Cotton and wheat crops could not follow one another and could not employ farm workers year round. These developments made it difficult to earn a livelihood from small scale farming and thus facilitated internal migration from rural areas to the big cities such as Istanbul, Ankara and İzmir with limited employment opportunities in the cities. The economic immigrants from mainland Turkey to the UK were first internal migrants in Turkey. Those who first migrated from villages to the big cities of Turkey tended to reside on the outskirts of those cities, and they built up so called *Gecekondu* ("gece" is night, and "kondu" denotes set down; as most of them were unlicensed constructions). Structural unemployment and general poverty forced many families to seek new possibilities. The absence of a universal social protection net in the form of social welfare or unemployment benefits created visions that could possibly only be realized outside of the country's borders. It was such processes that lay behind emigration from Turkey to Europe. Those who emigrated were in the first instance farmers and farm workers, some of whom had settled down in *gecekondu* areas in big cities.

In contrast to labour migration to other European countries during the post-war period, migration from both Cyprus and Turkey to Britain was neither organised, nor regulated by the government. Instead, migration had been facilitated by social networks, which had a primary role in organisational and regulatory aspects of migration (Change Institute, 2009, p.25).

Turkish employment in the UK

During the late 1960s and early 1970s, many skilled workers came from Turkey to the UK to work in the textile industry and were later joined by their families. In comparison to other unionised manufacturing industries that had been moved to low wage zones after the 1973-74 oil crises, the textile and clothing industry managed to survive until the 1990s as a result of outsourcing and employing undocumented immigrant labour force (Atay, 2010; Phizacklea, 1988). The employment of an undocumented labour force provided the owners with an opportunity to exploit the workforce (Phizacklea, 1988). The workers' demand for improve working conditions and payment were responded to by the owners with the threat of deportation or being sacked. The "collapse of the former Soviet Union opened up labour markets with cheap skilled labourers in the textile industry in Eastern Europe in the 1990s" (Strüder, 2003, p.23). Textile companies moved their production to Romania, Bulgaria and Turkey. The textile and clothing sector collapsed towards the end of the 1990s, and various other trades have taken its place in providing sources of work for CTK communities. These include the restaurant and catering businesses. The following empirical chapters mainly explore these two sectors. It is clear that there is a relationship between structural forces and the move of CTK communities into entrepreneurship, to become small-scale shop owners, and this will be investigated in the empirical analysis in later chapters.

There was a military coup in Turkey in 1980, which led some to flee the country with a number of them seeking political asylum in the UK. The military coup in Turkey in 1980 caused the second wave of Turkish migrant arrivals to the UK, this time mostly refugees made up of intellectuals, students, trade union activists and professionals from various backgrounds, with mainly urban origins (Erdemir and Vasta, 2007).

Until the 1990s, KT communities could find employment in the textile industry, and the decline of this industry had a serious impact on the economic well-being of the communities leading to mass unemployment among the CTK communities (Change Institute, 2009). Those of the older generation, the first migrants of the community who emigrated from rural areas in Turkey with a lack of education, did not have the skills to shift into another industry. Thus, some "drifted into long term unemployment or even crime" (Change Institute, 2009, p.33). Another consequence of the demise of textile industry was a sharp increase in the number of small and middle sized business shop owners in the community. The empirical chapters will provide a detailed analysis of how these changes were experienced amongst a group of current shop owners.

The IPPR (2007) data from the 2005-2006 Annual Population Survey asserts that 35 percent of the economically active working age Turkey-born, excluding Turkish Cypriots, are self-employed as compared to 13 per cent of the total UK working age population.

Since then, the economic well-being of the KT communities has developed significantly, and the KT economic presence in London and England is visible. The KT economic presence is most felt across Haringey's Green Lanes, Hackney's Stoke Newington and Kingsland Roads (Change Institute, 2009). In these areas, the communities have created an "array of Turkish shops, cafés, markets and business that will give you a little taste of Turkey" (BBC London, 2008). It was also evident during my pilot interviews that migrants from East European countries had found employment in the CTK owned catering enterprises.

Kurds

Finally, Kurdish migration from Turkey accelerated at the end of the 1980s because of the armed conflict between the Kurdistan Workers' Party (PKK) and the Turkish government. The intensification of the conflict displaced thousands of Kurdish people from eastern and South-Eastern Turkey (King et al., 2008).

Kurds, according to the Home Office and Refugee Council statistics (Home Office, 1997; Refugee Council, 1996) started to seek refugee status in the UK overwhelmingly in the 1988-1989 periods. This is due to the persecution of Alevi Kurds in the Sivas, Malatya and Maraş provinces of Turkey. Kurds were amongst the top ten groups seeking refuge in Britain between 1993 and 1996 (Refugee Council, 1996), a situation repeated in 1997 (Home Office, 1997). The number of Turkish nationals claiming asylum between 1989 and 2003 was 33,972, which represents 92 per cent of all applications from Turkey between 1980 and 2006 (Change Institute, 2009, p. 25).

The Kurdish migrants to the UK joined already existing networks of solidarity to help them settle and integrate to the new environment. They implemented the same strategy as the Turkish Cypriots and mainland Turks before them. This is largely a consequence of the refugee resettlement and ethnic minority policies of the British state. In other words, to be able to ease the various problems faced by the immigrants in the host country, the British state utilised co-ethnic associations and social networks (Wahlbeck, 1998). Housing was provided in the co-ethnic neighbourhoods. The pre-existing economy and community organisations in the Turkish Cypriot and Turkish community has facilitated the insertion of Kurds into already-existing economic networks and eased the hardship faced in adapting to their new country of settlement. Accordingly, the community organisations often provided a very wide range of services for their members and clients. Their activities range from advice on welfare, housing and asylum issues, translation, language and training courses to social and cultural activities (Griffiths,2000; Wahlbeck, 1998, p.221)

Kurdish employment in the UK

Like their Turkish counterpart, the Kurdish community had no access to employment in various manufacturing industries of the British economy due to the fact that they were late arrivals to the UK. The manufacturing jobs had already been moved out of London. As a consequence, in order to ease their economic hardship, they looked for employment opportunities within the ethnic enclave economy, such as in the textile industry. It is increasingly evident that there are two major areas for immigrant concentration in London: the inter city boroughs of Hackney, Haringey, Lambeth, Lewisham and Wandsworth, and the outer city boroughs of Brent, Ealing, Hounslow, and Waltham Forest (Sassen, 1991, p.271). These deprived boroughs of London hold the excluded ethnic minorities from professional employment. For instance, writing about "Polish migrant workers in London" Bill Jordan (2002, p. 11) states that London Poles have found work in textile factories, catering, cleaning and the building industry. The textile factories were mainly owned by Turkish Cypriots and Turkish immigrant entrepreneurs in North East London. As the textile industry was still present, with diminishing profits, in London until the midst of 1990s, many Kurdish people found employment in this sector. However, "many found it difficult to find steady employment and save money. This was partly due to the less favourable economic conditions they faced in the early 1990s. In particular, the textile industry – a sector which, over previous decades, had provided employment for many in the CTK communities– declined significantly" (King et al., 2008, p.10).

Conclusion

Business cycles shaped by the profit maximising strategies of capital can be the driving force behind immigrant entrepreneurialism. The processes in political economy resulted in de-industrialisation, moving manufacturing jobs out of the UK while an increase in both high and low end service sector employment become dominant in old industrial cities of the UK. The Thatcher era was characterised by de-regulation and de-industrialisation in the UK, which was a starting point for seeing support for the self-help enterprise culture. People strove to make a living by running their own businesses as self-employed entrepreneurs. It was a period that turned wage-labourers into self-employed business owners in large numbers (Strüder, 2003). Until the 1990s, employment in the KT communities were dominated by the textile industry, and the decline of this industry had a profound impact on the economic well-being of the communities, leading to mass unemployment among the CTK communities (Change Institute, 2009).

Even though the historical, social background of Turkish and Kurdish migrations to the UK is quite different in many ways, we can observe convergence in their labour market incorporation and in the ways in which they cope with the difficulties in their new environment. They all strategically mobilise resources via social and kin networks. New streams of migrants to the UK have successively joined the previously settled migrant communities in order to cope with marginalisation. The already settled migrant communities have helped form a bridge from the successive migrant community to wider society. Turks and Kurds are late arrivals compared to the Turkish-Cypriots, and were initially dependent on the Turkish-Cypriot community for assistance. The dispersed nature of Turkish Cypriot settlement in London is evidence of their access to the mainstream economy in the city, rather than dependence on the migrant enclaves. Today, Turkish Cypriots mostly hold professional jobs. They have become teachers, civil servants, pharmacists, doctors, dentists, accountants, lawyers, insurers and entrepreneurs.

Chapter Four:
Researching Turkish Entrepreneurs in London

In this chapter I discuss the methodological approach and research process. The aim is to answer the questions such as, which methodological approach is operationalised in this book, and how and by which research methods I collected and analysed the data. In order to do this, I will first state my research questions. Secondly, I will discuss my methodological approach to answering those questions. Thirdly, I will focus on the research techniques used to collect data with a view towards clarifying the reason why I employed critical inquiry with an emphasis on qualitative research as a technique.

As I have mentioned in the literature review section the main questions of this study are an attempt to shed light not only on the survival strategies of Turkish, and Kurdish ethnic minority businesses in London, but also on the reasons and ways in which ethnic minorities from less developed economies, particularly Turkish and Kurdish communities set up businesses. Accordingly, the main aims and objectives of the research could be listed as follows:

There is one specific aim and two sub-aims:

The main aim of this project is to assess why and how Turkish and Kurdish minorities have become entrepreneurs in London;

The two sub-aims related to the main aim are:

to test the applicability of collective resource mobilization as a theory in explaining why and how members of Turkish and Kurdish communities in London become entrepreneurs;

to assess the interplay between Turkish and Kurdish ethnic minority businesses and the institutional, political and socio-economic background.

Specific objectives include:

assessing the role of the family, kinship, co-ethnics, and institutional networks in explaining collective resource mobilisation for the formation and maintenance of immigrant firms;

evaluating the links between the global re-structuring of economy and Turkish and Kurdish ethnic minority business formation by focusing on changes in the occupational structure in CTK communities;

assessing the changes in employment experiences of CTK communities over time; how and why forms of employment have changed

comparing and contrasting changing employment experiences of CTK communities.

The interview schedule I used in this survey probe into aspects of pre-migration history, post-migration experience, changing employment experiences of CTK communities, paths to business ownership, survival strategies of CTK businesses, the role of networks in businesses, competition with chain stores, security within business premises. In addition, the interview structure was guided by the principle of understanding the connection between KT immigrants' changing plans and strategies of mobility, adaptation, and survival over time on the one hand, and how and why the restructuring of the global political economy fuelled the collective mobilization of resources of KT minorities on the other. I aimed to understand the role of the policies of the British state as a regulatory entity of the labour market in migrants' decisions. More specifically, I wanted to understand the entrepreneur's own sense of these policies, meanings, and definitions that people bring to their situations. Furthermore, the interview structure with members of the community organizations aimed to understand the link between organizations and the migrant communities, particularly how cultural, social and faith based organizations have contributed to the CTK communities generating resources to establish and run businesses. I wanted to learn the role of those organisations in CTK business life in London. In addition, if there is any role, how it has changed over time.

Consequently, critical realism with an emphasis on the qualitative research method in this project is considered the most appropriate approach as they are able to grasp in depth the material conditions and living experiences such as social, political and cultural factors, which have a significant impact on people's lives and perceptions.

My ontological and epistemological assumptions in this study could be defined as critical realism with a synthesis of induction and deduction methods. On this basis, my analysis will mostly depend on a perspective in which people's daily experiences and their material conditions are shaped and determined by class, gender, and race. In terms of a research strategy, I have mostly used a qualitative research approach because of its flexibility in fieldwork. Semi structured interviews are widely used with flexible design.

Preliminary fieldwork

I accomplished the initial collection of data in a relatively open and non-prescriptive manner. Initially, I decided to carry out pilot interviews. I had the opportunity to have informal chats with CTK community members, and conducted twenty-five semi-structured recorded pilot interviews. The first part of fieldwork took place during the summer of 2010 in northern boroughs of London such as Hackney and Haringey. The shops were approached where outdoor signs made it obvious to see and observe that it was an ethnic shop. The interviewees were chosen from KT entrepreneurs from various sectors such as florists, restaurant owners, music school owners, hair dressers, cab company owners and supermarket owners and all were conducted in Turkish. I utilised the pilot interviews to identify the codes for further thematic analysis in the main fieldwork.

The pilot interviews were designed to create a general idea about the demographic characteristics of business owners, their working conditions, how they set up and run their businesses and mobilize resources and finally how they use their networks and the "culture" of the country of origin as a collective resource.

I avoided any pre-conceived hypothesis while I was collecting data. The initial outcomes of this preliminary analysis would then feed back into further data collection oriented towards the exploration of particular themes. These preliminary interviews contributed a lot to the formation of an idea of the field, the background of the business owners, the kind of jobs, the sectors they are in and their living conditions. It also provided data to formulate my orientation, specific aims and objectives in this project. During the pilot interviews, I observed that CTK communities collectively mobilize resources to establish meaningful livelihoods.

Accordingly, the preliminary field-work has inductively generated knowledge for clarifying my research questions. That is to say, at this stage inductive methodology synthesise with deductive methodology to produce a theory generated from initial outcomes, which can then be tested. The initial outcomes generated themes to be explored further. The object of pilot interviews is to access further instances of themes identified in the initial data. In order to develop the themes in the pilot interviews, any new instances should be compared and contrasted with existing examples in order to enable these themes to be explored and elaborated fully. The codes of thematic analysis were those that arose from the textual data gathered in pilot interviews and fieldwork survey rather than pre-defined categories and themes. This is because of the nature of the study, as I employed a synthesis of the deductive and inductive approaches. The process began by analysing pilot interviews in order to focus on further themes to be researched. Then, I coded each transcript thoroughly, so that I identified and evidenced particular themes. This also ensured the reliability and validity of the interviews.

Thus, the structure of the book and proposed theory of collective resource mobilisation in explaining the research questions, to a large extent, has been generated by and is dependent on the codes that emerged during the preliminary field work.

Main fieldwork and the selection criteria of the interviewees

The selection criteria used for the inclusion of business owners to be interviewed could be summarized as follows. First, business owners from three ethnic groups, Turkish Cypriot, Turkish and Kurdish were chosen to be interviewed. Secondly, specific sectors were identified to represent three broad Kurdish, Turkish, and Turkish Cypriot business owners, namely catering. More particularly, the owners of off-licenses, supermarkets, coffee-shops, wholesalers and restaurants were chosen to be interviewed. The reason for choosing these sectors was that most people from the target groups find employment in these sectors (see the contextual background section). In addition, I used multiple entry points to the communities. Finally, the shopkeepers interviewed were drawn from London boroughs of Hackney and Haringey. Following the London Borough of Enfield, largest groups of the KT community members have concentrated in the boroughs of Hackney and Haringey as the KT population grew over the years from 26,000 in 1991 to over 180,000 in 2011 (Sirkeci & Esipova, 2013, p.6; Karan, 2015).

In order to gain research access to conduct interviews with the focus groups, I adopted several methods including observation, snowballing techniques, visiting business owners at their workplaces and using personal contacts. The snowballing technique is driven by the referral of one participant to another (Berg, 2007). In addition, I used the telephone to get in touch with some of my interviewees using directories such as Turkish Business Guides published by the London Turkish Gazette which cover the business world of the Turkish communities in London were very helpful for getting in touch with the interviewees, including off-license, supermarket, café-shop, restaurant and wholesale owners as well as members of community organizations. I also visited businesses as a customer to set-up an interview for a later date.

The fieldwork includes key informants from community organizations such as voluntary, social, cultural, faith based groups and the association for shop owners for CTK ethnic communities in London. In addition, I interviewed a shop designer who had set up almost one thousand shops such as off-licenses and supermarkets. While I was coding the interviews, Turkish Cypriot, Kurdish and Turkish small business owners joined together and founded an organisation called the "British Anatolian Craftsmen Union". I therefore considered it necessary to interview the chair of the union. Further, semi-structured interviews were conducted with small shop owners (including corner shops, supermarkets, kebab shops and restaurant owners). The selection was made with the idea that CTK communities migrated in different time periods mainly to North London with diverse labour market insertion characteristics. In total, forty interviews were conducted. The number of interviews conducted with Turkish, Kurdish and Turkish Cypriot business owners were respectively twelve, eight and six. The number of interviews conducted with key informants was fourteen. The real names of the interviewees have been changed in order to maintain their anonymity.

Business guides published annually by the London Turkish Gazette, which covers the business world of the Turkish communities, including Kurdish, Turkish and Turkish Cypriots in Britain, mainly in London, were helpful for accessing the contact details of the business owners. Those workplaces located in the London boroughs of Haringey and Hackney was called in order to set up an interview date. Another major method of gaining access to research in these districts was visiting the business owners at their workplaces.

Almost all of the interviews were conducted at the business owners' workplaces. Thus, this provided the opportunity for me to observe the location of the businesses, the size of the businesses, the decoration of the restaurants and coffee shops, the number of people employed and whether they are family members. These observations will be discussed in the following sections.

In terms of the gender balance of the interviewees, the interviewees who were accessed via telephone or random sampling appeared to be almost all men when I asked to speak with the owner of the businesses. 4 out of 40 interviewees were women and only one of these owned a shop. It was my observation during the fieldwork that, in most of the cases if the business was not big enough to hire workers, women family members assisted their husbands. In other words, in such low end businesses with low skilled intensive working hours, female labour-power is consumed within the family which also provided a competitive advantage to their businesses. In order to increase the profit margins in catering and retail business, long working hours and unpaid female labour has been utilized.

With regard to my positionality in this study, being a native Turkish speaking researcher helped me in gaining research access to conduct interviews with Turkish Cypriots, Kurdish and Turkish community members. Apart from one Turkish Cypriot interviewee, all interviews were conducted in Turkish. Using Turkish language served to give me insider qualities with respect to the KT communities in North London. This helped me in gaining research participants' trust and nurturing rapport. Since I share a common cultural and ethnic background with the research participants, I was able to understand the experiences of interviewees, historical processes affecting them in Turkey, and the implications behind many of the things they have told me. This helped me to generate meaningful follow up questions for clarifying issues important for the research purposes.

I believe my being a native Turkish speaker living in London was an advantage in carrying out fieldwork research with the Kurdish, Turkish and Turkish Cypriot key informants and catering and retail business owners. Most of them were hospitable and welcoming. They were pleased to see someone from their community interested in their working lives. They appreciated the fact that I was undertaking research into their working lives, and they had a chance to express their problems and grievances, and to describe their living conditions. In restaurants, coffee shops and even off-licences, I was generously offered lunch and dinner many times. People were very eager to talk about their experiences, feelings and working lives in the UK. I often had to interrupt the conversation in order to satisfy the interview schedule.

During the fieldwork, in some cases, my higher educational background was one of the issues that threw my insider position into question. Some of the informants got shy to talk to me because of their low educational status. This was an unanticipated insider problem that I had to shift between insider and outsider positions. I did not expect to be treated like an outsider. In order to switch my position, I downplayed my doctoral researcher status and told them that I do not have the skills to set up and run a business like theirs. I said, there are different difficulties in any kind of job and it is beyond my skills to do what they do for living. In so doing, I was able to balance humility and status in the encounter with some informants.

All interviews were recorded. The digital voice recorder allowed the research to capture the interviews in detail. Using digital voice recorded data provided transportable, repeatable resource allowed multiple hearings (Nikander, 2008). The interviews were recorded with the prior permission of the interviewees. The recordings were then transcribed verbatim into Turkish, and particular themes in the interview were selected to be translated into English. Verbatim transcription is "central to the reliability and validity, and veracity of qualitative data collection" (Halcomb et al., 2006, p.40).

Chapter Five:

Interests

As I mentioned in chapter 2, according to Tilly (1978) *interests* involve the perceived shared benefits likely to emerge to the group in question as a consequence of collective action As mentioned in the earlier chapters, this chapter aims to elaborate on the reasons for setting-up small firms in the KT communities. I will explain why KT people moved into, and are over represented in the catering and retail sectors.

There is very little, if any, research that has addressed the question of why KT people have become self-employed in such large numbers (Dawson et al, 2009). I argue that KT communities were aligned in their interest for setting-up small businesses. The alignment was a process that entailed increasing communication and an intensification of networking within the community via community organisations, interpersonal networks, and ethnic newspapers.

The second aim of the chapter is to examine the ways in which shared interests and experiences within the KT communities instrumentally paved the way for the construction of an identity called *Türkiyeli* (people from Turkey). I argue that identities and cultural repertoires brought from the home country are not fixed and stable, but rather are socially constructed, shifting, and open to redefinitions and reformulations (Yeros, 1999).

Changing employment prospects and shared interests in the Kurdish and Turkish communities

People may become self-employed for many different reasons. At one end of the possible spectrum, self-employment may provide desirable incentives such as the need for financial advancement, status and independence, flexible working hours and job satisfaction. At the other end of the spectrum, self-employment appears to be reluctantly chosen as the only available alternative for employment. Within this latter factor, self-employment is viewed as a "rational response to labour market obstacles" such as discrimination against ethnic minorities in paid-employment and blocked upward mobility (Clark and Drinkwater, 2000; Metcalf et al., 1996). Thus, two distinct sets of causal factors are investigated. The first of these is motivations. If the motivation to become self-employed falls into the former 'voluntarist' category then self-employment can be evaluated positively, providing the opportunity for individuals to improve their quality of life (Basu and Altinay, 2000; Curran et al., 1991; Dawson et al., 2009; Stokes, 2002; Storey et al., 1989). In other words, individuals pulled into self-employment could be defined as opportunity entrepreneurs who start-up businesses voluntarily and are mainly attracted into self-employment by perceived benefits.

On the other hand, individuals are also pushed into self-employment because of external factors such as labour market discrimination, job dissatisfaction, structural changes in the economy, and lack of available paid employment (Dawson et al., 2009; Goffee and Scase, 1995; Scase and Goffee, 1989; Kuratko and Hodgetts, 2001). Push grounds for self-employment are related to limited or no opportunities in finding a paid job. It is possible to call this group of self-employed people necessity entrepreneurs (Dawson et al., 2009).

For instance, Turkish and Kurdish communities were mainly employed in textile factories from the 1970s to the middle of the 1990s. However, they suddenly found themselves unemployed (See chapter 3). As one of the interviewee states,

> *In one week 1500 textile ateliers were shut down. The people who used to work in those ateliers were made idle (Ates, restaurant owner).*

The collapse of the textile industry has led to a search for a new means of survival within the KT communities. While they were pushed into self-employment, they also started to search for new places to set-up takeaways. Savings made during employment in the textile industry were not enough to set-up shops. Social capital was largely utilised to drive economic capital, i.e. co-ethnic partnership or lending financial capital to co-ethnic would-be business owners was common after the collapse of the textile industry. Esnaf, chair of a business organisation describes those days as such:

> *People started to search for new means of survival. Primarily, they were oriented towards businesses like off-licences, restaurants and coffee-shops. The capital generated by working in the textile industry, their savings together with the capital gathered by social solidarity were all directed towards investments in the service sector. They have demonstrated devastating boldness. Where did this courage originate from? They told themselves that we were suffering, and there were no opportunities for a good livelihood in Turkey. We had to do something here as we could not turn back to Turkey. The logic was like this: we came with our jacket and can turn back with it. We have nothing to lose. So, they established businesses in a society where they do not know the language in a very short period of time. In twenty years, we became a real economic force. Ninety per cent of us became successful. This is a very serious thing. We even came from rural parts of Turkey. They did not have any experience in trade (Esnaf, chair of a business organisation).*

While KT communities started to search for alternative means of livelihood, a big question during the middle of the 1990s was, what could they do to survive? As was stated in the chapter 3, the majority of the Kurdish and Turkish migrants to Britain were farm workers in Turkey. Thus, they had no experience of being small business owners prior to their arrival. In addition, the anxiety was increased because of their previous isolated working lives in the ethnically exclusive textile industry, which did not enable them to mix with British society. The dramatic and rapid decline of employment in the textile industry had caused uncertainty and insecurity within the KT communities. The idea of setting up small shops was also approached nervously. With no English skills and having no relationship with the broader society in their previous employment, they started to ask whether small business ownership was an alternative way of employment in which they could be successful. As Tufan mentions, he acquired the skills to maintain a shop next to his co-ethnics,

Initially, we (Turkiyeli people) started to work in textiles. We worked for several years. After the closure of textile factories we had to look around and we setup off-licences. Actually, it was not in people's mind to get into such jobs. People set-up their shops after looking at each other. People thought we can do it just as well. We do not have any profession. In the beginning, we were uneasy about it. What could a farmer do in London? Initially, we got really worried. We were not sure if we could do it or not. We thought of the possibility of being unsuccessful in the business. We have learnt the business from people who knew it (Tufan, male off-licence owner).

Moreover, there was a general tendency at that time for increasing numbers of the unemployed in the KT communities to start discussing their employment prospects, and anxiety was widespread during this time. Ates, a restaurant owner comments on the social background of the KT communities, changes in the British economy and the general feelings of Turkish and Kurdish people:

Starting from the end of 1960s, we can see emigration from Turkey. Almost all of these people worked in the textile business. In 1988, a large group of people came to the UK. Some of them were not politically motivated in Turkey. However, in order to have a resident permit they claimed refugee status in the UK. All the people came here from villages. They almost brought their chickens with them. They were of all ages. All of these people started to work in textiles. You did not see so many restaurants and off-licences in those days. Off-licences used to be owned by Indians and restaurants were owned by Greek Cypriots. People faltered as a result of the collapse of the textile industry. They faltered, and asked themselves what is going on, what we can do? They entered into off-licence business.

They then spread into the restaurant and coffee-shop businesses. In this way it has changed. Then, the children of the migrants grew up. As their grown-up children have better skills in English some of them entered into different sectors. However, a majority of migrants have stayed in the same place (Ates, restaurant owner)

Cinar's case, below, exemplifies the process of interest alignment in setting-up businesses. Initially, like other unemployed co-ethnics he had to look for opportunities in order to survive. Because of the low transferability of cultural capital in terms of English language competence and qualifications, the opportunity for finding employment in the mainstream labour market was limited. While he was unemployed the possibility of finding a job was discussed in friendship networks. He regularly attended a Kurdish-Turkish community organization, meeting with friends, discussing the possible alternatives, getting recommendations, sharing information for survival. Social networks were a means to "formulate shared meanings and definitions that people bring to their situation" (McAdam et al., 1996, p.5). Such micro-mobilisation of networks is necessary for collective resource mobilisation. It entails framing the possible further action for economic survival (Benford and Snow, 2000). Cinar's case is a clear example of a process the author of this book calls *interest alignment* towards business ownership. The interest in setting-up a shop and the possible benefits of it were rationally and jointly calculated with his co-ethnics and relatives. Setting up a shop as a viable means of survival is socially constructed and elaborated by the micro-mobilisation of networks. As Cinar mentions,

I started to search for opportunities after the collapse of the textile industry. You have to do that in order to survive. You have to earn your living. You evaluate in your mind the things they tell you and recommend. You choose the option that is suitable, the one to suit your conditions. Yet, your relative also plays a role in the direction you take. We were socializing at an association, passing time with friends there. My friends from the association recommended this shop to me. They informed me that the shop was for sale (Cinar, off-licence owner).

The KT communities' habitus to a large extent is characterised by "a sense of place in the social order" (Bourdieu, 1984, p. 471), an understanding of shared social environment of opportunities and constraints based on their social class. They internalised the opportunities and constraints that are at hand in their host environment. As Bourdieu (1984, p.471) asserts that

objective limits become a sense of limits, a practical anticipation of objective limits acquired by experience of objective limits, "a sense of one's place" which leads one to exclude oneself from the goods, persons, places and so forth from which one is excluded.

According to the narratives of the interviewees, their sense of place in the host society led to adjust their expectations for a successful means of livelihood in the small business ownership. Interest alignment in small business ownership was a result of the objective limits that become a sense of limits as a survival strategy.

Interest alignment, moreover, led to partnerships within the KT communities. The interviewees stated that textile factories had provided relatively high wages that they were not accustomed to in their homeland. This enabled them to accumulate capital that could be invested in business start-ups. The capital accumulated via working in the textile business was directed towards investments in coffee-shops, restaurants and off-licences in a very short period of time. Gules, a mini-market owner, describes the structural change in the economy for KT communities as such:

When I came to this neighbourhood there were few Turkish businesses. There were at most ten shops in total. We were working in the textile industry. 70 thousand people were working in textiles. The textile business was transferred to third world countries such as Poland, China, and Romania in order to benefit from cheap labour in those regions. The textile sector collapsed and 70 thousand people suddenly became unemployed. This happened in just one year. These people formed business partnerships to set up shops with their accumulated capital from the in textile industry. While there were four or five partners in the beginning, the number of partners has decreased gradually as they got bigger. Now, you can find take-away businesses in every village in England (Gules, mini-market owner).

One of the consequences of pushing KT textile workers into self-employment was that it has been felt in every corner in Britain. Aksoy, chair of a refugee organisation who used to work in a textile factory comments on the processes involved in setting-up small businesses:

People accumulated good money during their time working in the textile business. They have started to show their presence in two sectors since the mid-1990s. The first one is small groceries. Families came together to set-up a shop. The second one is kebab shops. Above all, while the number of kebab shops in London increased dramatically, there is no one small town from coastal towns to all other small towns outside of London that does not have a Kebab shop (Aksoy, chair at a refugee organisation).

In other words, the impact of de-industrialisation, more particularly the collapse of the textile industry, has doubly pushed KT communities, first to self-employment and second to outer London. As they could no longer find employment in London, setting up a take-away out of the city emerged as an option.

There were several reasons for this shift into retailing and catering. Firstly, Kurds and Turks initially had been oriented towards jobs that did not require English language competence. Thus, textile factories provided an environment wherein they could work collectively and earn a livelihood without needing to learn English. In other words, they were able to find employment in areas that did not require high levels of cultural capital in terms of language competence. As Cinar mentions:

> *When we came to the UK in 1989, we started to work in the textile business. There was nothing else that we could do. We didn't know English. After the collapse of the textile industry we got into such businesses (retailing and catering). My wife's relatives used to be here. They are also originally peasant. They didn't have detailed knowledge about here either. They worked in textiles as well (Cinar, off-licence owner).*

In addition, the intensive working lives of KT migrants in the textile industry did not enable them to acquire cultural capital in terms of language competence. While such a working environment has played a major role in strengthening the ties between and within KT communities, it was an obstacle to developing ties with British society. In this regard, working in the textile industry was one of the contributing factors in the development of bonding capital rather than bridging capital. As Gules comments,

> *The first generation emigrants from Turkey still cannot speak English. They entered into intensive working lives. Some people started to work straight after their arrival at the airport. They started to work immediately. As they entered such an intensive working life, they had serious problems adapting and integrating. They just concentrated on their working lives. You cannot find anyone who worked for a British factory or British farm (Gules, mini-market owner).*

Narts, owner of a business consultancy firm that deals with licence issues for KT shops mentions that the lack of English language competency was compensated by help from their children. In other words, the lack of institutionalised and embodied forms of cultural capital related to the host country was compensated by social capital. The lack of cultural capital was not only related to the English language, but also to a lack of knowledge about host country customs, rules and know how in dealing with the bureaucracy. Furthermore, he talks about the textile factory closures and how Turkish and Kurdish workers pushed into self-employment:

> *Because of the cheap labour in Romania and Bulgaria the textile industry has moved to those regions. Mainland Turks started to lose their jobs. When they lost their jobs, they started to think about what they could do with their hot cash. These men could not speak English. If something happened he asked his son or daughter for help. While they were searching for new opportunities, getting into the corner shop business came to mind. The simplest thing a man could do. Then, they thought they could sell take-away, kebabs. We have all established our own businesses. We were obliged to do this because we could not do anything else. Other ethnic groups do the same thing. In general, all ethnic groups are working in the service sector. You cannot find a Chinese factory owner. The situation is different for Cypriots. However, all migrant groups who came at the same time as us did not have any other choice (Narts, owner of a consultancy firm).*

In a very short time period of time, Kurds and Turks have managed to establish their businesses. *Turkish Catering News (2002),* a Turkish magazine has estimated the increase in the number of catering businesses to be from 200 at most in 1975 to 15,000 in 2001.The whole KT communities once almost entirely employed in the textile industry (London Medya, 2003), searched for a new means of survival and decided to invest in small business ownership. The decision process was dependent on consultations within the KT communities which resulted in an interest alignment for setting up businesses amongst many KT community members. This involved the framing process, in which acting collectively becomes possible as it mediates between networks mobilised for common ends and the opportunity structure. In order to act collectively for setting up businesses, as a minimum, people have to both aggregate around certain interests in their lives and feel optimistic about the fact that acting collectively could actually redress their situation. In other words, the absence of this cognitive process which brings and binds people together around certain interests would make the mobilisation process very difficult and probably impossible. However, according to the literature on ethnic minority entrepreneurship (see Light,1972; Kloosterman & Rath, 2003; Waldinger et al., 1990), the collective ethnic minority tendency towards, and interest in setting up businesses is assumed to be relatively unproblematic and to have existed prior to mobilisation rather than having been socially constructed and created by the mobilisation process.

The way to initiate business start-ups was to imitate co-ethnics who already had settled businesses. Co-ethnics from the same social background had initiated and exemplified the pathway towards small business ownership (Özaktanlar, 2003). Self-employment in the retail and catering sectors was a means of providing employment for the immediate and wider family as well as co-ethnics. Social networks were utilised in order to obtain cheap labour. Such social networks are social capital for business owners and are used for accumulating other forms of capital, such as economic capital. Below, Aksoy, chair of a community organisation exemplifies that the reciprocity between the business owner and the worker is shaped by the patron-client relationship. While the co-ethnic worker provides cheap labour, the business owner provides accommodation and pocket money. Moreover, at the end of the quote he states that, prior to their arrival to the UK; the KT community members lacked the necessary cultural capital to set-up and operate businesses. They have acquired the skills to run a business in London. Yet, the cultural capital related to running a business is shared with the whole community.

After the closure of textile factories we started to search for new opportunities. We went outside of London. Families went and set-up a supermarket. They sometimes needed three or four workers. They found them in London. They knew the workers' language, paid low wages and even paid wages two or three weeks late. The workers usually resided on the upper floor of the shop. That is how they have been successful. They learned such businesses here. Someone from the community learns how to run a business, and he or she can teach it to the whole community (Aksoy, chair of a community organisation and ex-textile worker).

As I mentioned earlier, the skills to set-up and maintain a business were acquired with the help of co-ethnics who were already running retail and catering businesses. Co-ethnic help in terms of skill transmission aims to ease the risk and anxiety related to ethnic entrepreneurship. Sahir, a coffee-shop owner who used to run a restaurant talks about his experience in the business. He became a role model for many KT would-be restaurant owners. This is important since after his experience, it became more feasible for many Kurds and Turkish migrants to consider opening a restaurant business as a possible means of livelihood. Such role models provided the necessary cultural capital for would-be restaurant owners. They transmitted the cultural capital for setting-up and running catering and retail businesses to co-ethnics, so that this could be a success. As he asserts,

The textile factories started to close down one by one. Ninety per cent of the Turkish speaking community suddenly encountered unemployment. As a consequence, they started to search for jobs in new areas which were feasible for them. Some of them have been successful. At least, they own small businesses that belong to them. Before this coffee-shop, I was running a coffee-restaurant. It was on Stoke Newington High Street. We opened that place together with a friend. It initiated the first example of a coffee-restaurant business to serve the Turkish community. Afterwards, lots of businesses were inspired by us. The Turkish community looked for new opportunities as a means of survival as they were sacked from the textile industry. People got into businesses that they could achieve. First shops, then kebab shops and coffee-restaurants became widespread. In that period, while we were thinking of new opportunities for employment, the most suitable thing to do seemed to be the coffee-restaurant business (Sahir, coffee-shop owner).

Almost all my interviewees stated there were almost no small business owners in the KT communities when they arrived in Britain. There were only Turkish Cypriots who owned chicken fast food businesses. CTK self-employment was not widespread as such. Small businesses in the retail and catering sectors were owned by Indians, Greek Cypriots and Pakistanis. There were no KT owned businesses when this interviewee arrived in the UK. As Cem mentions:

I came to this country in 1972. At that time, there were no Turkish business owners I know of in the community. Maybe there were some, but I didn't know them (Cem, chair of a community organization).

In addition, only one of my interviewees had been a small business owner prior to his arrival. They were not originally running small businesses in their country of origin. Skills like knowing how to run a small business are a form of cultural capital, which were developed in the UK. On arrival in the UK, my interviewees lacked the necessary cultural capital to run such businesses. Prior to their arrival their means of survival to a large extent, was animal husbandry and agriculture labour. Consequently, the theoretical argument (Yuengert, 1995) that asserts the causal relationship between prior cultural capital attainments related to business ownership in the home country facilitating transition into self-employment in the host country could not be validated in this study. That is to say, there is no relationship between shopkeepers' prior cultural capital and their transition into catering and retail business ownership.

While Turkish and Kurdish migrants to Britain had held employee positions in the textile industry until the mid-1990s, Turkish Cypriots as early arrivals provided jobs to Turkish and Kurdish communities. The Turkish Cypriot textile factory owners have also been affected by the de-industrialisation. However, Turkish Cypriots did not experience the collapse of the textile industry in the same way as Turks and Kurds. They were largely integrated into the UK class system. As Cem, chair of a community organisation states:

Several Turkish Cypriots had to close their businesses or went to Cyprus to invest. Some of them couldn't become successful in Cyprus and turned back to the UK. Second and third generations of Cypriot Turks did not continue to run their fathers' businesses. They are professionalised and became teachers, doctors, accountants and so on. At the same time, we can talk about newly emerging Kurdish and Turkish petite bourgeoisie during the same period. When I came here in 1972, there wasn't even one Turkish business that I know of. Maybe there was, but we didn't know it. It was during the Gulf war times in 1991 that Britain was in economic crises. Cypriot Turks had invested in Eastern Europe. They were planning to benefit from the cheap labour. More than ten textile employers returned to Cyprus. They could not trade between Northern Cyprus and Britain as Cypriot products were controlled by the embargo. They went into bankruptcy. Most of them quit the textile business. The children and grandchildren of this generation moved into professional jobs, becoming lawyers, accountants and so on. (Cem, chair at a community organization).

As I state in the introduction chapter, the value of the collective resource mobilisation theory in the context of ethnic small businesses is that it is as illuminating with regard to the absence of collectivism as it is to its presence. The theory argues that, in the first instance, a sense of common interest or interest alignment toward business ownership among the co-ethnics is necessary to move into catering and retail businesses. The interest alignment involves the shift from low segment of proletariat to petty bourgeoisie.

Turkish Cypriots did not move into businesses like shop ownership after de-industrialisation started at the end of 1970s. There was no interest alignment to move into small business ownership within the Turkish Cypriot community. The members of the Turkish Cypriot community, to a large extent, differed from the Kurdish and Turkish communities in terms of the validation of institutionalised cultural capital. They were second or third generation of migrants to the UK. The acquired cultural capital in the host country was transposed into economic capital via professional jobs. Thus, Turkish Cypriots, to a large extent, were neither pushed nor pulled into self-employment. However, as discussed above, Kurds and Turks started to look for new opportunities in self-employment. That is to say, Kurds and Turks were pushed towards different means of survival than Turkish Cypriots. As Tekstil states,

Kurds and Turks are identical to each other. Turkish Cypriots are not into such small business ownership. They generally live outside of London, for example in Enfield. They are not in small business ownership. They are anglicised. They are different. Opportunities for employment have changed since we came to this country. There was a textile industry before, now there is restaurant and shop ownership for Kurds and Turks (Tekstil, retried textile businessman).

When the closures of textile factories resulted in mass unemployment in the KT communities, shop ownership did not develop as a quick response within the entire Kurdish and Turkish communities. For instance, Turkish and Kurdish migrants who did not have close relatives from whom they could borrow financial capital could not set-up their own businesses, immediately. They had to work for businesses owned by their co-ethnics. Social capital was utilized to find employment in catering businesses, but not for gathering economic capital. Even though there was an interest in setting-up a shop, the lack of economic and social capital prevented some individuals from setting up businesses straight away. The degree of social capital acquired by Olmez was insufficient to transpose it to economic capital. Unlike his co-ethnics who acquired economic capital from their relatives, Olmez had to work for several co-ethnic business owners for a while to accumulate economic capital. As Erel (2010, p.654) states, "speaking of the cultural and social capital of an ethnic migrant group is not useful as it glosses over intra group hierarchical distinctions and exclusions". In Olmez's case, he was excluded from kinship networks from where he could acquire economic capital. This issue is also discussed in more detail in the next chapter. In addition, initially, Olmez had no cultural capital related to his current business, which is a mini-supermarket. He acquired the skills to run a business via his friends. Thus, social capital has transposed into cultural capital in Olmez's case.

All of us more or less were in the same condition. I was unemployed for three months. After three months I found a job as a dish-washer in a restaurant. It was a very miserable period. I did not have any close relatives in this country. Then, I worked for a restaurant in the kitchen for three – five months. Then, I used my connections. I got into a restaurant. It was hard work there. I left the job and started to work as a waiter in another Turkish restaurant for a year. People (the KT communities) started to seek new opportunities for living. During those days, such business ownership was attractive. Turks started setting-up restaurants, markets, off-licences and coffee-shops. Savings from the time in the textile industry and loans from connections were invested in such shops. I am one of them. It was the fear of being unemployed that directed us towards such jobs. I have partners. I set it up together with my friends. Actually, trade was not my business (Olmez, mini-market owner).

Furthermore, Olmez's case is an example of an individual reacting against the sojourning mentality. Olmez did not willingly suffer being a waged labourer; he had no choice other than to accept jobs with hard working conditions. Olmez's case exemplifies the fear of being unemployed as the motivating factor for becoming self-employed. He changed his job several times and started a new one, which had more favourable working conditions.

Relying on the support of relatives and home-town networks also became common among the KT people (Atay, 2006). In some cases, interviewees tried to overcome unemployment via job-centres. However, these rarely provided a solution. The wider economic environment has also played a key role in the decision to become self-employed in the catering and retail sectors.

The major institutions were unable to redress the unemployment problems of the KT communities. For instance, Carsi, a mini-market owner, talks about his humiliating experience at job centres. Actually, his experience at job-centres was a motivating factor in his decision to opt for self-employment.

We knew it was impossible to live without any job. I went to the job-centres. I said enough, and rather than going there, I could do my own work. If you are unemployed you go to the job centres to see if they are going to provide you with some money. We have to wait 4-5 hours in order to have a word with them. If it is possible, I don't want to go there and get unemployment benefit. Until now, we have not received any benefits. Thank God (Carsi, mini-market owner).

Accordingly, it is possible to state; the motivating factor for moving into self-employment for him was the lack of alternatives. He was pushed into self-employment because of the inability of the job centre to provide a job for him. He was pushed towards self-employment because of the negative external factors he faced in Britain.

While de-industrialisation has been a major factor for pushing the KT communities into self-employment, changes in the political economy in the UK are not the only factors which pushed Kurdish and Turkish communities into self-employment. After the decline of the textile industry, the majority of the interviewees were motivated to enter self-employment by push or negative factors due to their rural background and lower educational qualifications, which resulted in poor employment prospects. However, there is evidence that, even though 4 of the interviewees unlike the majority of interviewees in this study have received higher education and attained degrees in British universities, however, they were unable to find appropriate employment according to their educational qualifications. The case of Olcay, who is running a Kebab shop together with his immediate family, exemplifies the lack of opportunity for finding a paid or salaried job:

I came here from Istanbul. I also attained my university degree from the same school (referring to me), London Metropolitan University. I graduated with a degree in business administration. As I could not find a job, I got into the kebab business. Now, as you see, we are running a Kebab shop. It has been two weeks since we bought this shop (Olcay, Kebab shop owner).

The structural changes in the British economy have not only overwhelmingly affected the KT communities, but are also reflected in the background of community organisations' members. The profile and the interests of the members of the organisations have changed in a short period of time. Such changes reinforce support networks. As Karadag, member of a Turkish and Kurdish community organisation states:

The background of our members has been changing over the years. I mean, a member registered as a worker could become a self-employed business owner or could be unemployed. In fact, it is very flexible. The migrants of our community do not have a fixed position in this country. Their aim in coming to this country was to have better living conditions. There are also people obliged to migrate, but generally, the reason was economic. All the people I know have worked in textile factories. However, they all shut down. Due to such changes, their interests have changed towards setting up a shop. They also support each other. If someone wants to setup a shop they, people come together and loan money to a would-be entrepreneur. Then the others provide support. We see such solidarity within the community (Karadag, manager at a Kurdish -Turkish community organisation).

As Karadag mentions, the interest towards setting up businesses among the KT communities required the utilisation of social capital and the intensification of networks to acquire economic capital for setting-up shops.

The process of setting up businesses was discussed within the families and community. The main motivation for would-be shop owners was that there were already a number of successful examples of individuals who had been observed running businesses. They thought, if their co-ethnics have managed to setup a shop and could successfully run it, why could they not do so the same. The few successful examples in the catering and retail sectors encouraged many others in the KT communities to follow the same path. There were also failures. According to the dominant narrative of the business owners, in a very short time period, there was a rapid growth in the number of small businesses. As Ismet, a partner at coffee-shop mentions:

Coffee-shops started to appear in 1993. People provided support for would-be entrepreneurs. It all happened in the same period. Kebab shop and most of the corner shops flourished in the same period. When someone sets up a shop, why cannot I do the same thing, thinks another guy. Even at home, my wife told me for instance; even Mehmet has set up a shop, couldn't you... It was with such an ambition that lots of people were motivated to set up a shop (Ismet, partner in a coffee- shop).

The statement made by Ismet's wife exemplifies the gendered division of labour within the household. This assigns the husband the 'bread winner' role and considers the wife a 'care taker', responsible for duties such as looking after children, cooking and cleaning. However, such gendered roles are not stable and fixed, but are open to changes in a specific historical context (See the next section for further discussion).

Such a structural shift towards self-employment also has implications for peripheral services provided for small businesses. A shop designer and market consultant talks about the increased demand for her services. The structural changes in the political economy created job opportunities for Yetisal. The co-ethnic lack of cultural capital with respect shop design was utilised by Yetisal:

> *When I came to the UK, most of our community members were working in textiles. When people started to lose their jobs in the textile industry, they went into supermarket and kebab businesses. Our people oriented towards supermarket businesses. Also, kebab businesses became a new area for investment. Thus, the demand for the services I could provide increased at that time. This shift towards small business ownership resulted in job opportunities in my area (Yetisal, shop designer and market consultant).*

The above discussion mainly focuses on the structural factors that pushed Turkish and Kurdish migrants into self-employment. Self-employment was reluctantly chosen as the only available alternative for employment. "Self-employment was a rational response to labour market obstacles" (Clark and Drinkwater, 2000, p.1) and blocked upward mobility (Waldinger, 1986). For instance, racialized migrant professionals face discrimination in the labour market, are ascribed negative characteristics, and their skills are viewed sceptically (Bates, 1997; Kyriakides & Virdee, 2003).

The following section discusses the pull factors; in which self-employment provided the desirable incentives, such as flexible working hours, self-realisation, independence and job satisfaction.

Another argument for business start-ups is an individual's particular interests, such as the need for achievement according to educational credentials and the desire for autonomy or independence. Self-employment provides the desirable incentives for achieving particular interests, such as the need for financial advancement and independence, flexible working hours and job satisfaction. In other words, individuals in this category were pulled into self-employment, 'voluntarily' attracted by perceived benefits.

According to my findings in this research, there were two interviewees in this category. Both Zeytin and Kumkapi had university degrees from Turkey and first had developed the idea of starting their own businesses during their studies. It was their occupational choice to set-up their own businesses. Self-realisation and a desire to use their own skills, talents and abilities were their motivation, which pulled them into self-employment. Zeytin had employment experience in the catering business and was pulled into self-employment by the possible independence that it offers:

After I graduated from the university I worked at trading companies. I wanted to have my own business. While I was studying at the university, I also worked in a restaurant as a waiter. I knew the business. I wanted to be independent as well. That's why I decided to run my own business (Zeytin, restaurant owner).

Moreover, the employment trajectories of some participants in this study represent both push and pull factors during different time periods. The case of Sahir initially represents the necessity entrepreneur who has been pushed into self-employment due to textile factory closures. As his first experience in self-employment was too demanding, he was pulled into another small business that could provide more flexible working hours. Sahir reported that both greater control over his life and reserving time for his family were the major reasons for shifting from one business to another. His first business ownership in the catering sector ended because of its demanding working schedule. He decided to end his partnership and set up a new coffee bar-restaurant in order to reserve time for his family. As a machine technician in Turkey, Sahir could not find a job in accordance with his educational background. In other words, migrating to Britain has meant devaluing his human capital. His cultural capital could not be transferred across borders. Initially, he was able to find paid employment in the textile industry. Then, he was pushed into self-employment because of factory closures. However, because of the tense working conditions he decided to change his business, but to another sector. Consequently, it is possible to state that his first employment in Britain can be viewed as downward mobility in relation to his educational background, and he was pushed from being a textile factory employee into self-employment. His second business ownership in the catering business entails opportunity entrepreneurship. He was pulled by the flexible working conditions in his new coffee-shop. In his own words:

We opened our first business in 1998 and here in 2005. I met my partner at a community centre in the early days of my arrival in the UK. He was one of my close friends. I quit that business because of working too much. It was very tiring. In addition, we have a family. We are a family of four people. We don't earn so much in this business, but it covers our expenses. It is a meeting point for our friends. This makes us happy. We open at 7:30 a.m. and close at 6 p.m. Before, it was not like this. We used to open early in the morning and work until late at night 11-12 p.m. We are much better right now. We can spare time for our children. We recognized that we could not spend enough time with our children. Our children's' education is very important for us. We thought we will lose our children. We had to make a choice between money and our children. Thus, we sold that place and bought this one. In terms of the working schedule, this business is much better. We can spend time with our children in the evening (Sahir, coffee shop owner).

In addition, four interviewees have setup shops because of family reasons. Gulay and Aksoy set up businesses to provide employment for their sons. They were aware of the fact that their sons would not be able to find any paid employment apart from in the co-ethnic economy with low pay. The second generation's low levels of institutionalised cultural capital, i.e. low levels of formal education attainment prevented them from finding employment as waged labourers in the mainstream labour market. The parents' decision to set up shops for their children was considered the only alternative for a reasonable livelihood. In addition, the main motive to set up shops was to keep their children away from crime and gangs. As Gulay mentions:

I set-up this shop, because of my son. He did not attend at school. He did not finish his studies. Most of his friends from the same period did not study. It was clear to me that he didn't want to study. I told him that he should work somewhere. He got into a job in a supermarket. He was good at it. He does not have any skills. I had to open this off-licence. He knows what he is doing (Gulay, off-licence owner).

In conclusion, the decline in the textile industry in Britain has been the major contributing factor for the majority of KT people entering self-employment. The interviewees' rural background and lower educational qualifications were not the sole reason for their poor employment prospects in paid jobs. Labour market discrimination, pull factors and lack of paid jobs were also contributory reasons for stepping into self-employment. There is also evidence that poor educational qualifications and English skills were not the sole grounds for entering into self-employment. A lack of available paid employment became a major push towards self-employment for the KT communities.

In such circumstances, the chances of finding a meaningful livelihood were low. The Kurdish and the Turkish migrants to the UK were experiencing unemployment in the mid-1990s. They shared similar problems and grievances as discussed above. In the early days of settlement, grievances related to adapting to the host country, learning its customs and lifestyle played an important role in the conservation, dissolution, and emergence of newly constructed, ethnic attachment, namely "Türkiyeli" and/or "our people". These issues in the early days of the settlement were vital importance for connecting Kurdish and Turkish communities. The close proximity of their living spaces and workplaces together with existence of community organisations paved the way for the construction a shared meaning of ethnicity among the Kurdish and Turkish migrants. In the next section, I discuss how shared interests facilitated an instrumentalist account of ethnicity.

Interests and Constructivist account of ethnicity and culture

The aim of this section is to examine the ways in which shared interests and experiences within the Turkish and Kurdish communities instrumentally paved the way for the construction of an identity called "Türkiyeli". I argue that identities brought from the home country are not fixed, but that ethnic identities are socially constructed and open to redefinitions. I show that the first component of Tilly's (1978) collective resource mobilisation theory, namely interests, can provide an approach for analysing the dynamics within KT communities. Ethnic identities and the groupings such as Turks and Kurds can change over time as circumstances affecting their lives change, and interests and claims made by the group members change as well.

In the case of most of the Kurdish and Turkish migrants, the Turks form an earlier migrant group in the UK than Kurds and their migration experiences are quite different from each other (See chapter 3). However, they have experienced similar problems from the time immediately following their arrival until now. According to one of the key informants, Cem, who was working for the Kurdish-Turkish organisation Halkevi, most of them got in touch with the Halkevi (People's Home). Indeed, the physical building of the organization functioned as a home until the organisation's social workers could find accommodation for some Kurdish and Turkish migrants. Some of the migrants had to live in organisation's building for seven months. Initially, Halkevi provided services indiscriminately to Kurdish and Turkish migrants for various issues such as finding accommodation and jobs, translation, filling out forms and applications and much more. This was the period when large cohorts of migrants arrived at the end of 1980s. During that period, both the Turkish and Kurdish communities found themselves in a situation where everyone had similar tasks to perform in textile factories in North London. Ethnic community organisations such as Halkevi with its service provision to Turks and Kurds, and participation in the activities of the organisation played a role in shaping their own identities.

The collapse of the textile industry caused mass unemployment and a large part of the KT communities decided to setup shops as a survival strategy as discussed above. Those shared experiences and class position in the host country contributed to collective consciousness. It is possible to argue that already existing collective consciousness and ethnic ties supported ethnic business start-ups and operation. Kurdish and Turkish collective identity facilitated ethnic enterprises; processes in business start-ups and maintenance also support collective ethnic attachment. That is to say, ethnic networks and ethnic minority businesses are mutually supportive of each other.

The spatial proximity of working places, the physical closeness of factories and homes of Kurdish and Turkish migrants in the UK also reinforced internal cohesion and networks. Textile factories used to provide a livelihood for CTK communities where they did not have to mix with other ethnic groups. This contributed to the development of high levels of bonding capital, but hindered the acquisition of bridging capital. Factories were later replaced by shops as a dominant form of employment. That is to say, the public spaces, and issues that matter in their daily lives were shared by both Kurdish and Turkish communities, so they could socially construct a shared identity based on their class position, problems and the practices of their daily life. The proximity of home and workplaces has made it easier to develop collective belonging and feelings of solidarity. The hard working life resulted in the total isolation of the CTK communities from British society as ex-trade unionist Aksoy comments:

> *People used to wake up at 5 in the morning and hurry along to the textile businesses. They did not have any idea about the life in England. People went to the factories together not to lose their way. They got into buses together not to lose their way. They got out from the buses together. Because of this, people chose to live in certain places. Most of them used to work till 11-12 in the evening. Some were even sleeping on top of the machines (Aksoy, chair of a community organisation).*

As mentioned before, the manner of the settlement of Kurds and Turks did not allow them to mix easily with British people. The new arrivals had to establish close ties with already settled co-ethnics and Kurdish and Turkish community organisations in order to acquire information and overcome the basic problems they faced in their new destination.

The close proximity of ethnic groups and the existence of an earlier KT community, namely the Turkish Cypriots, helped both the Turkish and Kurdish communities to acquire information to solve their basic daily problems relating to various issues. The concentration of Turkish Cypriots, Kurdish and Turkish communities in North London made exchange of information relatively easy. Thus, it is clear that social capital acquired in their new destination was utilised to drive their cultural capital. The cultural capital acquired by the members of communities is bounded by the spatiality. As

Karadag, a Turkish Cypriot who is a chair of a Turkish Cypriot community organisation states,

> *Our people (Turkish and Kurdish people) are working in the service sector. They experience a ghetto life as they do not know the language and don't have any idea about the customs and what's going on in the society in general. Turks and Kurds are living in northern districts of London. Everybody settles next to their co-ethnics. Early arrivals provide information about their experiences, practical knowledge on how to accomplish something, job opportunities, settlement, welfare benefits, course of law, and how to take refuge. Because of such issues they have close ties (Karadag, manager of a community organisation).*

During the early years of settlement, these issues were the major interests of the KT communities. In order to find a solution to these problems, social capital was utilised to acquire information and the required resources. They could receive guidance in their own language in co-ethnic neighbourhoods, where the co-ethnic neighbourhoods provided a safety net in the new destination. Mobilisation of social networks towards these issues was the means for redressing their situation in London. Access to various resources and information about key issues was available in these neighbourhoods. An ethnic neighbourhood is instrumental for the mobilisation of ethnic networks for generating valuable resources, which could be more easily accessible in close proximity. On the basis of their interests, the KT communities established close ties. Kurdish and Turkish communities strategically form ties in order to achieve common ends. As Karadag states at the beginning of his quote, the expression "our people" corresponds to Kurdish and Turkish people. Such an ethnic attachment is formed on the basis of their interests.

Ethnic organizations have played a key role in forming solidarity networks and determining the beneficiaries of the services they provide. They provide their services to a large extent selectively and control their resources by excluding non-KT communities. Services are provided to the Kurdish and Turkish migrants under the ethnic identity *Türkiyeli*. *Türkiyeli* could be used as an umbrella term for all ethnic groups in Turkey. It encompasses Turkish migrants from Northern Cyprus, Turks and Kurds. As Erel (2010, p.655) mentions, starting from the 1980s, "this was a result of a political alliance to demand recognition and resources within the London multiculturalist local government framework". In consequence, the resources delivered via ethnic organisations did not specifically target a specific ethnic community based on primordialist account, such as Turks or Kurds. The individual benefits were distributed according to the constructivist account based on shared interests and the living conditions of the KT communities. Such an understanding created scripts of shared interests.

Thus, the constructivist approach to ethnic identity focuses not only on the circumstances facilitating ethnic identity like instrumentalism, but also on kinds of bonds those circumstances create based on primordial moorings (Cornell & Hartmann, 2007). In other words, while instrumentalism focuses the external structure promoting certain interests among groups, primordialism involves a sense of "peoplehood", "common origin", and "blood ties". Ethnic groups may be influenced by circumstantial factors but they also use skin colour, ancestry, place of origin, a cultural practice, morality to distinguish group members and non-members and draw a line between "us" and "them". The constructivist account put emphasis on the role agency in the making of an ethnic identity. Individuals and groups may re-shape their identity. As Cornell and Hartmann (2007, p.83) argue that,

It should be clear; then, that the constructivist account does not depart from circumstantialist claims about the fluidity and dynamism neither of ethnicity and race, nor from its claims about the critical role does that context play in collective identification and action. It adds to those claims a creative component, rescuing ethnicity and race from the prison of circumstance.

For instance, in addition to the organisation Halkevi mentioned above, another community organisation, Day-Mer – a Turkish and Kurdish Community Centre – provides several services to KT communities. Actually, its name Day-Mer is a combination of two words, 'Dayanışma Merkezi', which means Solidarity Centre. According to the organisation's web page, it provides "help, information, advice and advocacy on enquiries on a wide range of fields from welfare issues to setting up a small business and help with your enquiries about your existing business. In addition, our (Day-Mer) advice centre is OISC registered and advice on immigration, citizenship, housing, welfare, health, education, education is also provided" (Day-Mer, 2014). Day-Mer also runs a youth service with clubs for around 100 students. Moreover, 2014 marked the 25th anniversary of Day-Mer fest, which is the longest running festival in Hackney. According to Oktay Sahbaz from Day-Mer, "the biggest event of the festival is the Park Celebration which has been taking place at Clissold Park and 10-15 thousand people from all parts of the community".

Kurdish and Turkish groups with common interests have been organised in various ways to pursue those interests. They establish more or less exclusive institutions specifically aiming to solve the problems group members face. Group members are bound together by their dependence on, and participation in, these institutions. In the case of Day-Mer, the institution is supported by the TUC. External recognition and support provided by the TUC encourages Kurds and Turks to organise under one umbrella. Identity construction involves group members distinguishing between themselves and non-members. These institutions not only help group members to solve their problems but also embed their '*Türkiyeli*' identity in the organised social relationship. According to Erdemir and Vasta (2007, p.7), "the most popular way of self-identification among our respondents was the Turkish neologism 'Türkiyeli', literally meaning 'someone from Turkey'". This observation was also confirmed during the fieldwork for this book.

As I state earlier in the introduction, one of the contributions of this book is that the theory of collective resource mobilisation allows us to critique primordialism. The Kurdish and Turkish communities found themselves in a similar problematic situation in their host country, where they could socially construct and derive an identity and form attachments to each other as a result of the experiences and shared conditions in their lives. The tension and armed conflict between the Turkish state and Kurdish guerrillas does constitute a minor problem for the cooperation on various issues between Kurds and Turks in London. Moreover, the shared experiences, problems and interests bring Kurdish and Turkish people into constant contact in their daily lives. Situational interests and shared experiences common to the Kurdish and Turkish communities resulted in a collective consciousness with in both communities. It was common during the interviews to hear that Kurdish and Turkish communities in the UK were called "our people" or "Türkiyeli". One of my interviewees explains how situational problems, grievances and interests in their daily lives paved the way to a socially constructed shared identity and networks of solidarity:

There are lots of reasons that bind Turkish and Kurdish communities. The child of a Kurdish nationalist parent and child of a Turkish nationalist go to the same school. Child of a Kurdish nationalist and a Turkish nationalist go to the same school. They both experience the same problems. They become closer. For instance, both Turks and Kurds have to have a resident permit to stay in the UK. They had to use the same consultancy and translation services. They exchange information in their neighbourhoods. They live in the same ghettos. They have adaptation problems. Children have poor educational success. As they do not see any future in school life they search for new areas of existence. Some of them become gang members. Both Turks and Kurds face the same problems in hospitals and elsewhere. When people from various social backgrounds sit next to each other, they can support each other. Another example is the riots. All Turkish and Kurdish people supported each other. There is a political dissidence between Turks and Kurds in Turkey. The disintegration between Kurds and Turks is a problem in Turkey. Here, the shared common problems can bring people together (Zet, restaurant owner).

The ideological, religious, and ethnic differences that cause major conflicts in the home country rarely become salient in the host country. Interests in the host country bring different identities together. Instrumental identities could be observed within partnerships of Turkish-Kurdish, secular-religious migrants. For instance, non-religious Turkish wholesaler Sancak established a joint venture with a religious, Kurdish wholesaler in order to produce meat related products. The wholesalers aligned their interests for the joint venture even though their ethnic and religious identities are a potential source of conflict in their home country. The tensions in their home country do not appear to influence the community relations in the UK. Ethnic sentiments do not affect businesses. My informant Cem who is a Turkish Cypriot mentions that relations between the Greek and Turkish Cypriots in the 1970s in the UK were amicable and helpful to one another, even though Turkish invasion of Cyprus has taken place in 1974. Likewise, the relations between Kurds and Turks in the UK are amicable. The communities once had conflicting relations between each other in their home countries have amicable relations in their host countries due to the shared problems and interests they have in their new environment. The shared interests and problems are the main motive to establish bonds of cooperation for survival in the host country, where mainstream institutions and larger society could not provide safety networks for the newly arrived migrants. Thus, the Cyprus dispute between Greece and Turkey and tensions between Turks and Kurds in Turkey did not and do not create tensions between Greek and Turkish Cypriots and Kurds and Turks in the UK. In his own words,

> In 1974, there was a war between Greek and Turkish Cypriots. There was a political apathy between sides. However, our relations with Greek Cypriots in the UK were not like the relations between Turkish and Greek Cypriots in Cyprus in the 1970s. The elected Greek Cypriot local councillors in London had a great positive impact on us. In the UK, they do not have something to share. We (Turkish Cypriots) benefited a lot from Greek Cypriots in various spheres of life, such as in employment, housing and social life. This cooperation and amicable relations between Greek and Turkish Cypriots in the UK in the 1970s applies to the relations between Kurds and Turks in the UK (Cem, chair of a community organisation)

Cooperation between Kurdish and Turkish community members whose ideological orientations are conflicting is salient. Partnerships were instrumental in gathering the necessary economic capital to set-up shops and reduce the risk of failures. The interest alignment within the Kurdish and Turkish, secular and religious groupings paved the way for new forms of ethnic and religious ties. It should be noted that, newly constructed attachments between individuals with previously conflicting identities in the home country are instrumental and situational. It was instrumental and situational for the generation of resources for setting up and operating businesses. As Narts mentions, when the reason to act collectively disappears, the newly constructed ethnic networks and bonds also become weaker:

They either had to work as workers, or three to five of them had to unite to set up a business, create an opportunity to work. They gradually have become an economic power. Then, it is the rule of trade and capitalism. As they started to earn more, partnerships became smaller; they decreased to two and one. They didn't plan any of those things. There was no other choice. They do not know the language. I experienced adaptation problems. I could not work. In some cases, the people united to set up a shop were three or four relatives who employ their nephews. It was the same process as in our villages. They employed their relatives. All of them continue in the same way (Narts, owner of a consultancy firm).

The quote above also mentions the village scale collaboration. The interviewee links the village scale practices of solidarity to the partnerships in small business ownerships. Another major finding of the study is that cultural practices prevalent in village-scale collaborative production, (see the section on culturalist theories and *imece*), and the patron-client and patriarchal relationships attached to the mode of production, have initially been dissolved and reproduced according to the changes in the British economy. This clearly supports the constructivist account of ethnicity. The changes in circumstances alter the utility of those identities. As Cornell and Hartman (2007, p.61) state "both identity and action ... are mediated, if not determined, by the circumstances and contexts in which individuals and groups find themselves". In a similar vein, this confirms the Tilly (1977) theoretical model, in which shared interests facilitate unities such as partnerships in small business ownership. Interests promote a common identity and unifying structure among individuals in the Kurdish and Turkish populations based on primordial ties such as kinship and place of origin. Thus, ethnic ties and identities are powerful resources in times of need for mobilising KT community members on behalf of their interests. In other words, interests are a precondition for the mobilisation of networks for common ends. The theory of collective action argues that, in the first instance, a sense of common interests or interest alignment in setting-up businesses is required among co-ethnics. It deals with the framing of interest in a particular space and time.

Initially, the shift towards waged labour in factories, where all men and women had to perform the same tasks for equal wages, led to the changes in village-scale practices such as patron-client relationships and women's gendered roles performed for the reproduction of the family. It is asserted that the woman's role and position within the family is affected when they find employment as a waged labourer. This also increases their individual power and self-confidence (Karaoglan and Ökten, 2012).They had greater control over the budget. They could decide what to do with their earnings. For instance, one of the preliminary interviewees, who were hairdresser, stated that the shift from factory work to small household level businesses in the Kurdish and Turkish communities affected his business as well. He had more female customers when they were working in textile factories. The closure of factories in turn has pushed Kurdish and Turkish communities to set up small shops, to a large extent based on family labour where women's labour is unpaid and consumed within the family. Women started to work in coffee-shops, restaurants, and off-licences mainly helping their husbands. Thus, many women have lost their economic independence. In sum, it is possible to say that "all that is solid melts into air" (Marx and Engels, 2004), but that which has melted into air may once again become solid. That is to say, the home town culture may be dissolved in time due to changes that have taken place in the political economy, but once dissolved it is also possible that the practises may once again be reproduced. Consequently, cultural practises are not fixed and unchanging as the culturalist theories assert; but rather the mode of production can influence the relation of production and cultural practices as well. In addition, the reconstructed cultural practices in the new setting also have an impact on the means and relations of production such as access to capital, markets, labour and information as well as gender relations (see chapter 6). The theoretical and analytical models I discuss in chapter two assert that ethnic communities have a specific fixed mind set which is ahistorical. On the other hand, the components of the theory of collective action focus on the processes in interests, networks, mobilisation and opportunity structure. The processes in these components determine the extent of collective action and practices. In other words, collective practices and ethnic identity are a function of processes in these components.

Conclusion: Interest alignment and collective identity

The possibility of finding employment was discussed by newly created co-ethnic, kinship networks. Co-ethnics regularly attended a Kurdish-Turkish community organization, meeting with friends, discussing the possible alternatives, getting recommendations, and sharing information for survival. Social networks were a means to "formulate shared meanings and definitions that people brought to their situation" (McAdam, 1996, p.5). Such micro-mobilisation of networks is necessary for collective resource mobilisation. It entails framing the possible further action for economic survival. Micro-mobilisation in co-ethnic networks involves the process of *interest alignment* towards business ownership. Because of the risks associated with self-employment, feelings of anxiety were common among would-be entrepreneurs. The lack of cultural capital to communicate with customers was also a contributing factor for anxiety. However, the interest in setting-up a shop was a rationally calculated act made in consultation together for co-ethnics. Setting up a shop as a viable means of survival was a socially constructed and elaborated alternative for a means of survival through the micro-mobilisation of networks.

Another major finding of this section of the chapter is that the interest component of the theory of collective resource mobilisation allows us to critique primordialism. Kurdish and Turkish communities found themselves in a similar problematic situation in their host country, where they could socially construct and derive an ethnic attachment and connect to each other as a result of the experiences and shared conditions in their lives. This interest alignment on the issues that matter to them brought people and communities together and enhanced feelings of solidarity. The tension and armed conflict between the Turkish state and Kurdish guerrillas did not constitute a problem between Kurds and Turks in terms of their cooperation on various issues in London. Similarly, religious and secular wholesalers could establish a joint venture. The shared experiences, problems and interests, which brought Kurdish and Turkish people constantly into touch with each other in their daily lives. The interviewees explained how situational problems, grievances, and interests in their daily lives led them to create networks of solidarity, and new ethnic attachments. Situational interests and shared experiences common to Kurdish and Turkish communities resulted in collective consciousness with in both communities. During the interviews, it was common to hear that Kurdish and Turkish communities in the UK were referred to as "our people" or "Türkiyeli".

Ethnic groups strategically redefine their attachments according to whom they cooperate with (Bonacich and Modell, 1980, p.3). Turkish and Kurdish communities facing similar problems and sharing meanings and definitions around their situation strategically form ethnic ties in order to achieve common ends. This perspective underlines the constructivist idea of ethnicity in a sense that the assertion of "Türkiyeli" or "our people" by Kurdish and Turkish communities is instrumental in acquiring power and advancing interests.

New forms of ethnic attachments and interest alignment are not only limited to Kurdish and Turkish communities, but also observable between various ethnic groups. This is because of the shared meanings and definitions that different ethnic groups bring to their situation. The interest alignment between various ethnic groups is situational in the sense that they face the same problems and share a common class position. As Gules mentions,

We have a great social network. We prefer to work with Indians, Iranians, Philippians and Turks. In general, we prefer to work with them because we share the same destiny. We treat all migrants as if they are Turkish. We share the same situation, the same life, and the same conditions. The British state treats them in the same way it treats us. It exploits them in the same way as it exploits us. They do not differentiate when they exploit. Thus, we should not discriminate when we unite (Gules, mini-market owner).

The pull factors indicate that the values attached to self-employment are positive and complementary to entrepreneurial behaviour. The pull factors to set-up businesses are the desire to be independent, to use one's own skills, talents and abilities, self-realisation, a particular interest in the restaurant and food businesses, keeping children away from crime and gangs, and finally, as in the case of Sahir, work-family balance.

The push factors have led a large part of the mainland Kurdish Turkish communities to experience a common fate and thrown them into a similar situation, which also enabled them to develop a collective consciousness of their social reality. The increase in the number of catering businesses from 200 at most in 1975 to 15,000 in 2001 clearly indicates the collective fate. On the other hand, there were several factors which eased Turkish Cypriots' adaptation problems. First, Turkish Cypriots have a longer presence in the UK. It also corresponded to the existence of a welfare state, which provided better support networks. Furthermore, they were migrants from a former British colony. Finally, Turkish Cypriots attained mainstream employment in multicultural workplaces where the basic means of communication was the English language. All these factors have reflected on the prospects of second and third generations. Thus, it is possible to state that Turkish Cypriots were not thrown into the same situation after the demise of the textile industry.

The ethnic groups' interpretation of prospects for a livelihood in small business ownership is dependent on how they "locate, perceive, identify, and label occurrences within their life space and the world at large" (Snow et al., 1986, p. 464). The Turkish Cypriot community did not experience the interest alignment process in small business ownership. Interest alignment involves defining social reality and occurrences within their life space, and feasible alternatives for a livelihood such as small business ownership in the retail and catering sectors. Consequently, interest alignment not only shapes social reality, but also provides an action strategy for a possible means of survival.

As I mentioned in chapter two, the term interest alignment indicates the social constructivist view of the micro-mobilisation of tasks and processes and interpretations of experiences and grievances in their social context.

According to social movement literature, frame alignment refers to the "shared meanings and definitions that people bring to their situation" (McAdam et al., 2008, p.281). Without the framing process acting collectively would be impossible as it mediates between networks mobilised for common ends and opportunity structures. The framing process could be viewed as the generation and diffusion of interests directed towards mobilizing and/or counter-mobilising ideas and meanings, which is enabled or constrained by the cultural and social context (Benford and Snow, 2000). The term 'framing' provides an opportunity to examine the ways in which an ethnic identity is constructed and to understand the processes of interpretations of experiences and grievances in their social context.

For Turkish Cypriots, it was not possible to develop a collective consciousness with mainland Kurds and Turks for their social reality. The Turkish Cypriot community was not capable of creating a common script in response to the features of the social reality that confronted the mainland Turkish community. They did not have an interest alignment in small business ownership. Interest alignment in business ownership refers to the linkage of ethnic group and entrepreneurial orientations such that ethnic group interests, values and beliefs and entrepreneurial orientations, goals and ideology are congruent and complementary (Snow et al., 1986, p.464). Interest alignment through which networks and bonds of solidarity were utilised for business start-ups and maintenance with Turkish Cypriots after the demise of the textile industry was not possible. In other words, Turkish Cypriots have not participated, and are not participating, in solidarity bonds and the mobilisation of resources for survival in small business ownership.

On the other hand, people from mainland Turkey, Kurds and Turks alike had experienced a common fate, starting with their pre-migration experiences. They were thrown into a similar situation, which enabled them to develop a collective consciousness of their social reality. They had an interest alignment in small business ownership. The framing process enabled the generation and diffusion of interests directed towards the mobilisation of networks for small business ownership.

In the next chapter, I discuss the ways in which networks are mobilised for ethnic minority business ownership.

Chapter Six:
Social Networks and Mobilisation

As I mentioned in chapter two, mobilisation of networks involves the efforts by which Turkish and Kurdish community members acquire control over the resources needed for entrepreneurial action. It entails the collective control over capitals that, this study contends, facilitates ethnic business ownership and the strategic activation of forms of capital that ethnic business owners commonly confront. As Tilly (1978) states, the word *mobilisation* "...identifies the process by which a group goes from being a passive collection of individuals to an active participants in public life". It denotes the utilisation of strategically formed ethnic attachments to invoke economic interests.

More specifically, what I mean by the collective control over resources is the consumption of strategic information promoting ethnic businesses, economic capital, reliable and cheap labour, (re)-construction of ethnic identity and cultural practices, and protection of business premises by the ethnic community.

This chapter aims to assess the broad research question of how Turkish and Kurdish community members have become entrepreneurs and maintained their businesses as a livelihood in London. The specific objective related to this broad research question is to assess the role of the co-ethnic networks as well as community organisations in resolving various problems in the formation and maintenance of ethnic minority businesses. Kurdish and Turkish communities to a large extent encountered the same problems as mentioned earlier in chapter three. I argue that the problems related to economic capital, information, security, labour, skills, dispute resolution and claim making are addressed by the mobilisation of various kinds of capital such as social, cultural and economic capital. Thus, while the existing research mainly focuses on social networks that are activated merely for business start-ups (Aldrich, 1999; Granovetter, 1985; Johannisson, 1988; Larson, 1991; Light, 1972; Waldinger et al., 1990; Aldrich & Zimmer, 1986), this section not only focuses on the mobilisation of social capital that support the establishment of businesses, but also on how social networks are utilized in efforts to solve various problems in the maintenance of small businesses. These various maintenance problems include, providing security for the business premises, finding trustworthy workers, dispute resolution with partners and other businesses, liaising with the council and police for better business regulations, and finally the acquisition of information and skills for running their small businesses.

In addition, I suggest that the re-enactment and persistence of ethnic collective identity and practises are dependent upon structural changes characterizing British cities and the structure of the groups. The reproduction of Turkish village-scale collaboration, practices and values to deal with adverse circumstances appears in a post-industrial London. One of the most crucial traditions that has been re-enacted after immigration was *imece*. Several interviewees stated that the re-enactment of *imece*, which is village level collaboration played a role in overcoming various problems in starting-up and maintaining businesses (Esnaf, chair of a community organisation and wholesaler; Ismet, coffee shop owner; Narts, shop consultant; Yetisal, shop designer; Zet, restaurant owner).

For example, during weddings villagers engage in the activities of the ceremony. They participate in the preparation of the venue, of the food, including but not limited to the, construction of the new house for the newlyweds etc. This tradition reconstructed in the modern world where, in big cities, co-villagers would help each other in undertaking such tasks. *Imece* is a voluntary activity, yet has its unwritten rules and obligations. Particularly when members of the community are co-located, reciprocity is expected (Erginkaya, 2012, p.10).

Moreover, Paul Stirling (1965, p.30), who carried out ethnographic research in two Turkish villages between 1949 and 1994, expresses villagers solidarity in the protection of the boundaries of their land against neighbourhood villagers as such:

> *For the village, this territory is much more than an administrative area; - it is a symbol of village identity (de Planhol (1958) p. 340). If any other village attempts to use land lying within the village boundaries, people mobilise rapidly and are quite prepared to fight, with fire-arms if necessary. Even incursions by other villages' flocks or herds cause at the very least militant indignation. On one occasion, Sakaltutan animals crossed the frontier to Suleymanli, and the Suleymanli headman who happened to be passing on a horse, struck the shepherd in charge with his whip. Many Sakaltutan men talked of immediate armed attack. However, they were restrained by wiser counsel. I never witnessed mobilisation of this kind, but it is clear that all members are expected to defend the village regardless of the quarrels which constantly divide them. Not even lineages cross village frontiers, so that the village from the outside presents a solid front of loyalty. Its members are ready at all times to defend both its reputation and its territories.*

The quote exemplifies how social capital in a village was activated to protect villagers' economic interests and identity. As expressed, the territory of the village is more than an administrative area. It symbolises the identity of the village where economic interests are realised. The economic interests of the villagers are dependent on the land. Any incursions by neighbouring villagers to the territory imply an attack on the economic interests and identity of the village community. The collective mobilisation of the villagers to defend their territory is situational in times of incursions. It is the shared interest and interest alignment to defend the territory from incursions that causes people to form unities and which makes collective action possible. The territory is defended regardless of quarrels and disputes within the village community. Interests promote common identity and a unifying structure among the villagers.

The salience of many cultural practices and their transposition to a new setting after immigration do not come about spontaneously, but usually result from the structural conditions, so, in this sense, they are an emergent product (Portes and Sensenbrenner, 1993). As has been mentioned, KT people used to be wage labourers in the textile industry. It was de-industrialisation and wider structural changes in the British economy that facilitated a unified identity among Turkish and Kurdish people, collective resource mobilisation, the transposition of cultural practices and values, such as imece to the UK. The "fundamental source of solidarity is still situational" (ibid, p.1330), since it is the structural changes that took place in the British economy that activated dormant home customs. Hence, it is worth mentioning the re-enacted village level collaboration of imece in London.

The evidence I gathered in this study defends the idea that such home country village scale practices, such as *imece* and solidarity in various forms, have been transposed to the host country. As stated above, these collective actions are situational in the sense that the ethnic community acts collectively on specific issues for bettering living conditions and finding solutions to the existing problems that have been identified.

Esnaf, chair of a craftsmen's union and a wholesaler states;

> *We came here via social solidarity. We didn't know how the society functions; we could not open bank accounts. We didn't have residence permit. Thus, we could not apply for bank loans to set-up businesses. We could generate capital via the Anatolian tradition called imece. That was the way to set up businesses. If someone wants to set-up a shop, the amount of capital that she or he had was not enough. They gathered capital via their relatives, friends, and acquaintances. In time, those who gathered capital managed to earn money and provided loans to their acquaintances. (Esnaf, chair of a craftsmen's union an a wholesaler)*

While the above quote confines itself to the acquisition of economic capital the re-production of village scale collaboration is not limited to this. The Kurdish and Turkish community provides an excellent example of the reactivation of a cultural repertoire as an adaptation to structural changes in the economy. In other words, the cultural repertoire *imece* is based on village scale collaboration is brought from the home country. The transposition of *imece* to the new context is actually not only limited to capital acquisition, but also entails providing information, protection of business premises, providing free labour, gaining skills and training. The unwritten rule of *imece* is mutuality, reciprocity and underpinned by the threat of sanctions. The reconstruction of *imece* due to structural changes in the economy exemplifies the constructivist account of culture, which asserts that aspects of culture are changeable and situational depending on the circumstances in a particular time and space.

In the next section, I focus on the mobilisation of social networks to generate economic capital for setting-up businesses.

Economic capital and social networks

As I state earlier, economic capital refers to the resources that are immediately and directly convertible into money (Bourdieu, 1986). While it is important to make a distinction between economic, cultural, and social capital for analytical purposes, the boundaries between the capitals are fluid, as envisaged by Bourdieu (ibid). In modern differentiated societies, access to sources of income in the labour market depends on the class based resources such as "cultural capital in the form of educational credentials and social capital in the form of networks" (Swartz, 1997, p.74).

As Kurdish and Turkish migrants to the UK are relatively disadvantaged in the labour market, due to both limited cultural capital and the various forms of racism and discrimination they face, small business ownership has been a means of achieving economic and social mobility.

For instance, Yesil, who is running a mini supermarket in Harringay used to work for a bakery shop out of London, then set-up an off-licence, comments about the racism he had experienced:

We were running a small market out of London. It was not this big. There is racism out of London. No one can say that there is no racism. Verbal abuse, insult was common. I sold my shop because of racism. It was small but we could live on. They even attacked physically. 30 teenagers aged between 15-20 years old smashed our shop windows, threw eggs. I called the police; they said only kids (Yesil, mini-supermarket owner).

Kurdish and Turkish migrants have limited cultural capital because of their low English skills, agricultural working class background, low education and most of them originated from rural parts of Turkey and had not lived in a modern city prior to their arrival in London. Thus, they have been attracted to businesses characterized by low entry barriers. Low entry barriers include the necessary capital and technical requirements for setting up a business. Businesses such as textile manufacturing, restaurants, taxis, off-licences are such areas that provide a livelihood for Kurdish and Turkish migrants. In this section, I explore how interviewees acquired economic capital to open-up their shops.

First of all, according to the findings of this study, the major sources of capital for setting-up businesses appear to be family and co-ethnics. Both husband and wife can borrow economic capital from co-ethnics and relatives. The nuclear family is viewed as the economic unit. The participants of this study relied largely on their relatives, including extended family members as well as co-ethnics, or on a combination of their own resources and capital acquired via social networks. For instance, Cinar, an off-licence owner from Maras mentions the role networks played in the provision of financial capital and psychological support:

> *When I became unemployed because of the textile factory closure, I worked as a cab driver for a while. However, I didn't like it. It was not a job suitable to me. I become a partner in a small business with the support of my co-ethnics. I did not have any idea about running the business. It was hard times. I became depressed (Cinar, off-licence owner).*

Those shops owners are members of large families from Maras, Sivas, Malatya, Dersim, and Kayseri from where large cohorts of Kurdish and Turkish people migrated to the UK to a large extent in 1989. All of them are from rural parts of Turkey where the basic means of survival are animal husbandry and agriculture. In Bourdieu's words, the would-be entrepreneurs depended on "the size of the network connections he can effectively mobilize and on the volume of the capital possessed in his own right by each of those to whom he is connected" for setting up their shops. None of them had worked in a similar kind of self-employment prior to their arrival. When they arrived they were able to work in the textile industry and accumulate economic capital. As Akdeniz states:

> *When we came to this country the main source of livelihood was waged labour in the textile industry. Our people made serious money via the textile industry. After the collapse of the textile industry, even though they did not have any experience in small business ownership they set up shops with courage and with the financial capital accumulated during their time*

in the textile industry. We are generally in the service industry. Most businesses are owned by Turks (Akdeniz, mini-market owner).

They could work in the textile industry for a couple of years before the factories were closed down. After factory closures they had to mobilize resources via their social networks to open up shops. Halk, chair of a community organisation, speaks about the benefits of being a member of a co-ethnic network.

The Thatcherite policies from the end of the 1970s till the beginning of the 1990s resulted in massive unemployment, public spending cuts, factory closures and poverty. Thus, we started to search for alternative ways of livelihood. Our community was suitable for small business ownership. Its chemistry was appropriate for business, to set-up shops, even though the size could be small. Such kinds of organisational network do not exist in any other community. For instance, I do not think a Brazilian can borrow money from another Brazilian. On the other hand, I know one man who lends his relative £50,000. It is all based on trust, not a contract. If you are from Maras, you can do anything you want here (Halk, chair of a community organisation).

Olmez, who migrated from Maras to the UK in 1991, has worked in textile factories and in several restaurants. Now, he is a supermarket owner. He saw an advertisement in one of the Turkish weekly newspapers and bought his current shop from a co-ethnic in the year 2000. His case exemplifies the role of cultural and social capital in setting-up businesses, particularly in obtaining information and generating economic capital. Cultural capital, such as Turkish skills, helped him to obtain information about the sale of a shop, and his social capital was transposed in to economic capital. After repaying their debts, the successful entrepreneur provides economic capital to would-be entrepreneurs. Olmez had to change two partners while he was running the shop. Olmez's story is typical of most shop-keepers' cases:

People started to search for alternative opportunities after the factory closures. I was one of those. Turkish people entered off-licence, coffee-shop, restaurant, and market businesses. People who had £3-5 thousand, and the ones who could borrow £3-5 thousand from their relatives or co-ethnics, went into such businesses. It was the fear of becoming unemployed that oriented us to such businesses. We were affected by our surroundings. In reality, trade is not my business (Olmez, mini-market owner).

The case of Sahir, a male, university graduate from Istanbul, who is a coffee-shop owner, presents an example of how social capital or social networks can be converted into economic capital as with Olmez. He could not convert his institutionalised cultural capital into the British mainstream labour market. Yet, his case exemplifies the Kurdish and Turkish migrants who were not connected to any co-ethnic network prior to their arrival to the UK. Thus, his case enables us to exemplify the individualistic basis of Bourdieu's notion of capital when making a comparison between those with different portfolios of social, cultural and economic capital. It is important to note that he accumulated capital to finance his business start-up in his previous self-employment situation in which he was a partner in a restaurant. He acquired economic capital for his first business via working in the textile industry.

Sahir migrated to the UK in 1989 without any English skills. His case is typical of the hardship of Kurdish and Turkish migrants who were not connected to any co-ethnic network. A lack of social capital and of a support network intensified adaptation problems in the host country.

It was really hard not to know English. It was very hard to get into a culture you were not accustomed to. We didn't know the language. The lifestyle, homes, motorways were different. In various ways lots of things were different. Everything seemed wrong to me. However, you get used to it as time goes by. The hardest thing in our initial period in the UK was having no acquaintances and relatives. Because of not knowing English, you become dependent on a person when you have a health problem or need to deal with the council and public institutions. That was the difficulty we faced. I mean, you feel inferior. You are trying to tell your problems via someone else (Sahir, coffee-shop owner).

Three weeks after arriving with his wife, they started to look for jobs with the help of people they met at the airport. They were able to find employment in the textile industry where they worked for eight years. The working conditions in the textile industry were aggravated by extremely long hours. They used to work from eight in the morning to nine in the evening, 13-14 hours a day. It was in 2000 that he moved in to self-employment with the accumulated capital from the industry. His wife has started helping him as well as taking care of their children. As he is not a member of a big family from whom he can borrow money, he had to depend on his savings. However, he acquired social capital in community organisations.

I didn't borrow money from anyone or from an institution. However, our friends provided their support. One of my friends helped with decoration. Another architect friend planned and designed the coffee-shop. Some others painted it for free. Furthermore, all of our friends visited us. This gives you strength. If you have people around you who help, then life gets a bit easier. It is very important to have real friends. I haven't experienced financial problems, but for those of people who have, it is like this; if the business does not make any profits, and if you are in-depth, then your friends help you and say "take this money to clear your debt". This is important (Sahir, coffee-shop owner).

The above quote exemplifies a business owner lacking kinship and hometown networks who had to rely on friendship networks formed in the UK. Accordingly, Bourdieu's notion of various forms of capital enables us to analyse how one form of capital can be converted into another. They are subject to cycles and generate returns. One form of capital can be transposed into another. As Bourdieu (1987, p.4) comments:

Thus agents are distributed in the overall social space, in the first dimension according to the global volume of capital they possess, in the second dimension according to the composition of their capital, that is, according to the relative weight in their overall capital of the various forms of capital, especially economic and cultural, and in the third dimension according to the evolution in the time of the volume and composition of their capital, that is according to their trajectory in the social space.

In addition to Sahir, the situation of Zeytin and Ates is representative of similar cases of people from middle class backgrounds who do not have a big family or home-town network in London. That is to say, they could not rely on kinship and hometown network to borrow financial resources. As Bourdieu and Wacquant (1992, p.99) mention, "two individuals endowed with an equivalent overall capital can differ ... in that one holds a lot of economic capital and little cultural capital while the other has little economic capital and cultural assets". Furthermore, both Zeytin and Ates set up restaurants and coffee-shops for the purpose of selling it for a better price to a co-ethnic. They initially required little capital to transform the vacant places into fully furnished small businesses during the 1990s. The candidates for those small businesses were co-ethnic ex-textile factory workers who were able to accumulate capital to invest in new opportunities for a livelihood. Because almost all of the ex-textile factory workers were from rural parts of Turkey, they did not have the skills or knowledge to set-up a shop; they did not know how to acquire a licence, how to decorate a shop, where to find reasonably priced and good quality products. The new opportunities for livelihood during the first half of the 1990s were the catering and retail businesses, where not many skills are required to establish and maintain the businesses. Consequently, there was a market for those service providers. Thus, Zeytin and Ates functioned as middlemen between property owners and would-be entrepreneurs. In other words, the volume of social capital possessed by ex-textile factory workers enabled them to exchange the cultural capital of their co-ethnics. The sizes of the ethnic networks that could be effectively mobilised were rich in volume for mobilising economic capital, but weak in quality. Thus, ex-textile factory workers with greater social capital had to buy co-ethnics cultural capital. Zeytin and Ates used their cultural capital to extract economic capital. In this way, they managed to accumulate capital for setting up their own businesses.

Zeytin, 46 years old, a married male restaurant owner explains the disadvantages of not having an extended family network in London:

In this city, people who have an extended family network are in solidarity with each other. They provide soft loans to each other without any interest rates. It was a disadvantage for me as I do not have any relatives in London. I didn't have any accumulated capital. In the beginning, I mortgaged my home. This was how I obtained my first capital. That's how I started. I would be able to grow more quickly if I had an extended family in London. Things were much harder for me (Zeytin, restaurant owner).

Accordingly, during the 1990s, the number of kebab houses in London increased enormously (Sirkeci, 2016). In addition, it is now impossible to find a town outside of London where you can't find a kebab shop. Some people started a business called a "set-up and sale". They went to towns in the outside of London to set-up kebab shops. If setting-up the shop cost between £20,000-30,000, they turned over the shop for £120,000-130,000 pounds.

Whilst, businesses obtained capital through savings from their previous employment in the textile industry and catering, Turkish Cypriots were able find employment in the mainstream economy as they were earlier arrivals with competence in English language than the Turkish and Kurdish migrants to the UK. For instance, Doner's family, with British partners, was trading meat products between 1969 and 1988. The British partners were not interested in selling the company to Doner at that time. His partners retired in 1988 and he bought the meat processing company. Until then, they had been doing business with Kurdish and Turkish people, mainly selling kebab meat wholesale. While the company was selling mainstream British products before the 1990s, it was after a large Kurdish-Turkish population had settled in the UK, and following de-industrialisation, that the company started to sell ethnic kebab wholesale products. In a way, they were pulled by the opportunities in the kebab business. They voluntarily shifted their mainstream business to an ethnic business.

It was also common to shift from self-employment in off-licences to restaurant and take-away ownership or visa-versa. Thus, capital accumulation in one area became economic capital for investment in another area. For instance, Tutun, who came to the UK when he was eight years old in 1989, runs an off-licence.

Karan

His father used to work in textile factories. After two years of working in the textile industry he started to run a kebab shop. He had to hire a chef as he was not experienced in running a kebab shop. Tutun helped his father in the kebab shop as a child. He washed the dishes and cleaned the tables. In 1995, they bought the neighbour kebab shop in order to prevent competition with their business. They transformed it to a coffee shop. In 1998, they changed the coffee shop into an off-licence and sold their first kebab shop. As he states:

> *While we were running the kebab shop, another Turkish guy from Adiyaman opened a kebab shop next to us. He became bankrupt. Then, we bought it and we ran it as a coffee shop for three years. Two kebab shops were side by side. He opened the shop to us, so we bought it in order to prevent someone else running it as a kebab shop. Then, we sold our first kebab shop and changed the coffee shop into an off-licence (Tutun, off-licence owner)).*

Ziprot and Zeytin relied on a combination of personal savings gained from previous employment and property sold in the homeland.

Moreover, partnerships were a way of avoiding unemployment and entering into trade. It was attractive as two or more families could gather the necessary capital and labour force to start-up businesses. Self-employment seemed, to many, to be the only means of survival during these times. Accordingly, quite large numbers of businesses were owned by more than one person. Partnerships generally ended with the families' aim of owning their own shops. In other words, partnerships end when they achieve prosperity and collective self-help is no longer necessary.

Spor, a married male, owner of a mini-market started his business with two partners and he is still continuing with the same partners. They had to mobilise economic capital in order to prevent unemployment.

> *One of my partners is from my home town Elazig and the other one is from Istanbul. We met in a textile factory. I was working together with my current partner from Elazig. The other partner was working in a factory next to ours (Spor, mini-market owner).*

Kurdish and Turkish informants in this study did not have any business history in their early periods of arrival. Thus, bank loans did not emerge as an important source of financing at the initial start-up of the businesses. However, if they have subsequently had a good business record, bank loans were available to the participants when they wanted to shift from one business to another or expand. For instance, Olmez, a mini-supermarket owner decided to expand his business as he thought his current mini-supermarket did not have any chance to compete with chain stores. In his own words;

Three years ago, we thought small businesses could not compete and would shut down. We decided to get bank loans and we went into huge debt. We set up a second mini-supermarket. We undertook serious expenditure. But, we could not find what we were looking for. Expenditure tripled. The shop could not sustain itself. Now, we are trying to get rid of it. I have been living here for almost for eleven years and have reduced the number of shops to one. I do not know if we can survive. According to my predictions, small business owners will become bankrupt if things continue like this (Olmez, mini-market owner).

The above quote illustrates that the development of bridging capital to mainstream institutions in order to access economic capital from banks was only available to those who had a previous business history. Thus, bank loans were not a viable option for would-be business owners. It is a vicious circle for would-be entrepreneurs as they do not have a business history and are therefore not eligible for bank loans. And as they cannot access bank loans they will not acquire a business record via mainstream institutions.

Community organisations emerged as another source of capital acquisition for would-be entrepreneurs. Halkevi, one of the oldest Turkish-Kurdish community organisations in the UK, functioned as a credit rotating association during the 1990s. It was argued that, starting in 1989, the Kurdish armed guerrilla organisation the PKK encouraged Kurdish migration to European countries in order to obtain financial and political support from foreign countries (Laciner, 2000). In ten years, about 40,000 refugees settled in the UK (Atay, 2006, p.46). Halkevi used to have 90,000 members, including the Kurdish and Turkish migrants. As I was informed by my interviewee Cem who witnessed those times, the members of the organisation contributed the same amount of money every week. One member was allocated the whole sum at the end of the month. There was a lottery to decide which member would take the money. All of the candidates had to inform the organisation about the type of shop set-up. The institutionalised social capital embedded in the organisation was transposed into economic capital. This model of credit rotation was learned from the Jewish community. This clearly shows that individuals are capable to cut and mix from a variety of ethnic heritages and cultures to forge their shared interests embedded in the host society.

However, solidarity between community members is not without problems. Sometimes disputes between partners in a shop intensify and problems occur during the sale of the shop. One of the partners might exaggerate the value of the shop. In addition, loan money provided by co-ethnics may not be repaid. In order to deal with such problems, two community organisations held regular meetings every week. They are called a "peace and conflict resolution assembly" and "arbitration assemblies". According to the narrative expressed by the informants, the assembly treats everyone equally and is chosen from respected members of the community.

The service provided by the organisation sustains and institutionalises future collective resource mobilisations in ethnic minority businesses. Would-be partners do not hesitate to collaborate with the help the institutionalised relationships of mutual recognition. The sanctions imposed by the organisation prevent fraud. It is the social capital generated by the membership in the organisation which provides each of its members the service provided by the "peace and conflict resolution assembly". I will discuss this issue in detail in the third section of this chapter.

Furthermore, it was not without problems for would-be entrepreneurs to open a shop after acquiring the necessary capital. Would-be entrepreneurs require information about the possible options. The next section is on the role of social networks in providing information.

Information, setting up a business and social networks

Even under favourable conditions, migration is a harsh experience. The lack of a security net and friends together in an unfamiliar environment makes migrants vulnerable. Know-how becomes a valuable resource as they try to survive and adjust to their new environment. Accordingly, in this section, I will show that CTK people learn how to survive and adjust in the broader society through the contacts they establish in familiar environments.

Community organisations provide informative meetings for their communities on various issues related to health, welfare, migration, the problems of shopkeepers, and housing. There are several community organisations based on faith, cultural, political and hometown identity. Some organisations are inclusive in their covering of Kurdish and Turkish communities, supporting not only Turks, but also Kurds, East European and Central Asian Turkish speaking communities. Information and resources provided by the community organisations are exclusively used by its members. Some organisations are rich in their provision of resources. For instance, the network for the community organisation for the town of Maras – a city in Southern Turkey – provides considerable social capital. There is a large community from Maras and most of its members are self-employed shop owners. Support within the community organisation is provided exclusively to its members.

However, information on general welfare issues was first provided and transmitted by Turkish Cypriot organisations. Turkish Cypriots, first of all, were competent in the English language. They were under British colonial rule until 1960 and they had arrived in the UK before Kurdish and Turkish people. Community organisations filled out paperwork related to accounting for small businesses and general welfare issues like housing, school registration for children, benefits and so on. Kurdish and Turkish small businesses started to flourish during the first half of the 1990s, that is, after the collapse of the textile industry. Gradually, Turkish and Kurdish people have learned to keep accounting records for their small businesses. As, Halk, chair of a community organisation, explained, there are now lots of accountants and solicitors within the Kurdish and Turkish communities. Most shop keepers have relatives who provide such services for them free of charge. That is to say, small business owners need such supplementary services, which are provided within the community to run their businesses.

Until the 1990s, such services were provided by the Turkish Cypriot community organisations. In other words, there were few accountants or solicitors with a Kurdish-Turkish background. Consequently, it is possible to state there were inter-ethnic solidarity and a transfer of knowledge between late and early arrivals. Sezgin, chair of a Kurdish-Turkish community organisation talks about those early years:

> *There is a huge difference between Turkish Cypriots and the Kurdish-Turkish community. They arrived to the UK much earlier than us. When we arrived in the UK, they were already a settled community. They were integrated into society. In this sense, migrants from Turkey have benefited a lot from the experiences of Turkish Cypriots' community organisations. In addition, Turkish Cypriots provided jobs for the migrants from Turkey in textile factories. They provided a lot of assistance to the migrants from Turkey. Of course, every old lived experience feeds new experiences (Sezgin, chair of a Kurdish-Turkish community organisation).*

The above quote exemplifies the patron-client power relationship between the old settler Turkish Cypriot community and new Kurdish-Turkish arrivals. Thus, it is not the altruism or benevolence of Turkish Cypriots that provided assistance and jobs for the new Kurdish-Turkish arrivals, but rather such assistance and jobs provided by the Turkish Cypriots were exchanged for cheap labour provided by Kurdish and Turkish migrants. This pattern, to a large extent, was replicated within the Kurdish and Turkish communities in London. The majority of the interviewees developed their skills for small business ownership in co-ethnic businesses as workers. The social capital was utilised to access economic and cultural capital. Being a worker in a co-ethnic or family owned business is a step towards self-employment in the same sector. By the same token, it is a patron-client relationship which entails the exploitation of the co-ethnic worker until the worker sets up his or her own shop.

The difference between the Kurdish-Turkish and Turkish Cypriot communities can also be explained by their different labour market insertions.

While Turkish Cypriots were able to find employment in mainstream jobs, working together with English speaking colleagues, Kurdish and Turkish people were able to find jobs solely in the ethnic economy. Karahasan, chair of a Turkish Cypriot community organisation, speaks about the Turkish Cypriots relationship with the wider society.

> *Turkish Cypriots worked together with British, Nigerian, Italian and Greek communities in the factories. As they could find employment in various sectors they are dispersed and unrecognisable as a group (Karahasan, chair of a Turkish Cypriot community organisation).*

In all of the community organisations, employers looking for workers or unemployed community members looking for a job can leave a note on the notice board. Thus, community organisations provide a kind of social platform where small business owners can fulfil their needs in terms of human resources. Suleyman, a manager at an Islamic faith organisation, exemplifies the function of community organisations in bringing people face to face:

> *For instance, I migrate to this country and I want to set up a business. What do I need? I need an accountant. Our community organisation is a social platform. It is possible to find whatever you are looking for. We provide support to the people who need an accountant. We do not function as an agency for finding an accountant, but as a social platform we can orient people. Our audience may require a lawyer, an accountant, an estate agent, or an employee, and we can recommend some people. It is a word of mouth process. We can point to the relevant people (Suleyman, chair of an Islamic faith organisation).*

In addition, there are five newspapers in London, namely, Olay, Londra Gazete, Telgraf, Avrupa, Haber Newspaper, all of which have yellow pages providing information to small business owners on various subjects. Another source of information is co-ethnic networks. Co-ethics can recommend partnerships and provide information about favourable opportunities for new shop start-ups. Carsi exemplifies how home country networks facilitate new start-ups:

> *While I was searching for a shop, my current partner came with a proposal and said, if you are searching for a place, I and my brother can join forces with you. He had set aside some accumulated capital. We can also quit that shop. We can start a new business together. Things developed like this. We are three partners here (Carsi, mini-market owner)*

All would be entrepreneurs require the guidance and advice of their co-ethnics. Aksoy's (chair of a community organisation) experience reflects the general condition of would-be entrepreneurs who lack the cultural capital for starting up businesses. Aksoy, a left wing ex-trade union activist in Turkey, voluntarily provided guidance to his co-ethnics to show his solidarity:

As I was competent in the English language, lots of Kurdish and Turkish people used to come to me to ask if we can look at a shop outside of London. We would drive by car and go to look at a shop. We were working as voluntary consultants. We tried to help them. Housing, health care, school registration, problems at schools and translation services are some of the issues that community organisations deal with (Aksoy, chair of a community organisation).

Would-be entrepreneurs have to calculate the profit they could make before buying a business. Thus they need reliable information about the possible profit that they could make in a week. Would-be entrepreneurs have to acquire information about the potential of a new start-up in the area. Gules, 41 years old, married male, who owns a mini-market in Hendon explains how crucial it is to getter information about the potential of the shop before setting it up:

You can buy most of the shops, but you have to evaluate its potential. You choose according to its expenditures and income. You evaluate. You focus on the weekly income of the shop. Migrant workers from Turkey do not open a shop immediately without any analysis of the district. They examine the feasibility and the potential of a new start-up business in a district. What nationalities live in the district? What ethnicities exist? They gather such information from their co-ethnics and discuss the feasibility of a new start-up. They research the appropriate products that could be sold in the district. For instance, in our area, Hendon, there are no British. There are no Turks either. It is necessary to know the residents. It is necessary to know the potential of the residents. Predominantly 40% are Iranians. There are Polish, Chinese, and Japanese. Then there are Romanians and Czechs. Thus, we provide our service according to population. As we know the ethnicities of the residents, we found their wholesaler (Gules, mini-market owner).

Furthermore, newspapers in the Turkish language are useful for Kurdish and Turkish small business owners. They provide information about support services and their contact details for small business owners. They inform small business owners about issues related to their businesses. The support services are regularly advertised and provided by people with Kurdish and Turkish backgrounds. Shopkeepers want to work with Turkish-speaking service providers as they can communicate with them much more easily, and share the same culture and experiences. Cinar, 47 years old, married male, an ex-textile factory worker, who is running an off-licence at present and explains the role of newspapers in small Turkish businesses:

> *The newspapers in the Turkish language are very informative for me, as my understanding of the English language is poor. I can get various kinds of information. For instance, recently, I was looking for a consultant who works on licence issues. I just checked the pages and found an advert. Things like this. Again, recently, I was searching for a hygiene company for rat poison. I also follow some of the columnists who widen my perspective. The business was owned by a Cypriot. Someone from my home town who is a small shop owner recommended to me to buy it. My experienced co-ethnics in the business made suggestions about the essentials of the business. I have regular contact with my relatives who are in the same business. They have also passed through the same stages as me. We inform each other about the prices of goods (Cinar, off-licence owner).*

In summary, Kurdish and Turkish entrepreneurs mobilise formal and informal networks to gather information on various subjects from general welfare to business related issues as listed above. Social networks are utilised to gather information via word of mouth, community organisations, recommendations from friends, and newspapers. In addition, they could be essential for would-be entrepreneurs taking a decision whether or not to invest.

Dispute resolution and social networks

As I discuss in earlier sections of this chapter, to a large extent, Kurdish and Turkish businesses involve ethnic-solidarity and mobilize resources via their social networks in order to start-up and maintain businesses. For instance, information gathering, capital acquisition, service provision, and setting up a shop via partnerships is all accomplished through the mobilisation of social networks. Of course, cooperation and ethnic solidarity are not free of disputes and conflicts. Conflicts could arise from partnerships, loans provided within the community and setting-up the same kind of shop next to a co-ethnic shop owner. The ways in which such conflicts can be resolved are collective goods for the business owners that ensure the continuity of cooperation. Without any mechanisms for solving the conflicts, collaboration cannot be sustained in the future. For instance, the capital provided to a co-ethnic without any interest rates would have to be returned in order to ensure future capital from within the community. Then, the question, of what shopkeepers do in times of conflict has to be answered. Bardak, chair of a Kurdish organisation, sheds light on the issue of dispute resolution at the community organisation level:

> *The shop owners voluntarily apply to the assembly. One side of the dispute comes to our community organisation and makes an application.*

Sometimes both sides make an agreement and apply together. The assembly gathers once a week. They receive ten pounds. It consists of reputable elders (including men and women). The assembly has been working for 10 years. The members of the assembly change every year. It has been present for more than ten years, but it did not have any official recognition. It deals with various issues such as disputes within or between businesses and disputes within families. There are also youth and women's assemblies. Some of the disputes are solved via these assemblies. Community organisations have been present for more than a decade. They are respected by the people (Kurdish community). Members of the assembly change every year (Bardak, chair of a Kurdish community organisation).

While Aksoy's following statement is a clear example of capital accumulation by an imam via co-ethnic loan lenders. Conflict could arise from the non-repayment of the loan. Thus, it is also important to see the sanctions associated with the loan.

Let me tell you how our imam has opened his shop. He was from Pazarcik, Sivas. He just visited his countryman and collected £28.000 in two days. If he does not pay it back then it would be disgrace for him (Aksoy, chair of a refugee organisation).

Writing on indigenous participation in development projects in Sebat Bet Gurage of Ethiopia, Henry (2004) observes that disputes relating to development projects may be regulated by the Gurage customary law and can be enforced by a range of sanctions implemented by development associations. Non-compliance with the decision of the organisation is unusual, firstly due to trust vested in the associations and the perceived benefits from compliance, and secondly, as the threat of sanctions, without necessarily being implemented, underpins trust in social networks. The power of sanctions does not lie in their implementation but rather in their threat. Sanctions include ostracism, stigmatization, expulsion and forcing people to pay their fines by confiscating and selling property. As Henry (2004, p.150) further argues,

Ostracism is the ultimate sanction in Gurageland, as when invoked it becomes impossible for households to function socially and economically. The household is expelled from the community and, unable to receive any form of communal assistance, is excluded from all rural social affairs...Due to its severity, this sanction is very rarely if ever used in the development process, as the threat of ostracism is normally sufficient to ensure compliance.

Similarly, in the case of the imam, the sanction is related to the damage to the reputation of the borrower, which could be disgrace for him. In other words, if the loan is not repaid, then the borrower would be stigmatised and lose his social capital and he would possibly face social exclusion.

As I mention earlier, there are mainly two community organisations that work on dispute resolution amongst shopkeepers. Such a mechanism originated in the Jewish community. They call it "arbitration assemblies" (Cem, chair of a community organisation). My informant Cem, who used to work as a coordinator for a Kurdish and Turkish community organisation during the first half of the 1980s and currently holds a chair position at a community organisation said that they have learned lots of things from the Jewish community. In his own words:

> *You know, Halkevi was founded in 1984. Then it was moved from its small building to a larger one in Stoke Newington in 1986-7. Since then, disputes between and within families, as well as businesses have been resolved by peace commitie. I officially registered this committie to the legal community services. By the end of 1980s, large cohorts of emigrants from Turkey came to London. Cypriots and their organisations mobilise their efforts to help the Kurdish and Turkish migrants' from Turkey. Migrants from Turkey started to work in Hackney. Time to time, specifically with the establishment of Halkevi, relationships have been built with the Hackney councillors and asked for their help to resolve housing related problems, registration of children to schools and much more. Those people asked for help, ei. Ward Councillors were from Jewish origin. To know how and what tools...Jewish community practices, particularly their court system was exemplified by Turkish and Kurdish community organisations.*

Bardak, chair of a Kurdish community organisation explains how community organisations function as an institution for solving disputes between shop-keepers:

> *One of our services involves solving shopkeepers' disputes between partners in a shop and between shop owners themselves. In order to do this, we regularly hold a "peace and conflict resolution assembly". It is an assembly where the different sides of the dispute gather. The assembly decides which is the just and the unjust side. In some cases, the assembly prevents a would-be entrepreneur from opening a shop next to another co-ethnic. Even though the council gives permission for opening a shop in one region, the assembly sometimes prevents this. Another task of the assembly is to solve problems arising from loaned money. They try to solve the problems that occur during the sale of shops. Sometimes brothers bring cases. In some cases the turn-over of the shop is exaggerated. We generally*

put their relatives in the loop. Kinship ties are really important to them. They repay loans to avoid the shame of not paying. It is against the norms of the community not to pay back one's loan. Therefore, it is paid back. Otherwise, the debtor might be excluded from the community. No one will cooperate with that person again. If one shop owner will not pay back his debt, he cannot go back to his village. He might not get in to this building again. In this commission 90% of the cases are related to financial issues. The commission consists of nine honest, reputable people from every corner of Turkey (Bardak, chair of a community organisation).

Similar to the discussion about the implementation of customary law in development projects in Gurageland, the above quote by Bardak outlines norms underpinning social capital, i.e. a system of sanctions including shame and ostracism. Affiliation to the community organisation is a social capital that can be utilised in efforts to advocate loan providers' interests. Sanctions such as ostracism have a potentially devastating impact since the social and economic wellbeing of the debtor is still dependent on the ties with co-ethnics. This is largely a consequence of strong bonding capital within the community, while bridging capital, i.e. ties between the Kurdish and Turkish community and wider society, is weak.

However, as I mention in chapter two, one of the central problems of Putnam's concept of social capital is that it focuses on the integrative functions, which allow cooperation and coordination free from conflicts of interest. Thus, it does not able to analyse distrust and conflicts of interest.

Kazim, a 48 years old, married male, who owns a restaurant and an off-licence, demonstrates how being loyal to the informal agreements is crucial. The option of not being loyal to the agreement goes against unwritten customs. The very conditions that flourished and maintained small businesses involve mutual solidarity. If Kazim does not pay back the loan, the incident will be known by his relatives, and in the long run, no one will do business with him in the future. In addition, it should be kept in mind that these people are from the same village in Turkey. As Cem (chair of a community organisation) also states if a shop owner breaks his promise, then he cannot return to his village in Turkey.

According to us, words are deeds. It is a disgraceful act and I have a huge network. Because of this, not to pay back is not an option (Kazim, off-licence and restaurant owner).

Sahir, as I mention in previous sections, is not a member of a big family from whom he could acquire economic capital. But he talks about other businesses and the role of elders, respected people in dispute resolution:

I didn't borrow money from anyone related to the Turkish community. But some people cannot get their money back. They solve this problem via their own means such as community organisations or elderly people who have a reputation in the community try to solve the problem. (Sahir, coffee-shop owner).

Our people cannot find employment in mainstream jobs. As a consequence, they try to set-up businesses in the service industry like restaurants, off-licenses and so on. If there is a need for such a business in the district it is right to set-it up. If there is no need, then owners will share the existing potential. They cannot earn the same amount as before. The share of the cake will get smaller. This became a common problem. There are no regulations related to business premises. Then, the craftsmen's union or community organisations have to say no (Esnaf, chair of a craftsmen's union).

The above quote demonstrates the role of associations in preventing co-ethnics establishing businesses in direct competition with each other. A potential dispute that may arise due to competition between co-ethnics is prevented by the associations. In addition another community organisation has also started to provide dispute resolution services. As Cem states,

I was the one who formulated the "peace assembly" in Halkevi. I registered it with the community legal service. It was based on the Jewish community's arbitration assemblies. It provides a service for finding a solution to a dispute. The decision made by the community organizations have to be respected. It is not possible to question the decision of the assembly as shopkeepers are dependent on the organization for support provided regarding daily welfare issues. Yet, they open the shop with the financial help of the community organizations' cooperative. The peace assembly operates within the legal framework. Enforcement involves banishment, exclusion from the community in general. It shames the guilty party. He cannot return to his village in Turkey. He becomes a swindler, liar, and thief in the eyes of the community (Cem, chair of a community organization).

Kinship networks also play a role in dispute resolution. The peace assembly of the community organization can inform the relatives and co-villagers of the defendant who can have the greatest impact on him or her.

Community organisations emerge as intermediaries between the parties in the dispute. They are reliable and respected by the community. In addition, the involvement of community elders in dispute resolution is another influential community resource. This type of dispute resolution entails bonding capital

(Putnam, 1993). It reduces the risk of helping a co-ethnic and sustains future solidarity. It underpins trust between co-ethnics. Bonding capital guarantees compensation of any loss to a co-ethnic from cheating. Without such institutions, collective resource mobilisation would be impossible. It insures reciprocity and future collective collaboration.

Claim making and social networks

Claim making entails the mobilisation of social networks to engage shopkeepers' participation in achieving a specific goal. Claim making seeks to facilitate the improvement in conditions of work in self-employment through a range of interrelated actors such as decision and policy makers, professional groups, bureaucrats, technocrats, opinion leaders, CTK shopkeepers, the CTK community and community organisations. Thus, in this section, I focus on the needs felt by shopkeepers and the political opportunities and constraints for voicing their demands. Cem, a Turkish Cypriot who works in a community organisation as a consultant, explains the ways in which shop-keepers can mediate their claims:

> *It is solely community organisations who have relationships with the local government. Shop-keepers can only voice their demands via community organisations, namely Alevi Kultur, Halkevi, and Cypriots'. Apart from via these, there is no relationship with governmental bodies. As the local governments require the votes of the residents, they are in regular contact. (Cem, chair of a community organisation).*

Furthermore, competition within the community businesses and with chain stores pushes small business owners to employ smaller workforces and/or to work longer hours. The small shop-owners are forced to reduce their costs as the competition intensifies. In order to do that, exploitation of their labour power emerges as a way of keeping their business running. This, in return, leads to more severe 'imprisonment' with in their business. As a chair of a community organisation mentions:

> *Our people cannot participate to the meetings because of a lack of English skills. This is one of the biggest problems. The second problem is that our people do not hire workers. An increase in profit margins enables them to employ workers. If they do not employ workers they cannot leave the shop from early in the morning till late. They are imprisoned. Thus, they cannot even go to a course. For instance, the council used to provide free courses on hygiene at the workplace to shop owners. No one could attend (Cem, chair of a community organisation).*

Most of the shop owners complained about the business tax rates and parking regulations and competition with chain stores. However, they couldn't voice their demands via major political channels. This is due to the fact that they have weak social networks with mainstream British society in general. It exemplifies the weak cross-cutting ties, namely bridging capital with mainstream institutions. In order to assert influence, they have recently established a small business association. They collectively mobilise social networks to achieve change in local government policies. The chair of the British Anatolian Craftsmen Union explains the reason for establishing such an organisation:

> *We have gradually become a real economic force in Britain. We have a huge potential. However, we can't put pressure on the council and the government. Even though our contribution to the economy is huge, we provide lots of services and we pay too much tax, we can't get anything in return. We are just left alone with our problems (Esnaf, chair of a business union).*

Moreover, he further illustrates how Tilly's (1978) model of collective action operates with in the context of Turkish and Kurdish business owners in London. According to the theory of collective resource mobilisation, shared interests promote networks and unities, the intensity of networks facilitates increases mobilisation, and collective action is a function of all three components. As Esnaf asserts,

> *A community does not have any value if it is not organised. An organised society has a value. This is true for the whole world. The existing political system does not like the idea of an organised society. You have power if you are organised. You know what you can do with that power. You start to be considered seriously. You can solve your problems more easily. It was necessary to establish a professional union. There is a gap between community organisations and the shopkeepers. We required an organisation that deals with the problems of shopkeepers and applies pressures to the political structures. It was necessary to form a union of Anatolian shop-keepers. The aim of the union is as follows: It is going to voice the demands of the shopkeepers. The demands are related to council tax, electricity bills, parking regulations, regulatory by laws concerning chain stores, garbage collection. (Esnaf, chair of a business union).*

With regard to competition with chain stores small shopkeepers think that they have to force the council to implement measures against big chain stores. But, they are totally aware of the fact that their rivals are too big to fight with. Here is an expression of their view of chain stores:

> *Tesco, Sainsbury and other chain stores should be located in the out skirts of London where there is no parking problem, and where they cannot affect*

small shop-keepers. Over the last ten years, big chain stores have managed to remove and bypassed this regulation. Because of the liberal policies, they made agreements with governmental bodies aiming to remove the law. Their economic and political power does not have any limits. They are omnipotent in terms of their economic and political power. On the other hand, we have advantages too. We sell ethnic produce. It is the ethnic produce that keeps our businesses afloat. Their aim is to kill ethnic businesses. They want to get our share in the retail business. They systematically target us. Most of our members will have to shut down their businesses. They try to do this in a highly planned manner. They calculate the estimated turn-over of small shop owners and plan how much they could earn from them. They want to control the market. Lots of CTK people will have to put down their shutters. This is a result of being unorganized. If we become organized under this union and put pressure on local and central government, voice our concerns about unfair competition to the public, and then we can stop them. It is going to be the result of being unorganised as CTK shopkeepers. If we get organised, we can put pressure on the government and voice our concerns to the public that this is unjust competition. We are trying to fight against their expansion. We just learned that if an entrepreneur sets up a retail business, it should be eight minutes walking distance from the next existing ones. We have to inform our community. For instance, lately, we have collected 800 signatures to stop a chain store development in Haringey, which is a borough populated by our community shops. Reaction has been generated (Esnaf, chair of a business union).

Another example of collective action relates to high electricity bills. There is an alignment of interests within the Kurdish and Turkish business owners to have lower gas and electricity bills. As the chair of a craftsmen union explains, the business owners act collectively to realise lower bills:

In addition, the prices of electricity and gas are too expensive. However, if you have more than 200 members then you could have a bargaining power with companies. For instance, if you pay £2000 in a year, you can have a discount of up to £1000 (Esnaf, chair of a business union).

Apart from the newly established crafts union, none of the KT community organisations have been part of a protest that opposes the development of chain stores. A chair of a Turkish and Kurdish community organisation declared that their organisation has not been a part of any activity that opposes the development of chain stores next to KT businesses:

We didn't organise anything against chain stores up until now. There is one Tesco development project in North London. Shop owners and families living in the area spontaneously gathered to protest about the new Sainsbury's development. Up until now, we have not been part of any activism that deals with Tesco and small business ownership. We are involved with lots of issues like class based politics, austerity and other local issues (Sezgin, chair of a community organisation).

Furthermore, some of the socialist community organisations turned their backs on the problems of the Kurdish and Turkish business owners as mentioned above. While their members, to a large extent, consist of small business owners, their activities do not focus on any activism that deals with campaigning against the development of local chain stores. This could be explained by a lack of alignment of interests in the problems of KT business owners. As Collins (2000) states, "traditionally Marxist and socialist politics has held an antipathy towards the petit-bourgeoisie and the bourgeoisie. They were seen as class enemies". A number of the community organisations framed their activism within class based politics, i.e. the antagonism between waged labourers and owners of the means of production, austerity and other social issues. In so doing, they aligned their interests with waged labourers rather than with their members.

In conclusion, claim making entails bridging capital (Putnam, 1993) which facilitates pursuing support for the betterment of conditions of work in self-employment through a range of interrelated actors such as decision and policy makers, professional groups, bureaucrats, technocrats, opinion leaders and the KT business organisations and social networks. Kurdish and Turkish shop owners demand better business regulations regarding business rates, parking, garbage collection, electricity bills, and competition with chain stores. These issues are the class interests of Kurdish and Turkish business owners.

While bonding capital embedded within the Kurdish and Turkish communities is strong due to alignment of interests, relationships and trust within the close proximity of Kurdish and Turkish shops and neighbourhoods, it is possible to state that bridging capital that facilitates mobilisation for voicing demands to resolve a neighbourhood problem is weak. This is partly due to the fact that strong bonding capital does not automatically lead to bridging capital. While bonding capital is a preceding requirement for the development of bridging social capital (Ryan et al., 2008). Bridging social capital refers to cross-cutting ties where members of one group connect with members of another group to pursuing support and putting pressure on mainstream institutions. The lack transferability of migrants' cultural capital prevents Kurdish and Turkish business owners to voice their demands in the wider society.

Safety and ethnic networks

While being a shopkeeper allows some people to earn a living, it also involves costs, including, isolation, social 'imprisonment' (lack of time to take care of children or to attend educational and recreational activities), and social conflict with customers and the surrounding community.

The presence of Kurdish and Turkish communities in Britain is relatively new. They mainly settled in affordable impoverished areas that had previously been populated by migrants and minorities. These areas are mainly in North London such as Haringey and Hackney. Kurdish and Turkish groups do business in relatively less prosperous urban areas and isolated regions and conflicts between merchants and customers are common. In such locations, where money and jobs are scarce, where public spending cuts affect the population significantly, and where public services such as police and fire protection, garbage collection, and code enforcement are in short supply, and daily financial transactions often occur within a climate of tension and hostility, situations can yield humiliation and provoke violence (Gold, 2010). In such areas where money and jobs are scarce, the only symbols of wealth and representations of the desired consumer goods are businesses in their location. Protection from attacks, as well as theft and violence within the business premises are important considerations.

The case of the US demonstrates the fact that "financial transactions often occur within a climate of tension and hostility that can yield humiliation and provoke violence" (Gold, 2010, p.2). Daily police protection from attacks appears to be a crucial service provided to shopkeepers for maintaining their businesses. It may be impossible to recover from the damage caused by attacks. The cost burden for ethnic business owners could be beyond compensation. Consequently, security within the business premises is a major problem in districts with high crime rates.

Actually, this is a general concern for all Kurdish and Turkish shopkeepers in London in this study. They were all complaining about the security services provided by the police in general. The lack of security provision in migrant neighbourhoods leads Kurdish and Turkish community members to form unities. Consequently, business owners have to keep their eyes open and are ready to help each other. There is reciprocity between business owners in providing security for the business premises. As Ates, restaurant owner states,

> *We have to protect our living area. Police do nothing. There are some other shops close to us. We have an agreement. If something happens to one of us the other ones are going to help. There is a kind of solidarity between us (Ates, restaurant owner in Haringey).*

As Carsi, a mini-supermarket owner mentions, such incidents in everday life are common:

Recently, our van full of products has been emptied, robbed in 15 minutes. The material stolen from inside the van cost £2000. My camera recorded everything. Besides, there is another camera on the highway. We called the police. We cannot come, they said. What kind of security provider are you, my friend? According to my mind, police means security. I handed over a CD to the police. One week later I went to the police department. The CD I had given them had been lost, they said. Then, they called me and said we found the CD. I gave another CD to them. I shouted at them. I said, I am paying your monthly salary. If I pay £10,000 in a year, if I pay garbage fees, if I rescue 10 people from job centres and offer them a job, and pay their wages, if I am an employer here, then you should provide my security here. If you don't do this, leave it to us. They didn't do anything. This happens all the time when we are in trouble (Carsi, supermarket owner).

Accordingly, one aim during the fieldwork was to investigate the extent of police protection from attacks. At the time of the fieldwork of this book, safety at the shops emerged as an important problem for business owners following the riots across the UK in August, 2011. It was actually good timing to investigate the extent of police protection for KT businesses during the fieldwork as it coincided with four days of rioting in August 2011. Even though the riots were an exceptional case, it was an opportunity to assess the general police service provided for ethnic business owners.

For four days in August 2011 several streets of England experienced extensive property damage, mass looting and attack against the police. The shooting and killing of Mark Duggan in Tottenham Hale on the evening of Thursday August 4th has been the trigger for the subsequent riots. However, collective violence was not an immediate response. The collective violence broke out on the 6th of August after a peaceful crowd of no more than 100 people, made up of friends and family of Mark Duggan, gathered in front of Tottenham police station and demanded an explanation from the senior police officers. This was not provided and a 16 year old girl was pushed to the ground and hit with batons and shields by police. This was the spark that ignited four days of riots which spread very quickly throughout London's most socially deprived neighbourhoods. Hence, Kurdish and Turkish businesses had to face residents' frustration, even if they had no direct responsibility for its creation.

While the police were highly visible on the high value locations with expensive shops across the city, they were kept a low profile in Dalston, Stoke Newington, Tottenham, Green Lanes and Wood Green, where the majority of Turks and Kurds own businesses. It is also possible to state that most of the working class areas were neglected. "Unlike many high streets in the capital, where businesses brought down their shutters in the early afternoon to minimize the risk of looting, many of the restaurants and shops owned" by

Turkish and Kurdish people in those areas were defiantly open" (11 August 2011, Balkan Chronicle). During the riots, most of the premises were protected by men armed with baseball bats vowing to defend the shops from attack.

In the following sections, I will elaborate first on shopkeepers' perspectives on policing during the riots, and then argue that shop keepers have decided to take the law into their own hands to protect their businesses, not only during the riots, but also in daily transactions.

All of my interviewees were told by the police that they could not provide any protection against possible attacks. It was up to shopkeepers to decide whether to close their shops or stay open. Thus, "unlike many high streets in the capital, where businesses brought down the shutters in the early afternoon to minimize the risk of looting, many of the restaurants and shops owned by Turkish and Kurdish people in the London boroughs of Hackney and Haringey were defiantly open" (11 August 2011, Balkan Chronicle). Many business owners in these areas are run by Turks and Kurds, who defended their businesses and neighbourhoods from attacks. However, shopkeepers and their acquaintances "were forced to take the law into their own hands to defend homes and businesses across the capital" (9 August 2011, Daily Mail). During the riots, most of the premises were protected by men armed with baseball bats vowing to defend the shops from attack. It was permitted to hold and use baseball bats in case of attacks. They were left completely alone and they were aware of the fact that no protection would be provided by the police. They were in a self-help situation.

Several respondents stated that there was a conscious decision for police misconduct. It was asserted that, by keeping a low profile, the establishment aimed to change the public debate and divert attention from the causes of the riots. One of my respondent's, Olmez, a mini-supermarket owner, asserted that the reason for the police lack of ability to control the riots was their intention to pit communities against each other. He expressed his idea about police misconduct like this:

The police could control the riot in the beginning. However, they didn't do so deliberately. They wanted to create the image that there was a bunch of criminals behind the incident. Thus, it was a way to cover up the social causes underlying the events. It was said that no one in the government evaluated the incident in a way that placed its root cause in the policies of the government. The Turkish people tried to protect their businesses, but I did not like one BBC speaker saying 'I want to be Turkish'. We are migrants here. This country was built by blacks in reality. The political establishment wanted migrant communities to be pitted against each other. They wanted communities against each other (Olmez, mini-market owner).

What is clear in these narratives is that Kurdish and Turkish communities had to take matters into their own hands. Business owners experience constant insecurity at their business premises. The bonding capital within the Kurdish and Turkish communities is utilised for the provision of a security network within the neighbourhood. Such an emergent product is due to the lack of security services provided by the government bodies. Thus, strong ethnic ties are a consequence of the structural discrimination they experience in their daily lives.

Shop keepers, instead of blaming rioters for the destruction of stores, mostly focused on British institutions, such as the media, police and the government, blaming them for inciting tensions, reinforcing economic and political inequalities, and indirectly instigating urban violence. According to the interviewees, disputes are generally a product of the wider society's opportunity structure rather than racial, cultural, or ethnic factors per se.

According to Olmez, a mini-market owner, the eruption of violence was not a consequence of ethnic tension between communities, but rather of injustices in the society. Police misconduct was the major cause of the intensification of violence. He explains,

> *The police force did not want to prevent the riot, and paved the way for looting. It was all planed and conscious. Thus, several shopkeepers who I had chatted with were left alone to protect their shops. They were not racist against any community. Their main customers are blacks as well. I do not think that shopkeepers' reaction was racist. For instance, there are right wing Turkish people in London. Even, those people did not react in racist terms. Turkish shopkeepers' reaction to the rioters was right. If the political establishment continues with austerity measures, the consequences of such incidents will be worse. It is going to repeat itself, for sure. This was not the first time and it's not going to be the last. People are getting poorer. No one can blame them as they lost someone from their community. They, the blacks have the right to riot. Yet, they have been oppressed throughout history. If they had been submissive, things could get worse (Olmez, mini-market owner).*

As I mention earlier, the police kept a low profile in Hackney and Haringey. The findings of this study suggest that there was an overall lack of confidence in police conduct during the riots. This was expressed by a 37 years old shopkeeper, Carsi, as follows:

> *I said this to the police officer's face. They could suppress such events in two or three days with their 16,000 police force. They have the necessary equipment. If they can't stop rioters then there is something else behind it. They want to issue new suppressive laws.*

One shopkeeper stated "even though rioters mostly targeted big businesses, there was a conceived threat coming from rioters. Thus, big businesses such as Tesco have also benefited from Turkish mobilisation". It was the whole neighbourhood and their living space which was protected by the shopkeepers and the Turkish and Kurdish community, not just their individual shops. Such discussions prevalent within the Kurdish and Turkish communities socially define the resistance as being Turkish. It is their common perception that Turkish and Kurdish communities alike mobilized hand in hand to protect their neighbourhood and businesses.

One shopkeeper from Haringey asserted that the reason for the lack of ability of the police to control the riots was that they intended to set communities against each other. He expressed his view as follows:

The political establishment wanted migrant communities to pit against each other. They wanted to set communities against each other.

According to most shopkeepers, the riots were legitimate in essence as the government intensified the austerity measures. But, it was wrong to target small businesses as their owners originated from a working class background. They were aware of the fact that the rioters did not target their shops. As discussed earlier, the cultural practice of *imece*, which connotes collective mobilisation and action for various purposes, was transposed to this situation. Incursions into the neighbourhood activated mainly Kurdish and Turkish people to defend their community space, the territory they live in.

Thus, the collective need to protect their livelihoods brought shop owners and families closer together in some respects. The safety of their workplaces is a collective good for all shopkeepers. Because of the lack of police protection, they developed a sense of mutual aid and support networks. In times of need, they provide security for their neighbours. They have no choice but to depend on and keep an eye on each other.

The low profile of the police during the riots has been explained by the assumed police intention to force communities to face each other. Tensions between communities were prevented by backing the rioters, but not the looters. The Turkish and Kurdish community organisations stated at a press meeting that, if they have the right to riot, then we have to support them. We have to distinguish rioters from looters. According to the press statement,

The youth are one of the worst affected sections of society from the crisis in the world and the cuts that have been made as a result of the crisis. As a result of these cuts, 8 out of 13 Youth Services have been closed. And such cuts are not unique to Haringey. The removal or tightening of the conditions for being granted Education Maintenance Allowance (EMA), tuition fees going up to 9 thousand pounds, the low level of educational attainment in deprived areas, the removal of support from students who are experiencing problems in secondary schools or referring these students to other institutions are just some of the problems that are experienced by the youth. According to official figures the number of unemployed youths is 1 million. Youth unemployment in deprived areas, such as Haringey and Hackney, is higher. As a result of the cuts not only has there been an increase in the level of redundancies but there has also been an increase in unemployment levels and poverty levels. The stop and search practice by the police is very high in deprived areas and in areas where the migrants live. A black or ethnic youth is times more likely to be stopped and searched than a white youth. An egocentric and consumerist lifestyle has thus far been imposed on the youth. At a time when: poverty and unemployment have risen, the dream of educational achievement has vanished, the closure youth services where the youth express themselves socially and culturally has occurred, a rise in the level of police oppression has taken place, the vision for a better future has vanished. Such outbursts do take place and they're social outbursts. Let's not forget that the Turkish and Kurdish youth are also a part of the youth in this country and therefore Turkish and Kurdish youth and their future are also at stake as a result of such cuts.

Turkish and Kurdish Labourers and Traders Are Being Pitted Against the Black People

The members of our community, all of whom have been forced to flee from their homeland for economic or political reasons, are being pushed to oppose waves of riots. We are witnessing the development of an instinctive tendency to protect their small shops and, at times, to attack the youths. Surely the traders have the right to protect their shops. But such events should not be used to pit the Turkish and Kurdish community against the black community. Such an event should not be used to strengthen the prejudices that the oppressed and migrant communities have against each other. We, the people of Turkey and Kurdistan, should act in a prudent way and not fall for the trap of migrant communities being pitted against each other. Moreover, we should demand that those who killed Mark Duggan are found and held to account via the completion of the inquiry into his death (Turkish and Kurdish Community Organisations).

In Dalston, Turkish people took to the streets with sticks. It was not necessary as rioters didn't aim to attack Turkish and Kurdish shops; but rather targeted big companies. However, they were ready to safeguard their livelihoods in case of an attack due to the conceived threat coming from the rioters. Only a few shops of Kurdish and Turkish origin were looted. The majority of the rioters did not attack the Turkish shops. One of my interviewee's, Ismet, who was present at the Turkish and Kurdish mobilisation to defend the Dalston neighbourhood from attacks, chatted with some of the rioters. The rioters told him that they did not have any problems with Turkish shops. However, in order to prevent any possible damage, most of the shop owners did not close their shops. Similarly, Esnaf, charir of the British Anatolian Craftsmen Union mentions that,

> *The riots were started next to us. They were talking next to us, saying, let's go to Haringey and Hackney and smash the shops down. In the meantime, we told them not to do so as we also have shops there. They didn't touch the Turkish shops. A few Turkish shops were damaged. They mainly targeted the big companies of the state (Esnaf, chair of the British Anatolian Craftsmen Union).*

To summarise, the social capital of the KT communities have facilitated the provision of protection from possible attacks. The police force was not just unavailable during the riots but it also emerged that there was a general concern amongst Turkish shopkeepers that police did not take the security issues of the Kurdish and Turkish shopkeepers seriously at other times. This was considered to be due to there being a lack of police protection in general.

While migration literature widely utilises the concept of social networks to understand patterns of migration, settlement, employment and links with home (Castles and Miller, 1993; Jordan and Duvell, 2003), due to its loosely operationalised focus, there is little attention paid to the different forms of support they may provide to protect businesses. There is a broad perception that shopkeepers do not have equal access to the basic protective services provided by the state. They feel that they are discriminated against. The social networks had to be utilized to counter disadvantage and discrimination. In other words, network embeddedness is not a given condition or fixed in time and space, whenever the Kurdish and Turkish communities can mobilise to cope with marginalisation and disadvantage. It is rather strategically negotiated, validated, strengthened and dissolved in time and context.

Putnam's distinction between social capital based on bonding capital and bridging capital is useful for explaining the low validation of Kurdish and Turkish business owners' networks by the wider society. According to Putnam (1993), bonding social capital occurs among homogeneous populations, within a community like the KT communities. However, the relationships, and trust formed in close proximity to KT owned shops, which could be called bonding capital may not result in action addressing a neighbourhood problem. Bonding capital, thus, is requirement for the development of bridging social capital

(Ryan et al., 2008). Bridging social capital involves to attachments across groups, where members of one group connect with members of another group to seek support or acquire information (Larsen et al., 2004). According to Larsen et al. (2004, p.66), "examples of bridging social capital include calling a city department to voice a complaint about public services or forming a neighbourhood group to conduct a protest".

Putnam's distinction between bonding and bridging capital could be exemplified by the statement that the eleven Turkish and Kurdish community organisations made to the press and public on the 13th of August, 2011 (MR Zine, 2011). In their statement, they listed the actual reasons for the outburst by the youth and protest against the government.

According to Putnam's conceptualization of social capital, the mobilisation of KT shopkeepers on the streets to defend their livelihoods could be called bonding capital. It was largely dependent on to the relationships and trust and reciprocity formed within the close proximity of KT shopkeepers and with the community. Accordingly, the gathering of the Turkish and Kurdish Community organisations' to protest against the recent policies of governmental bodies could be called bridging capital. They acted on mainstream society's problems.

However, Putnam's conceptualisation does not explain why such networks of bonding or bridging capital have been formed in one area and not in another. The mechanism at work in this case could be labelled bounded solidarity (Portes and Sensenbrenner, 1993). Bounded solidarity depends on the emerging feelings of "we-ness" among those facing a similar challenging issue (Ibid). It points to a process rather than a given, fixed embeddedness. Individual self-interests in protecting their business premises were welded together into a higher level of consciousness that paved the way for shopkeepers taking to the streets and later to the Turkish and Kurdish organisations' statement. As a source of social capital, bounded solidarity derives from the situational reaction of a group of people experiencing common problems (Ibid). It is confrontation with the institutions of the host society that has created solidarity among KT shopkeepers.

Confrontation with the native society is situational. It is capable of activating not only attachments of national origin among immigrants but of facilitating such attachments where none existed before (Portes and Sensenbrenner, 1993). It is the contextual interests that constitute feelings of "we-ness". Zet, a restaurant owner, relates the ways in which Kurds and Turks come together and support each other:

There are lots of reasons that bond Turkish and Kurdish communities. The child of a Kurdish parent and the child of a Turkish nationalist go to the same school. They both experience the same problems. They become closer. For instance, both Turks and Kurds have to have resident permit to stay in the UK. They have to use the same consultancy and translation services. In their neighbourhoods they exchange information. They live in the same ghettos. They have adaptation problems. The children have poor educational success. As they do not see any future in school life, they look for new areas of existence. Some of them become gang members. Both Turks and Kurds face the same problems in hospitals and elsewhere. When the people from various social backgrounds, sit next to each other, they can support each other. Another example was the riots. All Turkish and Kurdish people supported each other. There is a political dissidence between Turks and Kurds in Turkey. This is a problem for Turkey. Here, the shared common problems can bring people together (Zet, restaurant owner).

It is important to note that while Turkish and Kurdish communities are fragmented and on some occasions have tense relationships because of the armed conflict in Turkey, the issues related to Turkish politics do not cause polarisation. The "fundamental source of solidarity is still situational", shaped by the daily needs of the community, "since it is the reality of discrimination and minority status that activates" (Portes and Sensenbrenner, 1993, p. 1330) bounded solidarity. This is also a clear example of reactivation of the village boundary defence mentioned earlier in this chapter. The social capital in the Kurdish and Turkish migrant neighbourhoods was activated to protect shop owners' economic interests. The territory of the neighbourhoods is more than an administrative area. It symbolises the identity of the Kurdish and Turkish communities where economic interests are realised. The economic interests of the shop owners are dependent on the land. Any attack by the rioters on the businesses is an implicit attack on the economic interests and identity of the KT communities. The collective mobilisation of the KT communities to defend their territory is situational in times of incidents such as theft and arson. The shared interest and interest alignment is to defend the territory from potential incidents, and this causes Kurdish and Turkish community members to form unities, which make collective action possible. The territory is defended regardless of quarrels and disputes within the neighbourhood communities. Interests promote a common identity and a unifying structure among the KT communities.

The lack of police protection provided to the shop keepers has been identified as one of the problems faced by the KT businesses. Another problem for them is competition with big chain stores. In the next section, I am going to focus on business planning regulations and competition.

Skills, training and social networks

Skills, training and work experience were important sources of cultural capital for the start-up process of the Turkish-Cypriot, Kurdish and Turkish interviewees. As they were inexperienced and had never been self-employed in their entire life, skills, work experience and training acquisition was one of the difficult challenges they had to face. All of my interviewees expressed that they did not have any prior experience in small business ownership. In other words, it was a courageous and risky act to setup a shop and entering into self-employment. Turkish and Kurdish catering and retail business owners in Britain gained skills and training in two main ways; very few gained them through formal education, either from formal academic training in hotel and catering management or in short term training courses in the food business. Informal training includes employment in catering and retail businesses. The second form is work experience gained in family and co-ethnic businesses and elsewhere.

As I mention earlier, the majority of the interviewees gained work experience in co-ethnic businesses as a worker. Being a worker in a co-ethnic or family owned business was a step towards self-employment in the same sector. It was a way to acquire the necessary skills for maintaining and accumulating the financial capital for starting a business. By the same token, it is a patron-client relationship which entails exploitation of the worker until the worker sets up his or her own shop.

Quite a few interviewees in the study held university degrees in various disciplines such as accounting, hotel and catering management, business administration, mathematics and computing. One businessman was trained at a technical school providing butchery and meat processing courses in London. However, of the eight caterers and retailer interviewees who had university degrees, only three, Doner, Halil and Kumkapi, had formal education in catering and hotel management. Doner and Halil are Turkish Cypriots whose families were also in the catering business in the UK. Halil's, (67 years old, married male) case exemplifies the general condition of Turkish Cypriots who received formal education in catering and retail businesses:

We came to London in 1957. I was in Cyprus previously. It was part of the British Empire, the Common-wealth. My father was in the British army during the Second World War. Then, my father came to London in 1953. Four years later, three sisters, I and my mother joined him in 1957. At that time I was seven years old. I was not fluent in English. As a young boy my father was a chef in London, in the catering business. My father was working for leading hotels at that time. He used to work at Charing Cross Hotel; he worked at the Strand Place Hotel. He worked at all the leading hotels in London at that time. But I went to the Westminster hotel school in

Vincent square in London. I graduated in hotel management in 1970 and then I finished my PhD in Cenova (a city in Italy). When I came back in 1971, I started my own business. I have been working from the age about 14 (Halil, restaurant owner).

In contrast to restaurant or coffee-shop ownership, off-licence ownership requires relatively less skills. Off-licence owners need to learn to arrange goods in a shop and from where and how they can acquire the wholesale products, marketing skills. Accounting services are provided within the KT communities. They generally gain experience about running a shop from co-ethnics who are in the same business, or from shop consultants. Most of them started to working as an employee in a shop. Carsi's case reflects the general condition of the interviewees who gained business experience through working in the restaurant, off-licence and mini-market businesses. It shows how cultural capital in running a business is transmitted from one co-ethnic to another.

After I completed the obligatory military service in Turkey I came to the UK via family unification in 2003. My wife was here. I started to work in off-licences. My wife's family was into such businesses. In general, the Turkish community is concentrated in the restaurant, supermarket and off-licence businesses. There is not much innovation in Turkish businesses. They do what they see at other Turkish businesses. When I came to the UK all the people I knew were in this shop keeping business. 90% of Turkish people in the UK work in shop keeping, kebab, or in the restaurant business. When I came to the UK, I saw that Turkish people were running off-licences and supermarkets. Generally they are not running a supermarket like us, but off-licences. I initially started· in off-licence businesses owned by 3-4 relatives. I worked there as if it was my own business. Here, I learned about the demands of the customers. Customers demand alternative options. My relatives didn't care about that. In that time, I acquired the necessary training. You learn by working in the business. I learned the business in my relatives businesses (Carsi, mini-market owner, 37 years old, male).

Given that many Kurdish and Turkish migrants to the UK lack the skills for running a take-away, restaurant or coffee-shop, it is not surprising that they have to hire the previous chefs if the shop is taken over from someone else, or they have to employ Kurdish or Turkish chefs if it is a new start-up. In addition, when children grow up, parents rely up them as translators and mediators in almost every facet of their lives. Translation and advice services were provided on issues related to welfare in the community organisations when Turkish and Kurdish migrants first arrived to the UK. However, as the number of new start-ups increased the shop owners required support institutions such as accountants, and law firms that to provide their services in Turkish. Carsi, 37 years old, married male who is a part owner of a supermarket exemplifies the ways in which the majority of the shop owners gained cultural capital.

Many immigrants to Britain from Cyprus arrived with a working knowledge of English as Cyprus used to be a British colony. As they were arrivals prior to the deindustrialisation, Cypriots were able to find employment as waged labourers in various sectors in Britain such as construction, the car industry and the dairy industry. Thus, they differ in terms of their backgrounds, skills and resources from Kurdish and Turkish people. English language competence is a big problem in running Turkish and Kurdish businesses. Cinar, a 47 years old, married male who owns an off-licence exemplifies the interviewees in this grouping:

> *We cannot establish good relationships with our customers. Since my level of English is elementary, conversations like hi, how are you, the weather is good or bad, are the limits of general conversations. However, there are some customers, like the elderly man who visited the shop a few minutes ago, who want to speak more. However, it's not possible to satisfy him as I can't get into a proper conversation with him. So, he goes away (Cinar, off-licence owner).*

Accordingly, the reliance on their children's labour is not only or even predominantly due to financial considerations such as benefiting from children's unpaid labour, but is also due to the children's roles as translators and mediators. Most of the parents had to rely on their children for English language assistance and guidance in almost every facet of life. They need their children's labour for public relations as an aspect of the business. This includes chatting with regulars, understanding what customers want, and sometimes listening to customers' personal problems. The cultural capital of children was utilized to maintain good relations with customers. Gulay, a 45 year old married woman who runs an off-licence, highlights the contribution of her son in terms of his language skills in running the business:

> *Of course, a smiling face is essential in this business. My son is brilliant at this. His English is proficient. It is necessary to maintain good relations with customers. It is very important to help when customers ask something. For instance, if one customer comes in and asks what brands of Vodka we stock, I can only name two. On the other hand, my son can show various products. I can't do this. My husband cannot either (Gulay, off-licence owner).*

Gulay's case exemplifies the English language competence level of first generation Kurdish and Turkish migrants to the UK. Even though she has been living in the UK for more than 25 years, she has difficulty in communicating with the wider society. This is due to the fact that they had only been able to find employment in the ethnic enclave economy with harsh working conditions. They have been 'imprisoned' by their working lives. Some Kurdish and Turkish migrants even started to work in textile factories immediately, right after their arrival. By the mid-1990s, the textile industry had collapsed and ethnic partnership became a major approach for setting up businesses selling ethnic products and targeting mainly migrants as their customers. Thus, they have been 'trapped' entirely within ethnic networks. Strong group solidarity and bonds within the Kurdish and Turkish communities can also impact group members in a negative way. Portes (1998) categorizes the negative impacts of social capital in four groups: exclusion of outsiders, excess claims on successful co-ethnic business owners, restrictions on personal freedoms, downward levelling norms.

Gulay's experience is typical of how kinship networks as social capital have been transformed into cultural capital within the family business. That is to say, the first generation of Kurdish and Turkish migrants acquire less cultural capital than their children to maintain their family business. As the child becomes mature, the child's social capital is ready to be used as cultural and economic capital in the form of labour power.

Finally, the acquisition of a 'health and hygiene' certificates for restaurants and a premises licence for off-licences and supermarkets are legal requirements in Britain for all catering and retail businesses. Thus, it is important to note that NARTS, the National Association of Turkish Restaurants, Takeaways and Supermarkets, acquired approximately 7000 licences via its training courses on food safety, health and safety and premises licences.

We provide services to shop keepers in their dealings with bureaucracy. But, our main job is to help them to have a personal license. For instance, if you want to sell food after 11:00 p.m. in this country you have to get a license from the council. We apply to the council for their license. We also get licenses to sell alcohol. We translated a personal license course from English to Turkish. We did it first. Now, it is available in Chinese, Polish and other languages. But, we started this first in 2005. Why I am saying this? Because until the 2000s, the owners of the shops sent their sons, daughters or some other relatives to the courts to get the license. These licenses were previously provided by the courts. Since they didn't know any English themselves, they couldn't have the licences in their own name. We provided the opportunity to obtain the licenses in their own names. Almost 7000 people have acquired their licenses via our services.

In other words, NARTS, owned by a Kurdish businessman utilises his cultural capital to derive economic capital. The would-be entrepreneurs lack the necessary knowledge to obtain a licence and are unable to deal with the bureaucracy. The lack of cultural capital of would-be shop keepers is utilised as an opportunity for NARTS.

In conclusion, social capital of would-be and existing Turkish and Kurdish business owners was utilised to acquire cultural capital, i.e. skills and training. Skills for running a business, work experience, translation, and advice and accountant services were all provided by social networks. It is the act of collective self-help of KT communities that provided information and skills to the would-be and existing business owners.

Workers, gender and social networks

For the Turkish and Kurdish caterers and retailers in London in this study, social capital played a key role in providing indirect economic capital such as labour support. The dire financial conditions of the shop keepers means they have to mobilise family members as employees. However, the working lives of the business owners do not differ from those of employees working in the shop. The shop-keepers participate in every step of the shop-keeping business. The working life of shopkeepers is shaped by social isolation, imprisonment and alienation stemming from long working hours associated with running small businesses (Sirkeci et al., 2016).

According to my interviews, most of the businesses in catering and retail are headed by males. Most of the shop-owners in this study stated that the contribution of their family in the form of labour support is essential. They had limited financial resources. Labour support from the family may include immediate family members: siblings, aunts and uncles, nephews and grandparents. Family members and co-ethnics have to engage in long working hours in order to remain competitive. As children get grown-up, the labour of wives and of teenage children becomes available. It is generally the women who take care of the children. Co-ethnics work for less than market wages as there are no other jobs available to them and they have to accept the wage that is offered by the shopkeeper. Patriarchal self-exploitation within the family and exploitation within ethnic networks reduces labour costs, which enables them to survive in the face of competition. Moreover, family and co-ethnic labour provides a particularly reliable workforce as they look after the business as if they owned it. Thus, family and co-ethnic labour embody a form of social capital that could be converted into economic capital in Turkish and Kurdish businesses.

In addition, Turkish born women, who work in small shops tended to be involved in their husband's businesses, perceiving themselves as building up a family business (Westwood & Bhachu, 1998, p.43; Change Institute, 2009, p.44). As Westwood and Bhachu mention, it is officially the man who is registered as managing the business, and in some cases the woman might be registered as his employee (Ibid). That is, the enterprise is conceived socially to be an extension of home. This is even physically true where the upper floor of the shop is used as a home. The family is an economic unit for migrants where they can acquire basic unpaid labour for migrant enterprises, which could provide them with the competitive advantage over native enterprises needed for survival.

Westwood and Bhachu further argued that "those ethnic groups deemed to be more 'successful' in the business world than others are characterized by social structures which give easier access to female labour subordinated to patriarchal control mechanisms" (Ibid, p.22). Accordingly, it is possible to argue that, the social relations within the family, shaped by the material base of the enterprise, are patriarchal, i.e. men have control over women's labour power. Solidarity between men and hierarchical relations between men and women enable men to dominate the business ownership. The control is sustained by "excluding women from access to necessary economically productive resources and by restricting women's sexuality" (Cockburn 1985, p.84, following Hartmann, 1979). Moreover, the control of labour power within the family does not only apply to the labour power of women. It also results in some parents actively discouraging their children from pursuing post school higher education, and encouraging them to take up the running of family businesses instead (Change Institute, 2009, p.8).

As I mention in the introduction, patriarchal relationships attached to the mode of production have initially been largely dissolved and restructured according to the changes in the British economy. Cultural practices are not fixed and stable. Initially, the shift towards waged labour in factories, where all men and women had to perform the same tasks for equal wages, led to the changes in village-scale practices such as patron-client relationships and male-headed households. It is asserted that the woman's role and position within the family is affected when they find employment as a waged labourer. This also increases their individual power and self-confidence (Karaoglan & Ökten, 2012). Female KT community members, to a large extent, had higher autonomy over their own earnings. However, the closure of the textile factories in turn has largely pushed the Kurdish and Turkish communities to set up small shops, to a large extent based on family labour where women's labour is unpaid and consumed within the family. As I mention in the methodology chapter, I conducted pilot interviews with people from various trades in the KT communities. One of the pilot interviewees has been a hairdresser in London for 30 years. The structural shift from employment in the textile factories to self-employment in the catering and retail businesses has affected his business. According to the hairdresser Haydar, employment in the textile factories provided equal wages for male and female members of the Turkish community. KT women had greater control over their own earnings and had a higher degree of independence with respect to their decisions:

> *Previously, (during employment in textile factories) the wife and husband alike used to work in the same factory. Our business during those years was good. Women could spend their earnings without any interference. They had greater independence (Haydar, hairdresser).*

The low level of women entrepreneurship in retail and catering businesses could be explained by a gender division of labour. Women started to work in coffee-shops, restaurants, and off-licences mainly helping their husbands (Tasiran, 2008). Small family businesses, which require intensive working hours with low profit margins in the retail and catering sectors, to a large extent are owned and run by men in London. Women labourers in the catering and retail businesses tend to be hidden, either working in the kitchen or supporting their husbands in running his business (Holgate et al., 2012; Inal, 2008; Phizacklea,1988; Strüder, 2001).

Networks connect veterans to newcomers, which enables the fast transmission of information about possible opportunities for businesses. Immigrants rely on connections with settlers to find shelter and work, and thus find themselves in the ethnic occupational and residential enclaves. It is clear that the residential areas where minorities are concentrated are determined by the locus of capital demanding cheap labour. For instance, with the textile industry until the 1990s in London, Hackney became the site for immigrant family location, and they subsequently established family networks to attract a second and third wave of immigrants (Petras, 2006). In the case of women who gave up waged labour in textile factories to participate in the running a business, few obtain a separate wage, even though there is an increase in money available for domestic expenditure. By changing the type of work, these women not only lose an independent source of income, and a large network of often female colleagues, but they also find themselves sucked backed into the kinship system which emphasises patrilaterality. Patriarchy could be defined as:

> *A set of social relations which has a material base and in which there are hierarchical relations between men and solidarity among them, which enables them in turn to dominate women. The material base of patriarchy is men's control over women's labour power. That control is maintained by excluding women from access to necessary economically productive*

resources and by restricting women's sexuality (Cockburn 1985:84, following Hartmann1979).

Turkish and Kurdish owned catering and retail businesses in this study are labour intensive enterprises that necessitate kinship and ethnic labour in order to increase competitive advantage in the market. Yetisal, a female shop designer and consultant who set-up more than 500 off-licences and supermarkets as Kurdish and Turkish business sector states:

Kurdish and Turkish businesses are generally family businesses. Family businesses are very important. The job potential they could provide does not fly away. They provide jobs for the family members. Money stays in the family. This is very important. A wage labourer in a shop does not receive less than £300. If you employ two workers, then you have to pay £600. Thus, employing workers increase the expenditures. Yet, it is also a bit dependent on the size of the shop. To my mind, family businesses are always better (Yetisal, shop designer and consultant).

Businesses like off-licences and takeaways require less labour power than CTK restaurants, wholesalers and large supermarkets. Thus, the necessary labour for running the business can be provided within the family in the former businesses, whereas outside labour may be required for the latter businesses. In larger CTK businesses, the division of labour for the family members may be different as they may play increasingly managerial roles.

Turkish Cypriot businesses were middle sized firms able to hire workers. For instance, Doner, who owns one of the biggest Kebab manufacturing companies, has two sons and they play managerial roles.

In addition, takeaways and off-licences do not require a skilled labour, whereas restaurants owners have to retain a good chef. Given the fact that there are lots of restaurants that serve Turkish cuisine, the cultural capital of chefs becomes a valuable resource. This is coupled with restrictions in the migration policy.

The issuing of government policy to restrict migration to the UK has led me to think that in five years, there is going to be a problem to find employees. I saw this. If the problem to find a good cook is going to be increased in the near future, I thought, I had to create a cuisine where everyone can work. The expenditures have increased. If you want to sell Turkish cuisine then you have to find experienced staff in that area. They do not come. You cannot bring them to work for you. I have raised several cook, but they went to some other place for a better salary. The other business owners offer better salaries. Even though the salaries they offer are high, they had to do so. They made investments into Turkish restaurants (Zeytin, restaurant owner).

Thus, it is possible to argue that the value of cultural capital of chefs is not independent from government policies. The value of cultural capital of chefs has increased due to the restrictions in the migration policy. The exchange value of chefs' labour has increased due of government policies.

Conclusion

In summary, my objective in this chapter was to explore the means of setting-up and maintaining small businesses. The main objective of this chapter is to answer the question of how KT communities acquire and utilise economic, cultural and social capital in setting-up and maintaining businesses in North London. The findings of this chapter suggest that KT communities managed to create self-help social networks and institutions. Resources required for the entrepreneurial action was generated to a large extent collectively. Kurdish and Turkish migrants to the UK responded, to a degree collectively to the conditions posed by de-industrialisation, such as unemployment. Ethnic institutions and social networks were established and strengthened in response to the welfare needs and interests of Kurdish and Turkish small business owners. Thus, in contrast to the individualistic conception of the entrepreneur as a risk taker who opens a business and attains success, in this chapter, I demonstrate the importance of collective resource mobilisation of economic, social and cultural capital in small business ownership. The salience of many collectivistic cultural practices and their transposition to a new setting after immigration was an essential resource for the KT communities. While village scale collectivistic cultural practices were, to a large extent, eroded during the textile industry years, when Turkish and Kurdish alike found employment as waged labourers, with the collapse of textile industry, unemployment and conditions in urban life activated collectivistic cultural practices such as *imece*. Thus, the facilitation and transposition of cultural practices should be understood in relation to the contextual socio-economic class position of KT communities. The strength and weakness of cultural ties in the KT communities is dependent on the mode of production and the degree of acquired economic, cultural and social capital.

With regard to police protection, the lack of it provided to the shop keepers has been identified as one of the problems faced by KT businesses. Social networks characterised by the KT communities' bonding social capital have facilitated the provision of protection from possible attacks. It is a bounded solidarity that depends on the emerging feelings of "we-ness" among those confronting similar difficult situations (Portes and Sensenbrenner, 1993).

According to the findings of the research, there is a link between Kurdish and Turkish groups' entrepreneurship and a strong sense of ethnic solidarity. Economic ties and obligations among the Kurdish and Turkish small business community in the UK strengthened their ethnic ties after deindustrialisation. They were once wage earners working in textile industry. As large numbers of Kurdish and Turkish families who migrated to the UK became unemployed due to de-industrialisation, they had to look for new opportunities for livelihoods in the mid-1990s. They were pushed into self-employment. As the mainstream labour market could not provide any meaningful opportunities for them, for various reasons such as discrimination, relatively low levels of education and limited English language abilities, shop ownership seemed to be a logical goal to work toward. They had to generate and mobilise entrepreneurial resources to set-up and maintain their small businesses. The mobilisation of resources via the ethnic networks and institutions include the provision of economic capital, information, favourable labour support, skills and training, safety within the business premises and neighbourhood, dispute resolution and pressuring the local government for better business regulations. The activation of social, cultural, and economic capital in order to set-up and maintain their businesses was a response to the conditions posed by de-industrialisation, such as unemployment.

As I discuss, we can identify several problems arising during the processes for setting up and maintaining shops. For all of the problems, class based resources such as cultural, social and economic capitals were mobilized to improve the shopkeepers' place in society. I suggest that all shopkeepers do not possess these capitals equally.

The ability to overcome these problems is dependent on the volume and quality of social capital. Shop owners from large co-ethnic networks managed to generate economic capital to set-up their businesses in a short period of time, while shop owners with no relatives utilised their cultural capital to generate capital to set up their shops. The transposable nature of Bourdieusian conceptualisation of capitals has been utilized by shop keepers to overcome various problems, as I discuss above.

Chapter Seven:
Opportunities and Constraints for KT Businesses

In this chapter of the book, I mainly focus on the wider institutional and economic context into which KT communities are inevitably inserted. The previous chapters' main focus was the micro level analysis of the mobilisation model. They illustrate the internal capacity for acting towards a common end by assessing the usage of different levels of economic, cultural and social capital. The capitals are utilized for the sake of setting up and maintaining catering and retail businesses.

On the other hand, in this section, my main concern is how the economic and institutional context as well as regulatory structures influence and interact with the business owners' agency. As Marx (1852, p.3) famously put it:

> *Men make their own history, but they do not make it as they please; they do not make it under self-selected circumstances, but under circumstances existing already, given and transmitted from the past.*

Similarly, would-be and existing business owners act according to their interests, albeit not in circumstances they choose. The wisdom, creativity and the resource mobilisation choices of Turkish and Kurdish business owners – agency- can only be understood and evaluated by focusing at the economic context and the legal regulatory framework – that is, structure. The ongoing interactions between business owners and the world around them determine not only the immediate outcomes of the businesses but also their development and potential influence over time. In this chapter, I discuss the external factors impacting on the processes of setting up and operating of ethnic businesses.

Changes in the economic structures
The key recognition in the economic opportunity perspective is that entrepreneurs' prospects for setting up particular shops, strategies for mobilising resources, and development of small businesses are context dependent. An analysis therefore has to direct its attention to the world outside of the Turkish and Kurdish business owners, on the assumption that exogenous factors inhibit or enhance business development prospects.

Tilly (1978)'s work asserts that opportunities could change over time, and argues that the notion of opportunities would explain the more general process of choosing strategies from a spectrum of possibilities. According to the application of Tilly's resource mobilisation theory in this book, tactics for resource mobilisation are a reflection of entrepreneurs optimising strategic opportunities in pursuit of particular ends at a particular time and place. Thus, I focus on how a range of factors including economic shifts, competition, legal regulatory framework, and protection from attacks impact on the Kurdish and Turkish business development and mobilisation of social, cultural and economic capital in North London.

As I have already mentioned, since the Second World War, global labour markets have changed in two main phases. In the first phase, large numbers of migrant workers were invited from developing countries to fill shortages of cheap labour to re-build the collapsed industry of Western European countries (Castles and Miller, 2003). Immigration has provided the capitalist class with cheap labour. However, the recession in the early 1970s shifted migration policy from recruiting to managing migration by favouring skilled migrants in advanced capitalist countries. The emergent global assembly line or transnationalisation of production during the early 1970s was a response to a labour movement that sustained higher wages and better working conditions in the advanced capitalist economies. That is to say, the profit maximizing strategies of transnational capital led to the re-structuring of the global economy. This entailed the movement of manufacturing jobs from advanced capitalist economies to lower wage zones, while de-industrialization involves the closure of plants, especially in the urban cores. This expansionist strategy, underpinned through international trade agreements to remove protective barriers, has provided the grounds for capital to move freely around the globe by "lowering of protective barriers and the subsequent penetration and domination of local markets by subsidised agriculture exporters and large-scale manufacturers" (Petras, 2006). This process goes hand in hand with the creation of a dispossessed surplus population which fuels migration streams and tighter migration controls. As Castles and Miller (1993, p.153) put it:

> The entry of the countries of the South into the international migration arena may be seen as an inevitable consequence of the increasing integration of these areas in the world economy and into global systems of international relations and cultural interchange.

Because of the macro structural factors the opportunity structures for new immigrants change over time. Consequently, the global political economy is especially significant in understanding changing migration patterns (Collins, 2003). It is also important in explaining changes in the labour market and new paths of immigrant labour market incorporation.

The structural change in global political economy, which necessitates the collaboration of each individual national state, has also called attention to the de-regulation of the labour markets in the British context. The restructuring of the political economy in the UK, particularly in London, is a micro-cosmos of the global political economy as the UK has been responsible for developing and exporting a particular model of economic organisation and social relations to the rest of the world (Wills et al., 2010).

In addition, it is also worth mentioning the shift from manufacturing to service sector employment in big metropolitan cities such as London. The increase in service sector employment corresponds especially to the rapid growth in those sectors associated with the activities of 'command and control', so called FIRE (finance, insurance, and real estate) industries (King, 1990; Massey, 2007; Sassen, 2001; Wills et al., 2010). Less well known is the extent of London's economic dependence on the lower end of service labour power, which is filled by service workers who were born abroad (Wills et al., 2010, p.29-30). According to the Greater London Authority, almost half (46 per cent) of London's 'elementary occupations' such as household domestics, contract cleaners, bottlers, canners, sandwich makers, postal workers, waiters, hotel housekeepers, traffic wardens, and hospital porters are filled by migrant workers (Spence, 2005, cited in Wills et al., 2010). It is this 'super-diversity' (Vertovec, 2006) that keeps London working and providing cheaper goods and services for millions of ordinary Londoners.

Furthermore, with the decline of the UK's textile industry, members of Turkish and Kurdish communities set-up businesses principally in the small retail and catering sectors (IPPR, 2007). These are particularly coffee shops, restaurants and kebab houses, alongside other more recently set up businesses such as estate agents, hairdressers and florists, and are family-run ventures with a growing level of competition (Thomson, 2006). Aksoy, who is a chair at a refugee organisation, was previously working in the textile industry and was also a trade unionist, comments below about employment in textile industry and its decline. His arrival to the UK in 1977 was earlier than most of the interviewees in this study. He was a union leader of the Turkish and Kurdish textile factory workers. He witnessed the decline of the textile industry. In his own words:

We (he and his wife) came here in 1977 when we were about 24-25 years old. We were looking for jobs. Turkish people, during this time, were working solely in textile factories. Until the middle of the 90s, the textile factories continued to be the major source of livelihood for Turkish people. For instance, this building used to be a textile factory. I was working here downstairs, in the finishing section, cutting thread. It was good money during those times. At that time, it was impossible to find an unemployed person on the street. They were providing jobs in the textile business when someone was unemployed. The tax office shut down the factories. They started to go abroad, to countries like Romania, Turkey and to the Far East. This building used to be a factory. I was working downstairs in the finishing department cutting thread. At that time I was also the union leader of textile workers for three years. Textile businesses had started in 1970 and ended in the mid-1990s (Aksoy, chair at a refugee organisation).

London Media Ltd provided a guide to CTK businesses in London in 2003. In their introduction they commented, "Since 1999 there has been evidence for a noticeable diversification in trades. Key informants confirmed that this has continuously happened since the collapse of the textile industry. Many Turks from mainland Turkey came to the UK, particularly London, in the 1970s and 1980s with textile skills, such as tailors, trimmers, in order to work in the textile industry. At that time, the establishments in the textile industry employed over 90 per cent of KT people. It is the collapse of the textile industry in western industrialised countries that pushed many Turkish people into self-employment" (cited in GLA, 2009, p.34). The report further argues that

"following the end of the textile trade various other trades have taken over, such as restaurants, fish and chip shops, kebab shops, cafés, supermarkets, minicab offices, off-licenses, import-export and various other trades" (ibid).

The above discussion emphasises the changing opportunity structure for the Turkish and Kurdish individuals in London during the 1990s. Accordingly, Tilly (1978)'s collective resource mobilisation asserts that opportunities could change over time. It explains how a range of factors including economic shifts, legal regulatory framework, the availability of elite allies and competition impacted on the members of the Turkish and Kurdish business owners' prospects for constructing interests, mobilising, employing particular economic strategies rather than others, affecting mainstream institutional policy. In the previous two empirical chapters 5 and 6, I analysed the response of the Kurdish and Turkish communities to the changes in the opportunity structures.

In he next section, I discuss the impact of legal regulatory framework on the economic opportunities of would be and existing Kurdish and Turkish business owners.

Legal regulatory framework

As discussed previously, ethnic business development is shaped not only by group characteristics, such as the acquired economic, cultural and social capital of its members but also by the surrounding commercial environment. As Kloosterman et al (1999, 257) argue that "wider economic and institutional context into which immigrants are inevitably also inserted" has a decisive role in ethnic business development.

The legal regulatory framework is another factor that draws the boundaries, constraints and opportunities for migrants businesses in England. According to the Food Standards Agency (2013) booklet, in order to "start a new catering business, or take one over, a would-be entrepreneur must register his/her premises with the environmental health service at their local authority at least 28 days before opening" (p.3).It further states, "this applies to most types of food business, including catering businesses run from home, and mobile or temporary premises such as stalls and vans" (ibid). The local authority should be contacted to gather information on how to register. If business owners run two or more ventures, they are required to register all of them.

Moreover, the general guidelines for businesses are as follows:

They might also need to register as self-employed and/or register for VAT. VAT stands for Value Added Tax. These registration processes are completely separate from registering their food premises. They will need to pay business rates on most premises. Licence is required if they want to sell or supply alcohol, sell hot food and drinks between 11pm and 5am, provide entertainment, such as theatre, cinema or some live, music performances, sell food from a stall or van on the street. They should contact their authority for information on all of these licences. If they are self-employed, they must register with HM Revenue & Customs within three months of becoming self-employed. As a self-employed person, they are responsible for paying their own tax and National Insurance contributions. They will need to fill in a tax return each year. Businesses that are 'VAT registered' charge VAT on the goods and services they provide. If their businesses have a turnover (not just profit) above the 'registration threshold', it must be VAT registered. From 1 April 2013, the registration threshold was set at £79,000 a year, but this is likely to change.

Almost all of my informants complain about the high business rates. The narratives emphasise the unfairness associated to council policy. They argue that it favours chain stores at their expense. It was asserted that high business rates are unfair as Kurdish and Turkish businesses operate in migrant concentrated districts, where profit margins are low. According to the interviewees, high business rates are one of the factors for business failures. Yesil, a mini-market owner in Haringey comments:

We complain about Haringey council. We pay more business rates than Oxford Street. They demand an amount we cannot pay. Because of this it is really hard to survive. Moreover, penalty rates...Haringey Council never tolerates...Thus, it direct customers there (referring chain stores).Customers should be able to park their car in front of our shop.

Camera records immediately. Penalty is £60.Thus, the number of customers decreases. Parking fee is 50-75 pence everywhere. In Haringey, it is £3. It was £1.90 and they raised it to £3.100% increase (Yesil, mini-market owner).

It is possible to state that the relatively lightly-regulated UK economic regime certainly encourages setting up retail and catering businesses. According to the House of Lords, "comparative indicators suggest that the regulatory environment in the UK is relatively supportive to business. A World Bank survey published in 2013 (covering the period June 2011 to May 2012), for example, places the UK seventh out of 185 in rankings for "the ease of doing business"" (House of Lords: Select Committee on Small and Medium Sized Enterprises, 2013, p.72). In contrast, for instance in Germany, self-employment in most crafts necessitates registration in the *Handwerksrolle* (Crafts Listing), which necessitates proof of professional competence, i.e. certification. In general, in comparison to the mainland European countries the "neo-liberal UK regime is less subject to interventionist state control" (Ram and Jones, 2008, p.62). Gules, a married mini-market owner, compares the legal regulatory framework of UK and Germany:

The UK is different from other European countries. It is possible to run a shop without residence permit in the UK. You have such an advantage. Thus, all of us have used this advantage. Now, one in two Turkish families owns a shop. This country is the forerunner of the free market economy. Thus, corner shops, small shops, supermarkets, small businesses like this are very widespread as compared to Germany, where there are big companies. It is a system where big companies are dominant. In this country, there are small businesses (Gules, mini-market owner).

Several interviewees in this study were irregular migrants when they set up their shops. The regulatory structure enabled them to set up shops and run them. Some members of the KT communities were able to run their businesses without being UK citizens. People without British citizenship living in the UK need to have leave to remain if they want to start a business.

In sum, in comparison to continental European countries like Germany, the UK has a liberal legal framework that provides incentives for would-be ethnic business owners. The opportunities for setting up shop encouraged new start-ups. However, according to the narratives gathered in this study, the council policy favours big chain stores with its high business rates and car parking policy.

Business competition

The number of specialist grocery stores has declined significantly since the 1950s (in the UK). The number of butchers and greengrocers declined from 40,000–45,000 each in the 1950s to fewer than 10,000 each by 2000. The number of bakeries declined from around 25,000 in 1950 to around 8,000 by 2000 and the number of fishmongers declined from around 10,000 to around 2,000 over the same period (The Competition Commission, 2008, p.34).

In all these sectors, the number of business owners has fallen by 90% since the 1950s, and at least 40% during the first decade of 2000 alone. Small independent shops have been driven out by <u>supermarkets, which now sell 97% of food in the UK, with four chains accounting for 76%</u> (Wilby, 2011).

Another external factor impacting on the prospects for the Kurdish and Turkish business development is the fierce competition from big supermarkets. Business development prospects of the Kurdish and Turkish catering and retail business owners are threatened by competitive market pressures, particularly from supermarkets.

In 2011, Sainsbury opened its first fresh kitchen shop offering cold and hot food. At the time, the Guardian reported that several others are also determined to take on the nation's sandwich shops and fast food chains head on. In other words, the competitive pressures of chain stores on the Kurdish and Turkish business owners are not only limited to retail businesses, but also to the catering businesses, such kebab shops and restaurants.

According to Esnaf, chair of a craftsmen association, the regulation for chain retail businesses is unfair:

Tesco, Sainsbury and other chain stores should be located in the out skirts of London It is unfair because, they do not pay any tax at all. Their head office is abroad. They are exempt from tax. On the other hand, there is no chance for us to carry our head office abroad. We pay tax. Secondly, they were not able open local stores before. They have changed the regulations. Now, they are everywhere (Esnaf, chair of a craftsmen organisation).

Tescopoly ("food poverty," n.d., para. 3-4) a campaigning NGO highlighting the negative impacts of retail chain stores' behaviour along its supply chains both in the UK and internationally, on small businesses, on communities and the environment, states,

More recently, and encouraged by government initiatives, supermarket chains have begun to set up stores in deprived areas. But this is not necessarily good news: New supermarket developments could result in the

loss of even more independent shops. It is often the most socially excluded and poorest groups who are most in need of the social and economic bedrock offered by independent neighbourhood shops and markets.

The development of chain stores is putting them directly into competition with ethnic businesses. The planning system for retail businesses in Britain allows local residents to have their say about the possible effects of chain store development. The guiding principles of the bureaucratic mechanism are quite simple and it is designed to provide opportunity for communities to voice their concerns (NEF, 2005).

However, my interviewee, Esnaf, chair of a craftsmen organisation, states that almost all of the applications have been accepted by the council and leading to complains from within the community about the lack of regulation of the retail sector:

> *The Turkish speaking community cannot find employment in mainstream businesses. Some of them are educated. But, still they cannot find jobs in the mainstream labour market. As a consequence, they set up businesses in the service industry such as convenience stores and restaurants. However, such businesses are over populated with surplus to requirement. Thus, businesses share the demand for such services and earn less than before. There is no regulation in England or in London. The Craftsmen Union or central government should say no. Councils let every applicant set up a shop since they aim to collect tax. It was not like this before. There used to be objections. There was a need for distance between shops. This condition for receiving a licence was removed after a while. This regulation was removed 15 years ago (Esnaf, chair of a craftsmen organisation).*

Actually, new developments of chain stores have had an impact upon existing independent Turkish and Kurdish shops. The pressures of over-competition with chain stores and within the Turkish community have been identified as one of the big problems. Supermarkets such as Tesco, Sainsbury, Asda, Aldi and Lidl are big players not just in the food industry. They have diversified their activities into different sectors, both into other branches of retail and into unrelated activities such as finance and travel. Supermarkets are now selling a wide range of items from clothes and flu vaccines to legal advice. The effects of the chain stores are enormous. As Thomson (2006, p.20) states that "competition has tightened margins with the effect that the work is increasingly casual, low-paid and subject to long hours".

In order to deal with the negative effects of large chain stores, a conference hosted by the National Association of Turkish Restaurants, Takeaways and Supermarkets (Narts) drew together business owners to discuss vital issues related to the question of how small Turkish and Kurdish owned businesses could fight back against the much larger supermarkets and how to ensure that they could compete against them. Halk, chair of a community organisation talks about the effects of big chain stores on family owned businesses:

There are lots of shop closures, undersold shops and low turnover. People became unemployed. They tried to work in other sectors. Lots of people are moving out of London. The number of people moving out of London is much more than before. Now, you can find a Turkish restaurant and a Kebab shop in every corner of England, even in the smallest town. This is because of competition. There are no good job opportunities in London. Generally, the family moves out of London. In their new destination, they live on the upper floor of the shop (Halk, chair of a community organisation).

In a similar vein, Narts, a shop consultancy firm owner comments on the effects of the aggressive market policies of chain stores:

The situation of corner shop owners is terrible now. It has been like this since 3-4 years, mainly because of the aggressive market policies of Tesco and Sainsbury. They have been opening small local stores in every neighbourhood. This killed a lot of corner shops, grocery stores and local independent shops. Now, independent shops are selling milk and bread. The development of chain supermarkets has affected the small stores and small craftsman enormously. Since two years, the sector has been in crises. In addition to the economic crises we have, the development of chain stores has contributed to the hardships of small craftsman as well. The small craftsmen are bleeding now (Narts, a shop consultancy firm owner).

Several interviewees have also mentioned the negative effects of economic crisis. It was argued that the government, in order to bail out banks, raised the price of electricity, gas and increased the business rates of businesses. I was told that the price of the economic crisis has been paid by the poor people, who did not contribute to it. Due to economic crisis many businesses had to close down. As Ramazan, a mini-market owner states,

Lot of businesses had to close down because of the economic crisis. The expenditures have increased too much. The business rates, electricity, gas etc. Small businesses cannot survive (Ramazan, mini-market owner).

Moreover, Ismet, a coffee shop owner mentions that the economic hardship in running his business is not limited to the increase in expenditures, but also related to the decreasing number of customers eating in his restaurant. In addition, he cannot increase the prices of the dishes due to the crisis. In his own words:

> *You cannot make the same price increase to the menu. Business rates have increased enormously. Gas, electricity and garbage collection and tax also increased a lot. People cut down their expenditures and do not eat out as before due to economic crisis. Lots of restaurant owners are in trouble. Many of them closed down (Ismet, coffee shop owner).*

The New Economics Foundation's (NEF) Clone Town Britain report, published in 2005, called attention to how the increasing expansion of large chain stores are homogenising British streets and people are left with identical high streets. As the report asserts that, "retail spaces once filled with a thriving mix of independent butchers, newsagents, tobacconists, pubs, bookshops, greengrocers and family-owned general stores are described as becoming filled with faceless supermarket retailers, fast-food chains, and global fashion outlets". According to my informants, the facelessness of supermarket retailers has an enormous impact on local communities in two ways. First, while independent shop owners are residents of the neighbourhood, where they run their businesses, they argue that the chain stores' headquarters are generally out of the country. In other words, independent shops contribute to the local economy. The money spent in them stays in the community. Chain stores do not have any responsibility to the community and all the profit they make is moved away from the borough. Accordingly, Tesco and Sainsbury's were both criticized for having subsidiaries based in low-tax countries and also for not fully acknowledging their UK profits (Campbell, 2013). According to the narratives of Kurdish and Turkish business owners, there are two distinct facets of chain and independent. Esnaf, who is a chair of a craftsmen association, explains my interviewees' concerns:

> *Why did we not call ourselves a business association, but craftsmen's association? Because being craftsmen entails an important culture. You cannot put businessmen and craftsmen into the same box. The work of craftsman starts with apprenticeship. It entails a certain culture. There is a kind of hierarchy between the craftsman and the apprentice. Some of our members are big business owners, but we all call ourselves craftsmen. We, to a large extent, target the cultural background of the people. In addition, craftsmen also have close ties with the community; we personally know our customers. Customers tell us their problems. If they do not have enough money on them they can postpone payment until a later date. There are emotional and social ties between shop owners and customers. It is a totally different mentality from how Tesco and other big chain stores operate. The customers of Tesco and others do not personally know the bosses. However, our craftsmen culture is not like this. It's not like this in*

Anatolia either. For instance, the customers can pay for their shopping on a monthly basis; the shop owner can open a pass book. This is solidarity. He can be unemployed, and the shop owner provides him with the necessary produce. On the other hand, a businessman can cut down a tree if he can't sell the shadow. This is the mentality of a businessman. Being a businessman is not moral. We prefer to be craftsmen. This is not related to the number of workers that we hire. We should not become savage (Esnaf, chair of craftsmen organisation).

What is clear from the quote above is that my interviewee draws a distinction between ethnic businesses and mainstream chain stores. In his view, while chain stores' only purpose is to make a profit with no personal relationships with the customers, the relationships that characterise ethnic shops could be defined by such features as social networks, cooperation, trust and mutual benefit. Ethnic shops have the potential to generate social capital in neighbourhoods. It is a relationship of mutual benefit as the shop owners can open a pass book and the customer can keep on shopping at the same shop. The shop becomes a public space where bonding social capital has been reproduced. Bonding social capital occurs within homogeneous groups featuring by trust, cooperation and reciprocity (Putnam, 2007). It is noteworthy to state that the bonding social capital could also be exclusionary, where non-members of the group would not be able to benefit from the resources provided by networks (Leonard, 2004). For instance, it may exclude neighbourhood members who do not share the same Turkish and Kurdish ethnic origin or those who have been excluded from the Kurdish and Turkish community. Secondly, as independent shops owners are residents of the borough, the shops themselves provide public spaces where residents meet and chit chat with each other and with the shop owner.

Competing economic and social capitals

According to Putnam's (1993) conceptualisation of bonding social capital, it is possible to assert that KT communities utilized high levels of bonding capital to maintain their shops. The newly built craftsmen union, as a response to the one of the factors of opportunity structure, market competition, is a form of bridging capital aiming to pressure on the council to have favourable business conditions for the Kurdish and Turkish small business owners. However, the level of bridging capital generated until recently was low for two reasons. Firstly, as my interviewee states, KT shop keepers' lack of information about regulations on business premises indicates that they could not connect with the council and/or any relevant institution to gain information. Secondly, the power differential between the bridging capital of KT shop keepers and the economic capital of chain store directors implies that the chain store directors have greater potential influence than the KT shop keepers, through which they were able to bypass regulations on chain stores. Thus, they were able to lower barriers for setting up local chain stores. As NARTS, shop consultant, comments,

Of course it's a free market economy. Everyone can open a shop everywhere. But, the government has to protect small businesses. Actually, the development of chain stores in every neighbourhood will kill small independent craftsmen. As we said, it's a free market economy. We cannot prevent this. But, there must be a control. If they would allow two or three chain stores in every neighbourhood this could be a solution, maybe. Indeed, this is a black hole. It doesn't matter how many people march on the street, whether they gather 10 thousand people, it doesn't change anything. The big business is going to open their store. They have a very strong lobby. The chain stores could not open any stores if Hackney council would not give plan permission and license. But, who runs the Hackney council? Labour. It doesn't matter whether the conservatives are in the council. These companies such as Tesco and Sainsbury donate to those parties. They are very strong. When the people who run the lobby campaign call the council for the development of a chain store in the neighbourhood, it is impossible to oppose this. It is important to know key people in the bureaucracy.

In other words, there is competition between the bridging social capital of independent stores and economic capital of chain stores seeking support from governmental bodies. The economic capital of chain store lawyers, accountants, lobbyists, strategic departments is more effective than that of the KT business owners' bridging capital. Olmez, a mini-market owner explains how the economic capital of big chain stores work for their benefit:

Many independent shops were closed down. They still continue to close down. You do not have any chance to compete with Tesco and Sainsbury's. Yet, the state has started to bailout banks. Banks are owned by big businesses. Big businesses started to open local stores everywhere. There is government support behind them. Shop owners like us had to close down. We expanded our business three years ago. We made lot of expenditure. Maybe, if you come back in two months, these two shops will be closed down. We had to close one of our shops. How long we can survive is another issue. Even though we support campaigns against Tesco and Sainsbury's development at street level, the government supports them. I support campaigns like "Say no to Sainsbury". Chain stores used to be open until five, at the latest until 7 or 8. Now they are open until 11, some of them 24 hours. They want to kill all independent shops that provide a livelihood. These are Tesco, Sainsbury's and ASDA (Olmez, mini-market owner).

In a similar vein, Carsi states,

> *The aim of Tesco Express in this area is to close all the local independent shops. The association for the protection of small businesses went to the Court of Appeal in order to oppose new developments of chain supermarkets. Now, there is a ban on opening a big Tesco. However, it got worse since they can open an Express now. It is not forbidden to open an Express. You cannot fully ban Tesco in this country. They are present in every district in London now. Customers look to the brand name I sponsored campaigns to stop developments of chain supermarkets. I published posters saying boycott Tesco, boycott Morrison and Sainsbury. I published 500 posters and one more poster saying "support your local shop" as well. There was a campaign run by English people called "my shop is your shop". We became a part of this campaign. We arranged meetings together with Hackney council. We couldn't gather more than 25 Turkish people. Our people are distanced from such things (Carsi, mini-market owner).*

The reason for being distanced from such campaigns could be discussed by one recent case of chain store development in the Stoke Newington district of North London. According to the web page of the campaign "Stokey Local" against the development of a new Sainsbury in the heart of Stoke Newington:

> *Sainsbury's wants to build a 24,000 sq.ft. store in Wilmer Place at 195-201 Stoke Newington High Street. The plans also include a 94 space car-park. However, residents and independent shop owners say the plans to build a Sainsbury's larger than the grocer's current premises a short bus ride up the road in Stamford Hill could force small grocery stores out of business. The site referred to as Wilmer Place is more properly referred to as the Wilmer Industrial Estate. This 0.5 hectare site is located in a Conservation Area on the corner of Stoke Newington Church Street and Stoke Newington High Street, beside Abney Park Cemetery, and is currently occupied by a private pay and display car park and a selection of buildings and extensions of 2, 3 and 4 stories in height. The developer has submitted a pre-planning document (known as a screening opinion) to Hackney Council in advance of a potential planning application to develop the Wilmer Place site. The screening opinion sets out why Newmark Property Investments feels that an Environmental Impact Assessment (EIA) is not justified for this development and the council has agreed and decided that an EIA will not be necessary. After a strong response from local residents, traders and councillors, the developers decided to redesign the proposal. The new proposal consists of;*

Building a supermarket with a retail area of 16,000 square feet, reduced from 24,000 square feet in the original proposal (by way of comparison, the proposed supermarket has about the same retail area as the existing Sainsbury's on Stamford Hill). Building 66 (an increase on the previously proposed 44) residential flats, of which a proportion will be affordable housing and family sized accommodation

In order for this development to happen as described it would be necessary to demolish 193 – 197 Stoke Newington High Street, buildings which lie within the Stoke Newington Conservation Area. One building would be demolished completely in order to make way for an entrance ramp to the underground car park. The other buildings would be demolished but their facades would be retained (The "proposal," n.d., para.3-4)

Groups like Hackney Unites and Stokey Local organised opposition to the renewed Sainsbury/Wilmer Place development. Stokey Local is largely a middle class British community response to the proposed development of a supermarket in Wilmer Place N16. They argued that the development has significant implications for the independent small business owners, local community, employment, transport & traffic, noise and safety and local heritage. One of my interviewees has signed the petition of Stokey Local. He expresses his grievance as follows:

The big retail chain companies are affecting our businesses in a negative way. Thus, in this area there is one local campaign group against big chain businesses. We signed a petition. They open branches everywhere. They are a cartel. They are a threat to small shop keepers. They are selling products much cheaper. They affect the small businesses in a negative way. Thus, small independent shops are forced to close their businesses. In various sectors those big companies hit small businesses. Because of such problems a campaign has been started by the community. However, we don't know whether it is going to be successful. Turkish shop keepers who are informed about these developments are in the campaign. Both the Turkish speaking community and other nationals face the same cost. So, I supported the cause which is against a new local branch of Sainsbury here (Sahir, coffee shop owner).

However, the people involved in the campaign, which involves leafleting, deciding further steps of protest, joining the consultations and giving press interviews, were mostly from a middle class indigenous British background and/or from a minority group that has been living in Britain for decades. Those Turkish speaking shopkeepers with grievances against chain stores lacked the cultural capital to be a part of the process. For instance, another interviewee, who owns an off-licence on the same street states,

The development of a Sainsbury's is going to affect our business. They are going to set-up their store next to us. They are going to sell the same products. Their offer is going to be better than ours. There is already one Sainsbury's a bit further away up the road and they are going to open another one. When we set-up this off-licence that Sainsbury's was not there. That Sainsbury's has affected our business, Iceland as well. In this area, just in front of us, a newsagent had to close down. Journalists from a TV channel came recently. They wanted to record an interview about the Sainsbury's. I cannot talk as such. It is hard. I refused and they went (Tutun, off-license owner).

Accordingly, Bourdieu's (1986) concept of cultural capital and Putnam's (1993) bridging social capital are interlinked with each other. The lack of cultural capital constitutes an obstacle for generating bridging capital which could be utilized to voice his/her demands to the mainstream institutions. As in the case of Tutun, a lack of cultural capital prevented him from expressing his concerns about the development of a Sainsbury. In other words, people with high levels of cultural capital in terms of English usage, lifestyle and code of conduct have a greater chance of activating bridging social capital to voice their grievances.

While Tilly (1978)'s work asserts that opportunities could change over time, the prospects for Kurdish and Turkish business development are largely dependent on the mobilisation of social, cultural and economic capital within the constraints set by these opportunities. The volume and quality of these capitals may inhibit or enhance the opportunities for ethnic business development. The case of Tutun exemplifies that the lack of host country cultural capital firstly was an obstacle to him articulating his interests and grievances. Secondly, it inhibits voicing claims that may achieve social change in business regulations, which support ethnic business development.

Disputes and grievances not only arise between KT shop owners and the mainstream institutions and companies, but also between the KT small business owners. As one of the interviewee states, concentration is in the KT business owners. Start-ups in the catering and retail sectors next to a co-ethnic shop diminish the margins of profit, and sometimes lead bankruptcy. As one interviewee states:

What happened is that our businesses mushroomed everywhere. Shops are opening next to each other. Thus, rates of profit are diminishing. If someone is doing good business in a neighbourhood in London we open a shop next to it rather than setting up a new one in another part of the UK.

It is like this in the take-away business as well. On the other hand, the number of customers in the area is not increasing. We are making the cake much smaller. No one is making money right now. There are only a few places making a profit.

KT community organisations are sometimes able to prevent competition between KT business owners by preventing new set-ups next by a co-ethnic small business owner. The bonding capital within the KT communities has been utilised to solve neighbourhood problems. The social capital within the community was utilised to come to a decision to which the parties have to agree. Such mechanisms for solving disputes between co-ethnics are crucial as parties can maintain their businesses without the risk of bankruptcy. Bardak, chair of a community organisation, mentions;

One of our services involves solving shopkeepers' disputes between partners of a shop and between shop owners themselves. In order to do this, we regularly hold "peace and conflict resolution assembly". It is an assembly where all sides of the dispute gather. The assembly decides the just and the unjust side. In some cases, the assembly prevents one would-be entrepreneur from opening a shop next to another co-ethnic. Even though the council gives permission to open a shop in one region the assembly sometimes prevents this. (Bardak, chair of a community organisation).

Another issue surrounding bonding social capital is government policy on migration. Governments can enhance or restrict the bonding social capital of KT small business owners by their migration policy. As I mention in chapter six, Zeytin had to change the type of restaurant he has been running for several years. The high number of Turkish and Kurdish owned restaurants with Turkish cuisine increased the value of cultural capital of Turkish cooks. He changed his restaurant menu. His restaurant offers Spanish cuisine at the moment. Thus, he employs chefs with Spanish cuisine cooking skills. Moreover, bonding social capital refers to the connections within a group and it is measured as ties to co-ethnics. Thus, government restrictions on migration policy affect transnational bonding social capital negatively. On the other hand, it affects bridging capital positively, that is, it enhances ties between different ethnic groups.

Competition and intensification of work

As I discuss previously, KT shop keepers imitated each other and by doing so they managed to set-up their shops. It was the experience of shop-keeping neighbours which partly motivated other KT people to set-up a shop. In a very short period of time, small businesses mushroomed, mainly in North London. Families joined and set-up shops. Green Lanes is the best example of this. The chain store companies did not have local branches that were open after 8 p.m. Companies such as Tesco and Sainsbury's have copied mini shop owners and started to open local small shops.

Another consequence of the expansion of chain stores is the intensification of the labour process in the independent shops. While products are supplied by more stores, the population demanding goods stayed largely unchanged. This in turn created competition between sellers. Thus, the market share for each retailer became smaller. The increases in competition and decreases in profit has led to independent shop owners having to consume more family labour and work longer hours and they are less able to hire workers as they need to reduce expenditures.

> *Tesco is a world giant. If you allow Tesco to open a branch next to an independent shop is there a chance for the independent shop to survive? Our only advantage is we sell ethnic produce. In addition, we owners of the businesses also work in the shops. The only way to survive is to work more. What's the consequence of this? People do not have a social life and cannot spend time with their children (Esnaf, chair of a craftsmen union)*

Intensification of work emerges as seemingly inevitable outcome of competition between KT shop owners and chain stores. In order to survive, many are no longer able to employ non family workers. As Tufan, a mini-supermarket owner mentions,

> *Nowadays, we do not employ any workers, only family members are working in the shop. Competition has intensified. Have a walk in this district. You can see that we are surrounded by businesses like ours. Things were not like this before. I have been in this shop for more than ten years. I used to employ workers. New shops were built next to already established shops (Tufan, mini-market owner).*

Moreover, shopkeepers in close proximity to each other are stuck in 'the prisoner's dilemma'. The quotation below shows why shopkeepers cannot cooperate, even if it is in their interest to comply with certain opening and closing hours.

> *We work almost 12 or 13 hours every day. As an employer, I work as well. There are lots of hardships, but we cannot prevent them. We clash and disagree with other shop owners. For instance, when I bought this shop, it was open 24 hours. I wanted to speak with other supermarket owners whose shops are next to us. We wanted to make an agreement about the opening hours. We said; let's close our shops at 10 or 11 pm. Two shop owners accepted, the other one did not. Yet, I also have customers coming*

at night. I do not want my customers shopping from another shop. We were forced to keep it open (Spor, mini-market owner).

In addition, more family members' labour is used in the shop or the already existing staff work longer hours. The long working hours in the shop leads to 'imprisonment' and isolation from the outside world. Imprisonment and isolation, thus, contribute to the inability to participate in the wider issues of society and to relate to them. Moreover, they cannot develop their skills, such as attending courses to improve their English language. For instance, it is difficult to leave their shops or reserve time for matters not related to them. Thus, this inhibits the development cultural and social capital of the Kurdish and Turkish business owners.

Competition and ethnic and indigenous taste

Chain stores are a real threat to shop owners. Migrant shop owners sell ethnic products, which gives them a small advantage and provides some protection against chain stores. As they target ethnic minority tastes, the products they provide differ from chain stores. In comparison to mega stores, local chain stores are relatively small. However, chain stores have also started to sell ethnic products in their mega stores. Some shops closed down as they were unable to compete. Thus, new development attempts by Tesco and Sainsbury and other large supermarket chains are opposed by the local community and small shop keepers and they have organised to oppose new branches of chain stores. Carsi, a mini-market owner in Haringey, expresses his concern about chain stores as follows:

Tesco Express is more expensive than local independent shops. However, big ones are cheaper. Because of the labour and rent costs at Tesco Express all the products are more expensive than us. On the other hand, when customers see name plates of Tesco, Sainsbury or Morrison, they do not see anything else. Name is very important. It doesn't matter how cheap your product is. Tesco and Sainsbury, especially Tesco does everything in order to dominate the market. Market entries of Tesco can steal half of the turn-over of independent shops in migrant populated districts. This is a threat. There is one 150 metres away.

What is clear in the above quote is that the symbolic capital associated with the Tesco products is higher than the products in the ethnic small businesses. The higher symbolic capital associated to the Tesco products have higher chance of exchange value in the market. Thus, symbolic capital associated to the Tesco products is exchanged with economic capital.

Nevertheless, the competitive advantage of the ethnic mini-market owned by Carsi is selling some different products than the chain stores. What makes chain stores impossible to compete with is that they are able to provide some products cheaper than the wholesalers. According to the narratives I gathered in this study, the reason for textile factory closures will be experienced in mini-supermarkets closures. In order to compete with chain stores or even to survive they have to work long hours. Because of the decrease in the margins of profit, they are unable to employ workers.

However, the products we sell differ from them. Because of this we can survive. For instance, we sell fresh meat and fruit, they don't. In general, they target British customers. We sell a variety of brands for the same product while they only sell one brand. Some products collide with one another. I also go and buy from there. They sell the products cheaper than the wholesalers. In order to protect the local independent shops, the council previously issued some measures. However, to my mind, the measures were not put in place correctly. If the association for the protection of small businesses barred big supermarket chains, it could also set up a condition for the small ones. I live in Hackney. Every 200-300 metres you can see an Express. This means that the whole district is in their hands, and you don't have any chance. While we buy the products more expensively than the wholesalers, they are selling the products much cheaper than the wholesalers. It is impossible to compete with them. Wholesalers are also competing amongst themselves. Ten years ago, we were meeting workers at the airport and bringing them from their countries. Today textile industry is finished. And ten years later, we could unfortunately say the same to the independent shops. The independent shops are going to close due to rising expenditures, falling turn-over and competition with big business. I mean, certain shops; the big ones will keep on working and in ten years I guess most of the independent shops will be closed. People's buying power is decreasing while economic conditions are getting worse. You have to demand cheap products when people's buying power decreases or you have to follow promotions. If you look carefully, there are 2 litre cokes over there. While I can buy one of them from £1.31, Tesco sells it from £1. When we need an extra worker, we increase our working hours. We have to face this hardship. Our life is certain, from home to work; from work to home. Sometimes we work for 12 hours; sometimes it goes up to 15 hours. We don't have anything else to do. Besides, politicians should issue safeguards in order to protect local, small independent shops. For instance, there should be 500 metres distance between every shop. In this way, the state can collect tax. If there is 10 metres between shops, this could not be achieved (Carsi, mini-market owner).

The Kurdish and Turkish individuals' prospect for business development and even chance of survival is highly determined by the council policy. The opportunity to survive is shaped by the competitive market conditions. The lack of elite allies, which could issue safeguards in order to protect local, small independent shops, is one of the factors impacting on the opportunity structure of the Kurdish and Turkish small business owners.

Independent mini-markets which offer largely ethnic products to their customers are not affected by the competition with chain stores. They target different customers. However, off-licences and mini-markets which offer the same type products with chain stores are more affected by competition as Cinar, an off-licence owner, states,

> *We cannot compete with chain stores. They sell some produce for half price the price of wholesalers. We can still survive as the shop is on people's way. However, no one buys wholesale. They come and buy just a bottle (Cinar, off licence owner).*

Akdeniz, a mini-market owner, which sells ethnic products to KT communities, states,

> *Chain stores do not threaten mini-markets like us (referring shops selling ethnic products), but businesses like off licences. Off-licences are small convenience stores that sell British products. On the other hand, we target ethnic taste, thus, they are not a threat for us. Tesco cannot sell the produce I sell because I have too many options and alternatives (Akdeniz, supermarket owner).*

Likewise, in Ramazan's words,

> *We do not have any relation with chain stores. We don't know them. They sell different produce. We sell different produce. We have different customers (Ramazan, mini-market owner).*

Moreover, Hallim is one of the oldest mini-markets in Haringey, mainly targeting Mediterranean customers. The only reason that Hallim has been able survival in this competitive market is that he targets the ethnic niche:

> *We cannot compete with them. We are on different tracks. We do not aim to compete and pull their customers into our shop. We sell Mediterranean and ethnic products (Hallim, mini-market owner).*

Independent mini-markets still have advantages in the retail business since they can target ethnic tastes. This means, they utilise social and cultural capital to understand their locality and gain an advantage over the supermarkets.

There is nothing in Tesco. You can only find traditional British products. On the other hand, Turkish speaking people prefer to shop from our shops. They can find their palate in our stores. Different ethnic groups can find their products in our stores. 7-8 ethnic groups can find their palate in our stores (Gules, supermarket owner).

However, as Narts contends, independent mini-markets will be in trouble if local chain stores start to sell ethnic products.

I recently read that ASDA has started a campaign. Customers will be able to get the same shopping basket they used to buy last year at a 10% discount. In response, Tesco made 30% discounts. What can Turkish shop keepers do? The only advantage of Turkish shop keepers is that they are providing ethnic products. This is the only advantage they have. When I go to a Tesco I can't buy Turkish lentils, Turkish yogurt or Turkish bulgur. The big crisis is going to happen if local chain stores start to sell ethnic products. It's going to happen like in Germany where chain stores started to sell ethnic products in neighbourhoods. There are already ethnic product departments in superstores. But, if Tesco Expresses and Sainsbury Local have ethnic product departments in their stores, then Turkish shops would be in real trouble. The council has not made any effort to protect local independent shops. They just don't care. There are some regulations to protect independent shops, but they are just on paper (Narts, shop consultant firm owner).

The location of a shop has considerable influence on its competitiveness, and can be a source of advantage. Independent shop owners try to secure a site where development of a chain store is not possible. As Gules mentions:

We do not compete with other chain stores. Besides, we are not powerful enough to compete with them. They are monopolies. They consider us competitors and open local Tesco and Sainsbury's. Just in London this year, 200 ASDAS are due to open. They bought estates. They even tried to buy our shop. We told them three times its value. They almost accepted it. Their only concern is to prevent us doing business. If you can seize a good place, which means chain stores do not have any chance to set up a shop next to your business, then your business is a success story. Ours is such a place. There are no chain stores or big shops next to or around us. Thus, we are a bit lucky and comfortable. However, they want to buy our place (Gules, mini-market owner).

According to Sancak, because of the chain store developments in London, the city has lost its number one location for investment for KT people. A greater number of people started to migrate to the other regions of the U.K

Turkish speaking businesses were largely located in London. Gradually, they started to move out of London. As market shares gradually became smaller, they started to diffuse out of London. Still, London is the major city for Turkish speaking people (Sancak, wholesaler).

The Turkish speaking community is generally based in London. But, people started to move out of London as well. It is getting harder and harder to live in London. It is harder to set-up and run a shop and rent prices are higher in every part of London. It is possible to pay £300 for a 3 bedroom flat. Is it possible to find a 2 bedroom flat in London? It is cheaper to live out of London. There is no competition in some places. In order to prevent unfair competition, the state should state, for instance "you have 1000 branches, enough". There are lots of small businesses which are at risk of closing down. At least five to 10 people are employed in independent shops. What will happen if they lose their jobs? When Tesco wants to set up a branch in Haringey, the council provides every help to them. They claim that they are going to develop the region, but, they just fill their pockets. They don't pay tax at all. Most of the big companies do the same thing. I pay 16 thousand pounds as business rates here (Yesil, supermarket owner).

As Yetisal, a shop designer and consultant states, the location of the shop is crucial. Kurdish and Turkish shop owners use their social and cultural capital to target ethnic tastes. They have an advantage over supermarkets which sells mainly British products. Likewise, the social capital generated in areas concentrated with the KT communities provides a safety net against racist attacks.

The location of the shop is crucial. Chain store developments may affect Turkish speaking businesses. It depends on the location. Some shops are affected and some are not. If it is an area populated by an ethnic minority, then it is probably not affected by a new chain store. On the other hand, if an independent shop sells produce like chocolate or alcohol, then it is hard to compete. As I said, the location of the shop is very important. We have discussed a lot the very issue of how to prevent the expansion of local, express style Tescos, Sainsbury's and ASDA. In addition, you can see big branches of Tesco and ASDA selling Polish, Turkish and Chinese produce. We have to stop their development. One of the consequences of local chain store expansion is the migration of the Turkish speaking community out of London. They face extreme racism in those places. Four or five months ago, I set up a supermarket selling ethnic products outside of London. There is serious racism. People do not want you to do something there. We have seen several incidents like this. We have seen smashed windows; we have seen assaults and verbal abuse. Almost all the businesses that I set up are out of London. Gradually, it has moved out (Yetisal, shop designer and consultant)

The location of a shop determines the level of bonding capital. For instance, in London, some boroughs are concentrated by KT people. According to Yetisal, if the shop is located in an area populated by co-ethnics, racism is not a serious threat to KT people.

The problem is competition. There are lot of ill-informed people. The most important thing in this business is to look at the kind of people living in the area. What ethnicities are living there? What will you sell? Who will you target? These questions are important. We held big meetings to discuss those questions? We tried to inform people. The location of the shop is crucial. It is more important than other things. For instance, when you go to Edmonton, it is possible to see six shops side by side. These shops were set up with capital accumulated over 20 or 30 years. Families united to gather capital and took loans from their acquaintances (Yetisal, shop designer and consultant).

Gules, a mini-market owner, talked about the effects of a newly developed Tesco on a Turkish supermarket owner. According to him, Tesco had an impact on his Turkish mini-supermarket for two months. After two months, the sales of the store returned to previous level.

Turkish speaking shops have an advantage. Places like Tesco sell exclusively British products. Their produce is uniform. They sell certain products. A new Tesco was opened in Stoke Newington recently. It is right across the Turkish supermarket Akdeniz. For two months it affected their business. Their profit decreased. After two months they started to do the same business as before. Akdeniz sells all ethnic products. Before, Tesco used to be open until 8 or 9. Now, they are open 24 hours. This is related to competition (Gules, mini-market owner).

While KT shopkeepers have grievances because of the overdevelopment of chain stores, it is possible to assert that KT political and cultural organisations have low levels of bridging capital. Low levels of bridging capital occur because they are not able to voice shopkeepers' grievances.

Conclusion

In this section, I discussed several external factors affecting KT businesses and the ways in which they try to cope with these issues. The factors I identified are legal regulation, police protection and competition with chain stores.

In terms of the regulatory frameworks, the UK economic regime is lightly-regulated. The legal framework does not prevent potential entrepreneurs from setting up their shops. On the contrary, it encourages the setting up of retail and catering businesses. In addition, "comparative indicators suggest that the regulatory environment in the UK is relatively supportive to business" (House of Lords: Select Committee on Small and Medium Sized Enterprises, 2013, p.72).

In terms of competition, the intensification of work emerges as an inevitable outcome of competition between KT shop owners and chain stores as well as within KT business owners. In order to survive, they are no longer able to hire workers. Chain stores are a real threat to shop owners. Migrant shop owners sell ethnic products, which gives them a slight advantage and provides a small protection against chain stores.

According to Putnam's (1993) conceptualisation of social capital, the chapter argues that KT communities utilised high levels of bonding capital to maintain their shops. However, the level of bridging capital generated was low for two reasons. First, the KT shop keepers' lack of information about regulations on business premises indicates that they are unable to connect with the council and/or any relevant institution to gain information. Second, the economic capital of chain stores is more effective than that of KT shopkeepers, whereby they are able bypass regulations on chain stores.

Chapter Eight:
Conclusion

I present the conclusion chapter of this study in four main sections. In the first section, I present the key themes that emerged from the study by revisiting the original research questions, highlighting the contributions of this study to our understanding, and stating the implications for the key literature on small business establishment and ownership. In the second section, I outline the original contributions of this research. An assessment of what I would do differently if I had the benefit of hindsight and the limitations of the present study are provided in the third section and suggestions for future research are outlined in the fourth section.

Revisiting the research aim and research questions

The results of this study are based on the data gathered from preliminary and main fieldwork studies on KT business owners and key persons in various community organisations -including cultural, faith based and political organisations –, and business consultants from Turkish, Kurdish and Turkish Cypriot origins. I generated 65 semi-structured face-to-face interviews in the field study in London in total. I conducted 25 interviews during the preliminary fieldwork with various small business owners in the service sector, including hair dressers, mini-cab owners, restaurant owners, florists and bookstore owners. I generated themes to be explored further from the initial outcomes of my preliminary fieldwork. The object of the pilot interviews was to access further instances of themes identified in the initial data. The codes of thematic analysis arose from the textual data gathered in pilot interviews rather than from focusing on predefined categories and themes. This is because of the nature of the study as I took a synthesis of deductive and inductive approaches. The process began with analysing pilot interviews in order to focus on further themes to be researched. Then, I coded each transcript thoroughly so that I could identify and evidence particular topics. The subjects I identified during the preliminary fieldwork were further examined in the main field-work, during which I carried 40 interviews were carried. The interviews I undertook were with participants from the catering and retail sectors and community organisations as well as business consultants within the KT communities. The main aim of this research was to explore the reasons for and the ways in which the KT communities manage to set up and maintain businesses in North London.

My first research question was: *why has the practice of becoming business owners arisen within the Turkish and Kurdish communities in London?* With respect to the reasons for the start-up, this study is concerned with the multi-level factors interacting on the macro, meso and micro levels.

With regard to macro level influences, the global re-structuring of the economy through structural adjustment programmes creates migratory flows of people and new surplus populations within both developing countries and advanced capitalist economies. According to Westwood and Bhachu (1988, p.6-7), these have been regulated and disciplined by the self-help ethos of minority entrepreneurship since the 1980s. The structural adjustment programmes de-regularised economies, and knowledge and information become essential assets of 'globalised' flexible production (Harvey, 1989; Sassen, 1991; Wilpert, 1998).

The displaced labour from the low income countries and the unemployed surplus population in advanced economies collectively mobilize resources to establish meaningful livelihoods in the host country (Petras, 2006). Business cycles shaped by the profit maximising strategies of capital can be the driving force behind immigrant entrepreneurialism. People strive to make a living by running their own businesses as self-employed entrepreneurs as a response. The Thatcherite era was characterised by de-regulation and de-industrialisation in the UK, and as such, is a starting point for the observation of support for the self-help enterprise culture. It was a period when wage-labourers turned into self-employed business owners in large numbers.

At the meso level, I suggest that the structural change in the global political economy which necessitates the collaboration of each individual national state has also called attention to the de-regulation of the labour markets in the British context. The restructuring of the political economy in the UK, particularly in London, is a micro-cosmos of the global change. The entire array of manufacturing locations has witnessed de-industrialisation, and manufacturing is no longer a defining characteristic of those places. While one of the consequences of restructuring is mass unemployment in the old industrial cities of the developed world, promotion of self-employment claimed to be a cure for the disturbances of restructuring.

Another meso level factor impacting the reasons for setting up businesses is that, in comparison to continental European countries like Germany, the UK has a liberal legal framework that provides incentives for would-be ethnic business owners. The regulatory framework regarding small business ownership encourages new start-ups.

In some instances, discrimination in the mainstream labour market has been identified as a factor contributing to business start-ups. Participants in this study who attained university degrees at a British university were unable to find employment according to their qualifications.

At the micro level, I have also demonstrated that push factors, namely the changes in the global political economy including the UK, have led the mainland KT communities largely to experience a common fate, and has thrown them into a similar situation, which also enabled them to develop a collective consciousness of their social reality. They had an alignment of interest in small business ownership. The framing process enabled Turkish and Kurdish communities to develop interests directed towards mobilizing ideas for business ownership.

Almost none of the participants' prior cultural capital was related to the catering and retail businesses. They had not had employment experience in those sectors, but rather animal husbandry and farming had been the means of survival in the home country. They had not acquired any work experience through working in small businesses. Consequently, it is possible to state that influences of the family or prior skills acquired in the home country did not constitute an important factor for becoming small business owners.

Furthermore, at the micro level, I have provided evidence that self-realisation, being independent and a desire to use one's own skills, talents and abilities were factors that pulled some participants of this study into self-employment. Unlike most of the participants in this study, these participants who were pulled into self-employment are from middle class backgrounds who acquired institutionalised cultural capital. They were voluntary entrepreneurs.

In addition, the power of collective resource mobilisation theory lies in its ability to explain the reasons for the Turkish Cypriot absence in catering and retail small business ownership. The findings of this study suggest that Turkish Cypriots did not have an interest alignment in small business ownership. Interest alignment involves a defining social reality and specific occurrences within their life, as well as feasible alternatives for a livelihood, such as small business ownership in the retail and catering sectors. Turkish Cypriots were not thrown into the same situation after the demise of the textile industry. This is largely due to the fact that the Turkish Cypriot presence in the UK goes back to earlier times, and they have attained a higher degree of cultural capital which enabled them to find employment in professional jobs.

In this book, I have shown that macro level factors such as changes in the global political economy; meso level factors like the national regulatory framework and economic structure, and micro level factors like community interests and individual class based resources such as cultural, social and economic capital, all interact to explain the presence and absence of Turkish Cypriot, Turkish and Kurdish groups in small business ownership. It is not solely macro, meso or micro level factors that determine the reasons for becoming ethnic minority business owners, but the interplay of these factors where varied permutations of their interaction lead to unique outcomes for individual participants.

Turning to my second research question on how KT communities acquire and utilise economic, cultural and social capital in setting-up and maintaining businesses in North London, the findings of my study suggest that KT communities managed to create self-help social networks and institutions. Resources required for the entrepreneurial action was generated to a large extent collectively. Kurdish and Turkish migrants to the UK responded, to a degree collectively to the conditions posed by de-industrialisation, such as unemployment. Ethnic institutions and social networks were established and strengthened in response to the welfare needs and interests of Kurdish and Turkish communities. Thus, in contrast to the individualistic conception of the entrepreneur as a risk taker (Brandstätter, 1997; Knight, 1921) who opens a business and attains success, this study demonstrated the importance of collective resource mobilisation in small business ownership. The salience of many collectivistic cultural practices and their transposition to a new setting after immigration was an essential resource for the KT communities. While village scale collectivistic cultural practices were, to a large extent, eroded during the textile industry years, when Turkish and Kurdish alike found employment as waged labourers, with the collapse of textile industry, unemployment and conditions in urban life activated collectivistic cultural practices such as *imece*. Thus, the facilitation and transposition of cultural practices should be understood in relation to the contextual socio-economic class position of KT communities. The strength and weakness of cultural ties in the KT communities is dependent on the mode of production and the degree of acquired economic, cultural and social capital.

More specifically, in terms of economic capital attainment to set up businesses, social capital appeared to be the main source of financial capital. Almost none of the business owners used bank loans. As recent migrants to the UK, Turks and Kurds had not possessed active bank accounts for the required period of time, so, they were not considered eligible candidates for bank loans. The participants of this study to a large extent relied on kinship networks composed of immediate and extended family members, hometown networks or a combination of their own resources and capital acquired via social networks. Partnerships with more than two co-ethnics were also common in order to generate the necessary capital to start-up a business. Collective interest alignment during the mid-1990s also provided the ground for partnerships. Co-ethnics without full amount of financial capital brought resources together for setting-up joint ventures. Moreover, business owners who were not a part of a huge family or a home town network received services for setting up shops free from friendship networks. This was also a reflection of the *imece* culture. Social capital as a class based resource played a crucial role in access to economic capital. A few shop owners who lacked relatives and hometown ties had to work for co-ethnics in order to accumulate start–up capital before setting up a shop. On the other hand, shop owners from large families and hometown networks were able to generate financial capital in a short period of time. The quality and volume of social capital attainment by each participant demonstrates the differences in social class.

Moreover, Halkevi, one of the oldest Turkish-Kurdish community organisations in the UK, functioned as a credit rotating association during the 1990s. The members of the Halkevi had collective interests. Halkevi used to have 90 thousand members. The members of the organisation contributed the same amount of money every week. One member, decided by lottery, received the whole amount at the end of the month. All the candidates had to inform the organisation about the type of shop they wanted to set-up. This model of credit rotation was copied from the Jewish community.

With regards to information and various services, the findings of the study suggest that Turkish Cypriots, as early arrivals to the UK were better equipped with cultural capital. They helped Kurdish and Turkish migrants to ease adaptation problems and have successfully set-up collectivist self-help institutions that provide services on a wide variety of issues such as health care, welfare, migration, problems of shopkeepers, translation, illiteracy, housing, school registration of children and extra courses to help KT children with their school work. Community organisations completed paperwork related to accounting for small businesses as well. Kurdish and Turkish small businesses started to flourish during the first half of the 1990s, after the collapse of textile industry. Gradually, Turkish and Kurdish people have learned to keep accounting records for small businesses. The supplementary services for small business owners are provided within the community. The collective interests of the KT communities were voiced, to a large extent, by community organisations. Notice boards and key persons within the community organisations provide a social platform where various needs could meet.

In addition, classifieds in five community newspapers in London provide information to small business owners on various subjects, including changes in business regulations, in their home country language. Another source of information is informal co-ethnic networks. Co-ethics can recommend partnerships and provide information about favourable opportunities, the prices of products and new shop start-ups. Moreover, co-ethnics provide information about favourable sites for investing in new small business ventures.

The lack of cultural and bridging capital, which could tie KT communities to mainstream institutions, has facilitated collective ethnic minority solidarity with regard to the sharing of information and provision of various services.

Collective institutions and informal networks play an important role in the resolution of disputes between business owners and community members. They reduce the risk of helping a co-ethnic and sustain future solidarity between them. Such mechanisms guarantee the compensation of any kind of loss to a co-ethnic through cheating. Assemblies and informal networks reflect the social capital embedded in the Turkish and Kurdish communities that ensure reciprocity and future collective collaboration.

With regards to claim making, competition between ethnic minority businesses and chain stores, high tax rates, parking regulations and security in the business premises are the major problems that the Turkish and Kurdish communities face. Kurdish and Turkish business owners can only mediate their claims via community organisations. In order to assert influence, they have recently established a small business association. They collectively mobilise social networks to achieve a change in government policies. However, they could not voice their demands via major political channels as they have weak social networks within mainstream British society in general. The cultural capital embedded within the KT communities is weak, which prevents them from running effective campaigns on various issues. In other words, if we combine Putnam's (1993) and Bourdieu's (1986) terminologies, the lack of cultural capital with respect to the host country has resulted in a lack of bridging capital. Furthermore, because of the long working hours, KT business owners are not able to reserve time to deal with the problems that matter the most to them.

In terms of safety, the business owners experience constant insecurity at their business premises. The bonding capital within the KT communities is utilised for the provision of security networks in the neighbourhoods. Such an emergent product is due to the lack of security services provided by the governmental bodies. Thus, the strong ethnic ties for the protection of business premises and neighbourhoods are a consequence of the structural discrimination they experience in their daily lives.

With regard to skills and training, very few Turkish and Kurdish catering and retail business owners in Britain gained skills and training through formal education, either from formal academic training in hotel and catering management or in short term training courses in the food business. The majority of the interviewees gained work experience in co-ethnic businesses as workers. Gaining catering and retail business management skills by working in a family or co-ethnic business exemplifies the transfer of social capital into cultural capital. The social capital of would-be and existing

Turkish and Kurdish business owners was utilised to acquire cultural capital, i.e. skills and training. Skills for running a business, work experience, translation, and advice and accountancy services were all provided by social networks. It is the act of collective self-help of the KT communities that provided information and skills to the would-be and existing business owners.

With respect to workers, the findings of the study suggest that most of the businesses in catering and retail are headed by males. Most of the shop-owners in this study stated that they rely on the contribution of their family in the form of labour support for maintaining the businesses. Their support is crucial as they have limited financial resources or because of the difficulty of finding trustworthy employees. Labour support from the family may include immediate family members: siblings, aunts and uncles, nephews and grandparents. Family members and co-ethnics have to engage in self-exploitation in order to remain competitive. As children grow-up, the labour of wives and of teenage children becomes available. Furthermore, co-ethnics work for less than market wages as there are no other jobs available to them and they have to accept the wage that is offered by the shopkeeper. Self-exploitation within the family and exploitation within ethnic networks reduces labour costs, which enables them to survive against competition. Moreover, family and co-ethnic labour provides a particularly reliable workforce. Thus, family and co-ethnic labour embodies a form of social capital that could be converted into economic capital in Turkish and Kurdish businesses.

I propose a systematic new approach to understand and analyse the ethnic minority business start-ups and maintenance activities in the Kurdish and Turkish communities in North London. I reveal that the business set up and maintenance activities of these groups of participants can be analysed and explained by the theory of collective resource mobilisation. Charles Tilly's (1978) work, namely collective resource mobilisation, offers the framework for discussion by bridging agency and structural approaches in ethnic business ownership.

Tilly's (ibid) theory of collective resource mobilisation has three components. Each component of collective action is understood to be a set of processes. Each component can vary and the degree of mobilisation and collective action are dependent on the processes and interactions between the three components. The Turkish and Kurdish communities' capacity to act collectively is likely to work as follows: In this elementary model, shared interests promote networks, the intensity of networks facilitates increased mobilisation, and collective resource mobilisation is a function of all three components.

The term "interests" is an analytical tool to understand on ethnic minority businesses and it is used in this context for the first time with this study.

Swedberg (2003, p.4) states, the use of interests provides the opportunity "that one would otherwise fail to understand *the strength* (emphasis original) that underlies an action", i.e. what makes members of Turkish and Kurdish communities in London small business owners. In so doing, it enables the discussion on globalisation as a contributing factor to the path for ethnic minority self-employment to be incorporated.

Secondly, the use of *interest alignment* contributes to explaining the reasons for setting up small businesses in the catering and retail sectors as a collective action in the Turkish and Kurdish communities and why this collective action, to a large extent, was not undertaken by the Turkish Cypriot community. The change in the character of shared interests with in the Turkish Cypriot community explains the reason for the lack small business ownership in the Turkish Cypriot community. The new generation holds professionalised jobs and do not have an interest in small business ownership in retail and catering sectors.

Thirdly, the operationalisation of Tilly (1978)'s collective resource mobilisation enables us to understand various forms of collective action, such as the acquisition of capital, information and skills, maintaining businesses, especially protecting business premises, collective bargaining with companies providing electricity and gas, voicing demands to government bodies, the employment of assemblies for dispute resolution, and campaigning against the development of chain stores. In other words, the realisation of interests also brings the social structure into the analysis of ethnic minority businesses.

Furthermore, another contribution of the book is its opposition to primordialist conceptualisations of ethnic identity based on people sharing a common national background or migration experiences (e.g. Waldinger, 1990). Jewish practices for dispute resolution have been incorporated to the practices community organisations of Kurdish and Turkish people. The shared experiences in the occupational structure and shared interests within different national backgrounds whose migration experiences correspond to different time periods could result in new alliances, ethnic attachments - such as Türkiyeli - and identity constructions that facilitate the building of networks utilised for entrepreneurship.

In a similar vein, the use of interests enables us to understand how the salience of many cultural practices is open to erosion and re-enactment. Another major contribution of the study to the study of ethnic minority business literature is that, the cultural practices transposed to the host country are understood as instrumental in overcoming adverse circumstances. While being wage labourers in the textile industry contributed to the dissolution of *imece* in the work place, small business ownership have led to the re-emergence of this collective practice.

Another major contribution of this project is related to the second component of collective resource mobilisation, namely social networks and mobilisation. The inequality of class based resources, such as social, cultural and economic capital acquired by Turkish and Kurdish business owners, has led to different strategies for setting-up businesses. The inequality of class based resources acquired by individuals led different strategies to acquire the needed capital to set up and maintain businesses. In other words, the study illustrates the interplay between different types of capital.

Limitations and suggestions for future research

There are six suggestions for future research: Firstly, the research could be built on by conducting a similar study with the owners of the failing retail and catering businesses. Secondly, a longitudinal dimension to the study, which would include interviews with the same participants about their business success, would have been valuable. Thirdly, interviews with business owners in relatively small towns outside of London, where the size of the KT population is relatively large, would have been valuable in order to compare and contrast the setting–up and maintenance activities of business owners. Fourthly, the gender dimensions of the subject in the study could be further examined. The current study has revealed that, in the catering and retail sectors, women have a more invisible position as helpers mostly to their husbands. Fifthly, a comparison between KT minority groups and other minorities within the same sectors, that is the retail and catering industries in Britain could prove useful. Sixthly, a study focusing on the second generation KT community members could be undertaken to compare and contrast the differences and similarities to the first generation of the KT community members.

In this book, I propose that collective resource mobilisation as an appropriate theoretical tool for understanding the reasons for business formation and the ways in which Turkish and Kurdish communities have managed to set-up and maintain them.

References

Abadan-Unat, N. (1995). Turkish migration to Europe. In R. Cohen (Ed.), *The Cambridge Survey of World Migration* (pp. 279-84). Cambridge: Cambridge University Press.

Abercrombie, N & Warde, A. (Eds). (1994). *Contemporary British society*. Cambridge : Polity Press.

Aldrich, H. (1999). *Organizations evolving*. London: Sage.

Aldrich, H., Ward, R., & Waldinger, R. (1985). Minority business development in industrial society. *European Studies Newsletter* 14 (4), 4-8

Aldrich, H. & Waldinger, R. (1990). Ethnicity and entrepreneurship. *Annual Review of Sociology*, 16, 111-35.

Aldrich, H. & Zimmer, C. (1986). Entrepreneurship through social networks. In R. Smilor & D. Sexton (Eds.), *The Art of Science of Entrepreneurship* (pp. 3-23). New York: Ballinger.

Altinay, L. (2008). The relationship between an entrepreneur's culture and the entrepreneurial behaviour of the firm. *Journal of Small Business and Enterprise Development*, 15 (1), 111-129.

Altınay, L. & Altınay, E. (2006). Determinants of ethnic minority entrepreneurial growth in the catering sector. *The Service Industries Journal*, 26 (2), 203-221.

Altinay, L. & Altinay, E. (2008). Factors influencing business growth: The rise of Turkish entrepreneurship in the UK. *International Journal of Entrepreneurial Behaviour & Research* 14 (1), 24-46.

Andersen, E. G. (1990). *The three worlds of welfare capitalism*. London: Polity.

Andersen, E. G. (1999). *The social foundations of postindustrial economies*. Oxford University Press.

Anthias, F. & Cederberg, M. (2006). State of the art theoretical Perspectives and Debates in the UK, Integration of Female Immigrants in Labour Market and Society. Policy Assessment and Policy Recommendations, WP4. Retrieved from http://www .femipol.uni-frankfurt.de/docs/working_papers/state_of_the_ art/UK.pdf.

Anthias, F. & Cederberg, M. (2009). Using ethnic bonds in self-employment and the issue of social capital. *Journal of Ethnic and Migration Studies*, 35(6), 901–917.

Atay,T. (2006). *İngiltere'de Türkçe yaşamak: Türkler, Kürtler, Kıbrıslılar*. Ankara: Dipnot Yayınları.

Atay,T. (2010). Ethnicity within ethnicity' among the Turkish-Speaking immigrants in London. *Insight Turkey*, 12 (1), 39-44

Auster, E. & Aldrich H. (1984). Small business vulnerability, ethnic enclaves and ethnic enterprise. In R. Ward and R. Jenkins (Eds.) *Ethnic Communities in Business: Strategies for Economic Survival* (pp. 39-54). Cambridge: Cambridge University Press.

Balkan Chronicle. (2011 August, 11).Turkish shopkeepers protect streets from London rioters. *Balkan Chronicle*. Retrieved from http://www.balkanchronicle.com/index.php/world/world-news/europe/1310-turkish-shopkeepers-protect-streets-from-london-rioters

Basch, L. G., Glick Schiller, N. & Szanton Blanc, C. (1994). *Nations unbound: transnational projects, postcolonial predicaments, and deterritorialized nation-states*. Amsterdam: Gordon and Breach.

Basu, A. (1998). An exploration of entrepreneurial activity among Asian small businesses in Britain. *Small Business Economics*, 10, 313-326.

Basu, A. & Altinay, E. (2000). An exploratory study of Turkish Cypriot small businesses in London. Paper presented at the *Third International Congress on Cyprus Studies*, Gazimagusa, November 13-17.

Basu, A. & Altınay, E. (2001). Culture and entrepreneurship: A study of ethnic entrepreneurship in London. Discussion Papers in Economics and Management, Series A, 13 (2000 / 01), The University of Reading.

Economic Survival Strategies of Turkish Migrants in London

Basu, A. & Altinay, E. (2002). The interaction between culture and entrepreneurship in London's immigrant business. *International Small Business Journal*, 20 (4), 371-394.

Bates, T. (1989). The changing nature of minority business: a comparative analysis of Asian, non-minority, and black-owned businesses. *The Review of Black Political Economy*, 18, 25-42.

Bates, T. (1997). *Race, self-employment, and upward mobility. An illusive American Dream.* Washington: The Woodrow Wilson Center Press.

Bates, T. (1999). Existing self-employment: An analysis of Asian immigrant-owned small businesses. *Small Business Economics*, 13, 171-183.

Bayart, J. F., Ellis, S., and Hibou, B. (1999). *The criminalization of the state in Africa.* Oxford: James Currey.

Baycan- Levent, T., E. Masurel, P. Nijkamp. (2003). Diversity in entrepreneurship: ethnic and female roles in urban economic life. *International Journal of Social Economics*, 30 (11), 1131-1161.

Baycan-Levent, T., A. A., Gülümser, S., Kundak, P., Nijkamp, and M., Sahin. (2003). Diversity and ethnic entrepreneurship: Dialogue through exchanges in the economic arena. Sustainable Development in a Diverse World (SUS.DIV) Position paper of research task 4.4. Retrieved from http://www.susdiv.org/upload les/RT4_4_PP_Tuzin.pdf.

Baycan-Levent, T., Masurel, E., Nijkamp, P. (2006). Gender differences in ethnic entrepreneurship. *International Journal of Entrepreneurship and Innovation Management*, 6 (3), 173-190.

Bell, D. (1975). Ethnicity and social change. In N. Glazer & D. P. Moynihan (Eds.), *Ethnicity: Theory and practice* (pp. 169-70). Cambridge: Harvard University Press.

Benford, R. D., & Snow, D. A. (2000). Framing processes and social movements: An overview and assessment. *Annual Review of Sociology*, 26, 611-639

Berg, B. L. (2007). *Qualitative Research Methods for the Social Sciences.* Boston: Pearson International Edition.

Berk, F. (1972). *A Study of the Turkish Cypriot community in Haringey, with particular reference to its background, its structure and changes taking place within it*, MPhil thesis, York: Department of Social Policy, University of York.

Bhatti, F. M. (1981). *Turkish Cypriots in London.* Birmingham: Centre for the Study of Islam and Christian Relations.

Blanchflower, D. and Oswald, A. (1991). Self-Employment and Mrs. Thatcher's Enterprise Culture. *CEP* Working Paper, No. 30.

Boissevain, J., J. Blauschkee, H. Grotenberg, I. Joseph, I. Light, M. Sway, R. Waldinger and P. Werbner. (1990). Ethnic Entrepreneurs and Ethnic Strategies. In: R. Waldinger, et al. (Eds.), *Ethnic Entrepreneurs: Immigrant Business in Industrial Societies* (pp. 131-157). Newbury Park, California: Sage Publications Inc.

Bonacich, E. (1973). A theory of middleman minorities. *American Sociological Review*, 38, 583-594.

Bonacich, E. (1987). 'Making it' in America: A social evolution of the ethics of immigrant entrepreneurship. *Social Perspectives*, 30, 446-66

Bonacich, E., and Modell, J. (1980). *The economic basis of ethnic solidarity: Small business in the Japanese American community.* Berkeley: University of California Press.

Bourdieu, P. (1984). *Distinction: A social critique of the judgement of taste.* London: Routledge.

Bourdieu, Pierre (1986). The forms of capital. In, J. G. Richardson. (Ed.), *Handbook of Theory and Research for the Sociology of Education* (pp. 241-58). New York: Greenwood.

Bourdieu, P. (1987). What makes a social class? On the theoretical and practical existence of groups. *Berkeley Journal of Sociology*, 32, 1–17.

Bourdieu, P. & Wacquant, L. (1992). *An invitation to reflective sociology.* Cambridge: Polity Press.

Brah, A. & Phoenix, A. (2004). Ain't I a woman? Revisiting intersectionality. *Journal of International Women's Studies*, 5 (3), 75-86.

Brandstätter, H. (1997). Becoming an entrepreneur – a question of personality structure? *Journal of Economic Psychology*, 18, 157–177.

Burrows, R. (ed). (1991). *Deciphering the enterprise culture: Entrepreneurship, petty capitalism and the restructuring of Britain*. London: Routledge

Business Link. (2012). The no nonsense guide to government rules and regulations for setting-up your business. London: *Business Link for London*, 2012 edition. Retrieved from https://secure.investni.com/static/library/invest-ni/documents/no-nonsense-guide-to-government-regulations-for-setting-up-your-business.pdf

Cam, S. (2006). Ethnicisation of temporary jobs in Britain. Cardiff: Cardiff University, School of Social Sciences Working Paper Series 80

Canefe, N. (2002). Markers of Turkish Cypriot history in the diaspora. *Rethinking History*, 6 (1), 57-76.

Calhoun, C. (1997). *Nationalism*. Buckhingham: Open University Press

Campbell, P. (2013 June 14). Retail giants including Tesco, Sainsbury's and John Lewis criticised over their tax affairs by new campaign. *This is Money*. Retrieved from http://www.thisismoney.co.uk/money/news/article-2341910/Retail-giants-tax-affairs-criticised-new-campaign.html

Carling, J., Bivand E. M. & Ezzati, R. (2014). Beyond the insider-outsider divide in migration research. *Migration Studies, 2* (1), 36-54.

Cassarino, J-P.(1997). *The theories of ethnic entrepreneurship, and alternative arguments of social action and network analysis.* Florence: EUISPS Working Papers

Castells, M. (1989). *The informational city, information technology, economic restructuring, and the urban-regional process*. Oxford UK, Cambridge MA: Basil Blackwell

Castles, S., & Miller, M. J. (1993). *The age of migration: International population movements in the modern world*. New York: The Guilford Press.

Castles, S. & Kosack, G. (1972). The function of labour immigration in Western European capitalism. *New Left Review, 73*, 3-21.

Castles, S., Booth, H. & Wallace, T. (1984). *Here for good: Western Europe's New Ethnic Minorities*. London: Pluto Press.

Castles, S., Loughna, S. & Crawley, H. (2003). *States of conflict: Causes and patterns of forced migration to the EU and policy responses.* London: Institute of Public Policy Research.

Chai, S. (1996). A theory of ethnic group boundaries. *Nations and Nationalisms*, 2 (2),281-307

Chan, K. B., Ong, J. H. (1995). The Many Faces of Immigrant Entrepreneurship. In R. Cohen (Ed.), *The Cambridge Survey of World Migration* (pp. 523-531). Cambridge: Cambridge University Press.

Clark, K. & Drinkwater, S. (2000). Pushed out or pulled in? Ethnic minority self-employment in England and Wales. *Labour Economics*, 7, 603-628.

Cockburn, Cynthia. (1981). The material of male power. *Feminist Review, 9*, 41-58.

Collins, J. (2000). Ethnicity, gender and Australian entrepreneurs: Rethinking Marxist views on Small Business. *Journal of Social Change and Critical Inquiry*, 2, 137-49

Collins, J. (2003). *Ethnic entrepreneurship in Australia.* Willy Brandt Series of Working Papers in International Migration and Ethnic Relations 1/02

Collins, J., K. Gibson, C. Alcorso, D. Tait, & S. Castles. (1995). *A shop full of dreams: Ethnic small business in Australia.* Sydney and London: Pluto Press.

Cornell, S., and Hartmann, D. (2007). *Ethnicity and race: Making identities in a changing world.* Thousand Oaks, CA: Pine Forge Press.

Coştu, Y., Turan, S. (2009). İngiltere'deki Türk camileri ve entegrasyon sürecine sosyo-kültürel katkıları. *Dinbilimleri Akademik Araştırma Dergisi*, 4, 35-52. Retrieved from http://dergipark.ulakbim.gov.tr/daad/article/viewFile/5000077093/5000071131

Crotty, M. (2005). *The foundations of social research: Meaning and perspective in the research process.* London: Sage Publications.

Curran, J., Blackburn, R. A. & Woods, A. (1991). Profiles of the small enterprise in the service sector. Kingston upon Thames, ESRC Centre for Research on Small Service Sector Enterprises, Kingston University.

Daily Mail. (2011 August 9). We don't do water cannon, we rely on consent: May rules out tough action as vigilantes are forced to defend. *Daily Mail.* Retrieved from http://www.dailymail.co.uk/news/article-2023932/London-riots-2011-Theresa-May-rules-tough-action-vigilantes-defend-shops.html

Dawson C, Henley A, Latreille P. (2009). Why do individuals choose self-employment? *IZA Discussion Paper*, 3974, 1-39

Day-Mer. *General Advice Services.* Retreived from http://www.daymer.org/content/general-advice-services.

D'Angelo, A., Galip, O., Kaye, N., and Lorinc, M. (2013). *Welfare needs of Turkish and Kurdish communities in London.* A Community based research project, SPRC Middlesex University and Day-Mer. (London). Retrieved from http://sprc.info/wp-content/uploads/2012/07/Welfare-Needs-of-Turkish-and- Kurdish-Communities-in-London-A-community-Based-Research-project.- Preliminary-report.pdf

DCLG (Department for Communities and Local Government). (2009). *The Turkish and Turkish Cypriot Muslim community in England, understanding muslim ethnic communities.* London: Change Institute, Department for Communities and Local Government. Retrieved from http://webarchive.nationalarchives.gov.uk/20120919132719/www.communities.gov.uk/doc uments/communities/pdf/1203710.pdf

Dedeoglu, S. (2014). *Migrants, work and social integration: Women's labour in the Turkish ethnic economy.* London: Palgrave Macmillan.

Dhaliwal, S. & Kangis, P. (2006). Asians in the UK: genders, generations, and enterprise. *Equal Opportunities International, 25*(2), 92-108.

Dicken, P. (2010). *Global Shift: Mapping the Changing Contours of the World Economy.* London: Sage Publications Ltd.

Drori, I. & Lerner, M. (2002). The Dynamics of Limited Breaking out: The case of the Arab Manufacturing Businesses in Israel. *Entrepreneurship and Regional Development*, 14, 135-154.

Drori, I., Honig, B. & Ginsberg, A. (2008). *Toward a practical theory of transnational entrepreneurship: understanding the habitus of cross-cultural affiliation.* Paper presented at the annual meeting of the SASE Annual Conference, Temple University, Philadelphia, PA, USA.

Duffield, M. (2005). *Human security: linking development and security in an age of terror.* Paper was presented at 11th European Association of Development Research and Training Institutes (EADI) conference, "Insecurity and Development"

Dulce, M.S., Mackoy, R., Curci, R. (2009). Socio-economic ethnic entrepreneurship development theories: An analysis of Hispanic business enterproses in central Indiana. *Journal of the Indiana Academy of the Social Sciences*, 13, 97-111

Düvell, F. (2010). Turkish migration to the UK. Retrieved from http://www.compas. ox.ac.uk/fileadmin/files/Publications/Reports/6_Turks_UK.pdf

Eller, J., and Coughlan, R. (1996). The poverty of primordialism. In J. Hutchinson & A.D. Smith (Eds.), *Ethnicity* (pp.45-51). Oxford: Oxford University Press.

Engelen, E. (2001). Breaking-in and breaking-out: A Weberian approach to entrepreneurial opportunities. *Journal of Ethnic and Migration Studies*, 27 (2), 203-223.

Enneli, P., Modood, T. & Bradley, H. (2005). *Young Turks and Kurds: A set of 'invisible' disadvantaged groups.* York: Joseph Roundtree Foundation.

Erdemir, A & Vasta, E. (2007). *Differentiating irregularity and solidarity: Turkish Immigrants at Work in London.* COMPAS Working Paper Series, WS-07-42. Retrieved from https://www.compas.ox.ac.uk/media/WP-2007-042-Erdemir-Vasta_Work_London_Turkish.pdf

Erginkaya, C.K. (2012). *Housing cooperatives as a tool of urban development in Adana.*A MA thesis. Middle East Technical University: Ankara

Erel, U. (2010). Migrating cultural capital: Bourdieu. *Sociology,* 44 (4), 642-660.

Evans, S. (1980). *Personal politics: The roots of women's liberation in the civil rights movement and the New Left.* New York: Vintage Books.

Fainstein S, Gordon I & Harloe M. (1992). *Divided cities: New York and London in the contemporary world.* Oxford: Blackwell.

Fielding, A. (1993). Mass migration and economic re-structuring. In R. King (Ed.), *Mass migration in Europe* (pp. 5-18). London: Belhaven Press.

Fine, B. (2004). Globalisation or panglossianisation?: A critical response to Keith Griffin. *Development and Change,* 35 (3), 583-589.

Food Standards Agency. (2013). Starting up: your first steps to run a catering business, London: Business Link. Retrieved from https://www.food.gov.uk/sites/default/files/multimedia/pdfs/publication/starting-up-booklet.pdf

Gabriel, Y. (1988). *Working lives in catering.* London: Routledge and Kegan Paul.

Giddens A. (1990). *The consequences of modernity.* Cambridge: Polity Press,

Giddens A. (2002). *Runaway world. How globalization is reshaping our lives.* London: Profile Books:

Gitmez, A.S. (1979). *Dışgöç Öyküsü.* Ankara: Maya Matbaacılık ve Yayıncılık.

GLA. (2009) *Turkish, Kurdish and Turkish Cypriot communities in London.* GLA Publications.

Goffee, R. & Scase, R. (1995). *Corporate realities: The dynamics of large and small organisations.* London: Routledge.

Goffman, E. (1974). *Frame analysis: An essay on the organization of experience.* Cambridge, Mass: Harvard University Press.

Gold, S.J. (2010). *The store in the hood: A century of ethnic business and conflict.* Lanham, MD: Rowman & Littlefield Publishers.

Granovetter, Mark. (1985). Economic action and social structure: The problem of embeddedness. *American Journal of Sociology,* 91, 481-510.

Griffiths, D. (2000). Fragmentation and consolidation: The contrasting cases of Somali and Kurdish refugees in London. *Journal of Refugee Studies,* 13(3),281-302.

Haberfellner, R. (2003). The case of Austria: Immigrant self-employment in a highly regulated economy. In R. Kloosterman & J. Rath (Eds.), *Immigrant Entrepreneurs.Venturing Abroad in the Age of Globalization* (pp. 213-232). Oxford/New York: Berg/University of New York Press.

Halcomb, E. J., & Davidson, P. M. (2006). Is verbatim transcription of interview data always necessary? *Applied Nursing Research,* 19, 38–42.

Hall, S. (2000). Conclusion: the Multi-cultural question. In B. Hesse (Ed.), *Un/Settled Multiculturalisms: Diasporas, Entanglements, 'Transruptions'* (pp.209-241). London: Zed Books

Harvey, D. (1989). *The condition of postmodernity.* Oxford: Blackwell.

Harvey, D. (2007). Neoliberalism as a creative destruction. *The Annals of the American Academy of Political and Social Science,* 610, 22–44.

Hartmann, Heidi L. (1976). Capitalism, patriarchy, and job segregation by Sex. *Signs,* 1,137-169.

Held, D., A. McGrew, D. Goldblatt, & J. Perraton. (1999). *Global Transformations: Politics, Economics and Culture.* Polity and Stanford University Press.

Held, D. & A. McGrew (2003). The great globalization debate: An introduction. In David Held and A. McGrew (Eds.), *The Global Transformations Reader an Introduction to the Globalization Debate* (pp. 1-50). Cambridge: Polity.

Henry, L. (2004). Citizenship, morality and participatory development: The case of Sebat Bet Gurage. In Mohan, G. and Hickey, S. (Eds), *Participation from tyranny to transformation* (pp. 140-156). London: Zed.

Hofstede, G. (1991). *Cultures and organizations: Software of the mind.* London: McGraw-Hill.

Holgate, J., Keles, J., Pollert, A., Kumarappen, L. (2012). Workplace problems among Kurdish workers in London: Experiences of an 'invisible' community and the role of community organisations as support networks. *Journal of Ethnic and Migration Studies,* 38(4), 595-612.

Home Office. (1997). *Asylum statistics.* Home Office Statistical Bulletin, Government statistical office

House of Commons: Select committee on small and medium sized enterprises (2013). *Roads to Success: SME Exports Report.* HL 131, 2012-2013. London: HMSO.

Hutchinson, J., & Smith, A.D. (1996). Introduction. In J. Hutchinson & A. Smith (eds.). *Ethnicity* (pp.3-16). Oxford: Oxford University Press.

ILO. (1974). Some growing employment problems in Europe. *Second European Regional Conference.* Geneva

İnal, G. (2007). Why do minorities launch businesses in Britain? *International Journal of Business and Globalisation,* 1(1), 51-59.

İnal, G. (2007b). *A comparative study of the reasons for and means of setting-up a small business: the case of Turkish Cypriot restaurateurs and lawyers in North Cyprus and Britain.* Ph.D. diss.,Queen Mary, University of London.

Inal, G. & Özkan, M. (2009). A Comparative Study on Career Choice Influences of Turkish Cypriot restauranteurs in North Cyprus and the UK. In Özbilgin, Mustafa F & Malach-Pines, Ayala (eds.). *Career Choice In Management And Entrepreneurship.* Cheltenham, Edward Elgar.

Inal, G & Karatas-Ozkan, M. (2011). Multi-layered analysis of Turkish Cypriot female solicitors' career trajectory in North London, *Equality, Diversity and Inclusion: An International Journal,* 30(6), 510 – 523.

Inal, G., & Yasin, N. (2010). Minority in a minority: A case study of a female Turkish Cypriot entrepreneur in Britain. *Kadin/Woman 2000,* 11(2), 1-40.

International Labour Organisation. (1974). *Record of the Second European European Regional Conference.* Geneva: International Labour Organisation.

Jenkins, J.Craig. (2008). Resource mobilization theory and the study of social movements. In V, Ruggiero, and N. Montagna (eds), *Social Movements: A Reader* (pp.118-127). London and New York: Routledge.

Johannisson, B. (1988). Business formation: A network approach. *Scandinavian Journal of Management,* 4(3-4), 83-99.

Jordan, B. (2002). 'Polish migrant workers in London: Mobility, labour markets and the prospects for democratic development'. Paper presented at the *'Beyond transition: Development Perspectives and Dilemmas' Conference,* Warsaw, 12–13 April 2002.

Jordan, B, & Duvell, F. (2003). *Migration: The boundaries of equality and justice.* Cambridge: Polity.

Karan, O. (2015). Collective resource mobilisation for economic survival within the Turkish speaking communities in London. *PhD Dissertation.* London Metropolitan University.

Karaoğlan, D., & Ökten, C. (2012). Labor force participation of married women in Turkey: Is there an added or a discouraged worker effect?. *IZA Discussion Paper* No. 6616.

Kim, Y-H., & Short, J.R. (2008). *Cities and economics.* New York, NY: Routledge.

King, A.D. (1990). *Global cities: post-imperialism and the internationalization of London.* *London:* Routledge.

King, R. & Bridal, J. (1982). The changing distribution of Cypriots in London. *Etudes Migrants,* 19(65), 93-121.

King, R., Thomson, M., Mai, N. & Keles Y. (2008). 'Turks' *in London: Shades of invisibility and the shifting relevance of policy in the migration process*. Sussex: University of Sussex. Working Paper No. 51.

Kloosterman, R. (2000). Immigrant entrepreneurship and the institutional context: A theoretical exploration. In Rath, J. (Ed.), *Immigrant Businesses: The Economic, Political and Social Environment* (pp. 90-106). London: Macmillan.

Kloosterman, R.C. & Rath, J. (2001). Immigrant entrepreneurs in advanced economies: Mixed embeddedness further explored. *Special Issue on Immigrant Entrepreneurship, Journal of Ethnic and Migration Studie*s, 27(2), 189-202.

Kloosterman, R.C. & Rath, J. (2003). *Immigrant entrepreneurs: Venturing abroad in the age of globalization.* Oxford/New York: Berg,

Kloosterman, R.C., Van der Leun, J.P., & Rath, J. (1999). Mixed embeddedness, migrant entrepreneurship and informal economic activities. *International Journal of Urban and Regional Research*, 23(2,) 253-267.

Knight, F. H. (1921). *Risk, Uncertainty and Profit*. New York: Houghton Mifflin

Kofman,E., Lukes,S., D'Angelo, A., & Montagna, N. (2009). *The equality implications of being a migrant in Britain.* Equality and Human Rights Commission, London. Research Report 19.

Kossoudji, S. A. & Ranney, S. I. (1984). The Labor Market Experience of Female Migrants: The Case of Temporary Mexican Migration to the United States. *International Migration Review,* 18, 1120-1143.

Küçükcan, T. (1999). *Politics of ethnicity, identity and religion: Turkish Muslims in Britain.* Ashgate Publishing Ltd.

Kuratko, D. F. & Hodgetts, R. M. (2001). *Entrepreneurship: A contemporary approach.* New York: Harcourt College Publishers.

Kyriakides, C. & Virdee, S. (2003). Migrant Labour, Racism and the British National Health Service. *Ethnicity & Health*, 8(4), 283–305.

Laçiner, S. (2000). *Açık kapı politikası'ndan yabancı düşmanlığı'na: İngiltere'de ırkçılık, dış göç ve ırk ilişkileri.* Ankara: ASAM Yayınları.

Ladbury, S. (1979). *Turkish Cypriots in London: Economy, Society, Culture and Change*, PhD thesis. London: University of London.

Ladbury, S. (1984). Choice, chance or no alternative? Turkish Cypriots in London. In Ward, R. and Jenkins, R. (Eds.) *Ethnic Communities in Business: Strategies for Economic Survival* (pp. 105-263). Cambridge: Cambridge University Press.

Landolt, P. (2001). Salvadoran economic transnationalism: Embedded strategies for household maintenance, Immigrant Incorporation and Entrepreneurial Expansion. *Special Issue on New Research and Theory on Immigrant Transnationalism*, 1(3), 217-242.

Larsen, L., Harlan, S.L., Bolin, B., Hackett, E.J., Hope, D., Kirby, A., Nelson, A., Rex,T.R., & Wolf, S. (2004). Bonding and bridging: Understanding the relationship between social capital and civic action. *Journal of Planning Education and Research,* 24, 64-77.

Larson, A. (1991). Partner networks: Leveraging external ties to improve entrepreneurial performance. *Journal of Business Venturing*, 6, 173-188.

Lassalle, P. (2008). *Ethnic minority entrepreneurs: communities, social capital, actors strategies.* Retrieved from www.uws.ac.uk/workarea/downloadasset.aspx?id=2147488702

Leonard, M. (2004). Bonding and Bridging Social Capital: Reflections from Belfast. *Sociology*, 38 (5), 927-945.

Light, I. (1972). *Ethnic enterprise in America: Business and welfare among Chinese, Japanese, and Blacks.* Berkeley, Los Angeles, and London: University of California Press

Light, Ivan. (2004). Immigration and ethnic economies in giant cities. *International Social Science Journal,* 56(181), 385-398.

Light, I. & Bonacich, E. (1988). *Immigrant entrepreneurs: Koreans in Los Angeles.* Los Angeles: University of California Press.

Economic Survival Strategies of Turkish Migrants in London

Light, I. & Gold, S. J. (2000). *Ethnic economies*. San Diego: Academic Press.

Light, I., & Rosenstein, C. (1995) *Race, ethnicity and entrepreneurship in urban America*. New York, NY: Aldine de Gruyter.

London Medya. (2003). *London Medya Business Guide 2003*. London.

Luxemburg, R. (2003) *The accumulation of capital*. London: Routledge and Kegan Paul Ltd.

Mars, G., & Ward, R.(1984). Ethnic business development in Britain: opportunities and Resources. In R. Ward & R. Jenkins (Eds.), *Ethnic Communities in Business: Strategies for Economic Survival* (pp.1-20). Cambridge: Cambridge University Press.

Marx, K. (1852). *The eighteenth brumaire of Louis Bonaparte*. Retrieved from: https://www.marxists.org/archive/marx/works/1852/18th-brumaire/ch01.htm.

Marx, K., & Engels, F. (2004). *Manifesto of the Communist Party*. Moscow: Progress Publishers.

Massey, D. (2007). *World city*. Bristol: Polity Press.

Massey, D. S. & España, F. G. (1987). The social process of international migration. *Science*, 237, 733-738.

Masurel, E., Nijkamp, P., Taştan, M. and Vindigni, G. (2003). Motivations and performance conditions for ethnic entrepreneurship. *Growth and Change*, 33(2), 238-260.

McAdam, D. (1982). *Political process and the development of Black insurgency, 1930-1970*. Chicago: University of Chicago Press.

McAdam, A., McCarthy, J.D., Zald, M.N. (2008). Comparative perspectives on social movements. In V, Ruggiero, and N. Montagna (Eds.), *Social Movements: A Reader* (pp.279-288). London and New York: Routledge.

McAdam, Doug, John D. McCarthy, and Mayer N. Zald. (1996). Introduction: Opportunities, mobilizing structures, and framing processes - Toward a synthetic, comparative perspective on social movements. In *Comparative Perspectives on Social Movements: Political Opportunities, Mobilizing Structures, and Cultural Framings* (pp.1-20). Cambridge: Cambridge University Press.

McDougall, P., Shane, S. & Oviatt, B. (1994). Explaining the formation of international new ventures: The limits of theories from international business Research. *Journal of Business Venturing*, 9(6), 469-487.

McEvoy, D., & Hafeez, K. (2009). Ethnic enclaves or middleman minority?: Regional patterns of ethnic minority entrepreneurship in Britain. *International Journal of Business and Globalisation*, 3(1), 94 -110.

Meagher, K. (2005). Social capital or analytical liability?: Social networks and African informal economies. *Global networks*, 5 (3), 217-238.

Mehmet Ali, A. (1991). The Turkish speech community. In S. Alladina & V. Edwards (Eds.), *Multilingualism in the British Isles Vol 1* (pp.202-213). London: Longman.

Mehmet Ali, A. (2001). *Turkish speaking communities and education: No delight*, London: Fatal Publications.

Metcalf, H., Modood, T. and Virdee, S. (1996). *Asian self-employment: The interaction of culture and economics in England*. London: Policy Studies Institute.

Min, P.G. (1996). *Caught in the Middle: Korean Communities in New York and Los Angeles*. Berkeley: University of California Press.

Min, P.G. (2008). *Ethnic Solidarity for Economic Survival: Korean Greengrocers in New York City*. New York: Russell Sage Foundation.

Moch, Leslie Page. (1992). *Moving Europeans: Migration in Western Europe since 1650*. Bloomington: Indiana University Press.

MR Zine. (2011 August 14). Turkish and Kurdish labourers and traders must refuse to Be pitted against the Black people. *MR Zine*. Retrieved from http://mrzine.monthlyreview.org/2011/uk140811.html

NEF (New Economics Foundation). (2005). *Clone town Britain: The loss of local identity on the nation's high streets*. London: NEF.

Nikander, P. (2008). Working with transcripts and translated data. *Qualitative Research in Psychology*, 5 (3), 225-231.

Oakley, R. (1970). The Cypriots in Britain. *Race Today*, 2, 99-102.

Oakley, R. (1979). Family, kinship and patronage: The Cypriot migration to Britain. In V. S. Khan (Ed.), *Studies in Ethnicity: Minority Families in Britain, Support and Stress* (pp.13-34). London: Macmillan Press.

Oakley, A. (1981). Interviewing women: a contradiction in terms. In H. Roberts (Ed.), *Doing feminist research* (pp.30-62). London: Routledge & Kegan Paul.

OECD. (2010). *Open for Business: Migrant Entrepreneurship in OECD countries*. Paris: OECD Publishing.

Özaktanlar U. (2003). *Researching Turkish Businesses in London: International Institute for Culture, Tourism and Development*. London Metropolitan University. Retrieved from www.londonmet.ac.uk/iictd.

Pang, C.L. & Rath, J. (2006). *The Force of Regulation in the Land of the Free. The Persistence of Chinatown, Washington D.C. as a Symbolic Ethnic Enclave*. In M. Lounsbury & M. Ruef (Eds.).Volume of RSO (Research in the Sociology of Organizations). Greenwich, CT: JAI Press.

Panitch, L., & Gindin, S. (2005). Superintending Global Capital. *New Left Review*, 35, 101-123

Pécoud, A. (2002a). "Weltoffenheit schafft Jobs": Turkish Entrepreneurship and Multiculturalism in Berlin. *International Journal of Urban and Regional Research*, 26 (3), 494-507.

Pécoud, A. (2002b). Cosmopolitanism and Business among German-Turks in Berlin. *Journal of the Society for the Anthropology of Europe*, 2 (3), 2–12.

Pécoud, A. (2004). Do immigrants have a business culture? The Political Epistemology of fieldwork in Berlin's Turkish economy. *Journal of the Society for the Anthropology of Europe*, 4 (2), 19-25.

Petras, E.M. (1981). The global labour market in the modern world-economy. In M.M. Kritz, C.B.Keely, and S.M. Tomasi (Eds.), *Global trends in migration: theory and research on inter-national population movements* (pp. 44–63). Staten Island, NY: Center for Migration Studies.

Petras, J. (2006). *Following the Profits and Escaping the Debts: International Immigration and Imperial-Centered Accumulation*. Dissident Voice (Aug. 8, 2006) Retrieved from http://www.dissidentvoice.org/Aug06/Petras08.htm

Phizacklea, A. (1988). Entrepreneurship, Ethnicity and Gender. In S. Westwood & P. Bhachu (Eds.), *Enterprising Women* (pp.20-33). London and New York: Routledge.

Piore, M. (1979). *Birds of Passage: Migrant Labor and Industrial Societies*. New York: Cambridge University Press.

Portes, A. (1995). Economic Sociology and the Sociology of immigration: A Conceptual Overview. In A. Portes (Ed.), *The Economic Sociology of Immigration* (pp.1-41). New York: Russell Sage Foundation.

Portes, A. (1998). Social capital: Its origins and applications in modern sociology. *Annual Review of Sociology*, 24 (1), 1-24.

Portes, A. (2001). Introduction: The Debates and Significance of Immigrant Transnationalism. *In Global Networks*, 1 (3), 181-194.

Portes, A. & Manning, R.D. (1986). The immigrant enclave: Theory and empirical examples. In S. Olzak and J. Nagel (Eds.), *Competitive Ethnic Relations* (pp.47–68). New York: Academic Press.

Portes, A. & Bach, R. L. (1985*). Latin Journey: Cuban and Mexican Immigrants in the United States*. Berkeley: University of California Press.

Portes, A., Guarnizo, L.E & Haller, W. (2002). Transnational Entrepreneurs: An Alternative form of Immigrant Economic Adaptation. *American Sociological Review*, 67, 278-298.

Portes, A. & Sensenbrenner, J. (1993). Embeddedness and Immigration: Notes on the social determinants of economic action. *American Journal of Sociology*, 98, 1320 – 1350.

Potts, R., Simms, A., & Kjell, P. (2005). Clone town Britain: The survey results on the bland state of the nation. *New Economic Foundation.*

Putnam, R. (1993). The prosperous community: social capital and public life, *American Prospect*, 13, 35 – 42.

Putnam, R. (2000). *Bowling alone: The collapse and revival of American Community.* New York: Simon & Schuster.

Putnam, R. (2007). E Pluribus Unum: Civic engagement in a diverse and changing society. *Scandinavian Political Studies*, 30 (2), 134-167.

Raghuram, P., Henry, L. & Bornat, J. (2010). Difference and Distinction? : Non-migrant and Migrant Networks. *Sociology,* 44 (4), 623-641.

Rainnie, A. (1991). Small firms: Between the Enterprise Culture and "New Times". In R. Burrows (Ed.), *Deciphering the enterprise culture. Entrepreneurship, Petty Capitalism and the Restructuring of Britain* (pp.176-199). London: Routledge.

Ram, M. (1992). Coping with Racism: Asian Employers in the Inner-City. *Work, Employment and Society*, 6 (4), 601-618.

Ram, M. & Jones, T. (2008). Ethnic Minority Business: Review of Research and Policy. In O. C. Reis & J. Rath (Eds.), Migrações Journal - Special Issue on Immigrant Entrepreneurship (pp. 61-71*).* October 2008, n. 3, Lisbon: ACIDI.

Rath, J. (1998). The informal economy as bastard sphere of social integration. In E. Eichenhofer & P. Marschalck (Eds.), *Migration und Illegalität* (pp. 117–136). Osnabrück: Rasch Verlag,

Rath, J. (2000). Immigrant Businesses and their Economic, Politico-Institutional and Social Environment. In Rath, J. (ed.), *Immigrant Business: The Economic, Political and Social Environment* (pp.1-19). Basingstoke, Macmillan.

Rath, J. (Ed.) (2002). *Unraveling the Rag Trade: Immigrant Entrepreneurship in Seven World Cities.*Berg Publishers, Oxford.

Rath, J. (2000b). A Game of Ethnic Musical Chairs? Immigrant Businesses and the Formation and Succession of Niches in the Amsterdam Economy. In S. Body Gendrot & M. Martiniello (Eds.). *Minorities in European Cities.The Dynamics of Social Integration and Social Exclusion at the Neighbourhood Level* (pp. 26-43). Macmillan Press, Houndmills, Basingstoke, Hampshire.

Rath, J. (2006). Entrepreneurship among Migrants and Returnees: creating New Opportunities. Available at: http://www.un.org/esa/population/migration/turin/Symposium_Turin_files/P05_Rath.pdf. (Date of access: 08/05/2011).

Rath, J. (2007). The Transformation of Ethnic Neighborhoods into Places of Leisure and Consumption. *IMES Working Paper 144,* 1-19.

Rath, J. & Kloosterman, R. (2002). Working on the fringes: immigrant businesses, economic integration and informal practices. Retrieved from: http://users.fmg.uva.nl/jrath/downloads/@rath%20NUTEK.pdf.

Refugee council. (1996). *Asylum statistics 1986-1996.* London: Refugee Council

Robins, K. & Aksoy, A. (2001). From spaces of identity to mental spaces: lessons from Turkish-Cypriot cultural experience in Britain. *Journal of Ethnic and Migration Studies*, 27(4), 685-711.

Rosenberg, J. (2000). Globalization Theory: A Post Mortem. *International Politics*, 42, 2-74.

Ryan, L., Sales, R., Tilki, M., & Siara, B. (2008). Social networks, social support and social capital: The experiences of recent polish migrants in London. *Sociology,* 42 (4), 672–90.

Sanders, J. M. and Nee, V. (1996). Immigrant self-employment: The family as social capital and value of human capital. *American Sociological Review*, 61(2), 231-249.

Sassen, S. (1988). *The mobility of labor and capital: A Study in International Investment and Labor Flow*. Cambridge: Cambridge University Press.

Sassen, S. (2013). *Global cities: London, New York, Tokyo*. Princeton: Princeton University.

Scarman, Lord J. (1981). *The Brixton Disorders*, 10–12th April. London: HMSO.

Scase, T. (2000). The enterprise culture: The socio-economic context of small firms. In Carter et al. *Enterprise and Small Business*. London. Prentice Hall, pp 32-47.

Scase, R. & Goffee, R. (1989). *The real world of the small business owner*. London and New York: Routledge.

Scholte, J. A. (2000). *Globalization: A critical introduction*. New York: St. Martin's Press.

Shane, S.A. & Venkataraman, S. (2000). The promise of entrepreneurship as a field of research. *Academy of Management Review*, 25, 217-226.

Silverman, D. (2005). *Doing qualitative research*. London: Sage Publications.

Simmel, G. (1971). *On Individuality and Other Social Forms*. London: The University of Chicago Press.

Simon, G. (1993). Immigrant entrepreneurs in France. In I. Light and P. Bhachu, *Immigration and Entrepreneurship: Culture, Capital, and Ethnic Networks* (pp.124-139). New Brunswick: Transaction Publishers.

Sirkeci, I. (2016). Transnational Doner kebab taking over the UK. *Transnational Marketing Journal*, 4(2). Retrieved from http://tplondon.com/journal/index.php/tmj/ article/ viewFile/762/550

Sirkeci, I., Bilecen, T., Coştu, Y., Dedeoğlu, S., Kesici, M.R., Şeker, B.D., Tilbe, F., Unutulmaz, K.O. (2016). *Little Turkey in Great Britain*. London: Transnational Press London.

Sirkeci, I., & Esipova, N. (2013). Turkish migration in Europe and desire to migrate to and from Turkey. *Border Crossing*, 3(1), 1-13. Retrieved from http://tplondon.com/journal/index. php/bc/article/view/89

Siu, P.C.P. (1952). The Sojourner. *American Journal of Sociology*, 58, 1, 34-44.

Snape, D. & Spencer, L. (2003). The foundations of qualitative research. In J. Ritchie & J. Lewis (Eds.), *Qualitative Research Practice* (pp.1-23). London: Sage Publications.

Snow, D. A. (2008). Frame Alignment Processes, Micromobilization, and Movement Participation. In Ruggiero, V., and Montagna, N (eds). Social Movements: A Reader. Routledge: New York.

Snow, D. A., E. B. R, Worden, S. K., & Bendord, R. D. (1986). Frame alignment processes, micromobilization and movement participation. *American Sociological Review*, 51, 464-81.

Sonmez, Y., & McDonald, S. (2008). *Turkish labour migration: Turkey-Germany migration corridor*. Paper prepared for *the* 11th Global Economic Analysis Conference, "Future of Global Economy", Marina Congress Centre, Helsinki, Finland.

Sowell, T. (1995). *Race and culture: A world view*. New York: Basic Books.

Srinivasan, S. (1995). *The south asian petite bourgeoisie in Britain*. Aldershot: Avebury.

Standing, G. (1999). *Global labour flexibility: Seeking distributive justice*. London and New York: Macmillan.

Stirling, P. (1994). *Turkish Village*. London: Weidenfeld and Nicolson.

Stokes, D. R. (2002). *Small Business Management*. London: Continuum.

Storey, D., Watson, R. & Wynarczyk, P. (1989). *Fast growth small businesses: Case studies of 40 small firms in North East England*. Department of Employment Research Paper, No. 67.

Strüder, I. (2001). *Migrant self-employment in a European global city – the importance of gendered power relations and performances of belonging for Turkish women in London*. Research Paper 74, London: Department of Geography, London School of Economics and Political Science.

Strüder, I. (2003). *Do concepts of ethnic economies explain existing minority enterprises? The Turkish speaking economies in London*. Research papers in Environmental and Spatial Analysis Series, 88, 1-34.

Swedberg, R. (2003). *Principles of Economic Sociology*. New Jersey: Princeton University Press.

Swartz, D. (1997). *Culture and power: The sociology of Pierre Bourdieu.* Chicago: University of Chicago Press.

Tasiran, C.A. (2013). *Turkish speaking population in the UK.* An Unpublished Study Based on Annual Population Survey.

Tasiran, H. (2008). *Emigration, Work and Identity: Emigrant women from Turkey at work in Gothemburg and London.* Incomplete PhD Thesis. Cardiff University: UK.

Tatli, A., Vassilopoulou, J., Ozbilgin, M.F. (2014). A Bourdieuan Relational Perspective for Entrepreneurship Research. *Journal of Small Business Management,* 52(4), 54-69

Terjesen, S. & Elam, A. (2009). Transnational entrepreneurs' Venture Internationalisation Strategies: A Practice Theory Approach. *Entrepreneurship: Theory and Practice,* 33 (6), 1093-1120.

Terzano, K.R. (2010). Demographic change and neighbourhood satisfaction: The case of little italy, Cleveland. *Policy & The Environment,* 41, 45-50.

Tescopoly. *Campaign tolls.* Retrieved from http://www.tescopoly.org/faq

Tescopoly. *Food poverty.* Retrieved from http://www.tescopoly.org/food-poverty

The Competition Commission. (2008). *The supply of groceries in the UK market investigation.* Retrieved from http://www.waronwant.org/attachments/The%20 Competition%20Commission%20Final%20Report.pdf

Thomson, M. (2006). *Immigration to the UK: The case of Turks,* University of Sussex, Sussex Centre for Migration Research: Report prepared for the Research Project, MIGSYS.

Tilly, C. (1973). *Do communities act?* Michagan: University of Michagan. Retrieved from http://faculty.ycp.edu/~sjacob/SOC340/Supplemental%20Readings/Do %20Communities%20Act%20Tilly.pdf

Tilly, C. (1977). *From mobilization to revolution.* Michigan: University of Michigan.

Tilly, C. (1978). Studying social movements/Studying collective Action. *International Symposium on the Organizing of Women.* Stockholm.7-8 February.

Trupp, A. (2015). Agency, social capital, and mied embeddedness among akha ethnic minority street vendors in Thailand's tourist areas. *Sojourn: Journal of Social Issues in Southeast Asia,* 30 (3), 780-818

Turkish Catering News. (2002). *İngiltere'de Kebab Ticareti.*

Turner, R. (1995). *The british economy in transition: From the old to the new?* London: Routledge.

Ülker, B. (2004). *Entreprenerial Practices of Turkish Immigrants in Berlin.* Unpublished MA Thesis. METU: Turkey.

Vasta, E. (2004). *Informal employment and immigrant networks: a review paper.* Centre on Migration, Policy and Society Working Paper No. 2, University of Oxford.

Vermeersch, P. (2011). Theories of ethnic mobilization: Overview and recent trends. In G. Brown & A Langer (Eds.). *The Elgar Companion to Civil War and Fragile States* (pp. 223-239). Cheltenham: Edgar Elgar Publishing.

Vertovec, S. (2006).The emergence of super-diversity in Britain. In Research on immigration and integration in the metropolis, Vol. No. 06-14: Working Paper Series: Vancouver Centre of Excellence.

Volary, T. (2007). Ethnic entrepreneurship: a theoretical framework. In L.-P. Dana. (Ed.), *Handbook of Research on Ethnic Entrepreneurship: A Co-Evolutionary View on Resource Management* (pp. 30-41). Northampton, MA: Edward Elgar Publishing,

Wahlbeck, O. (1998). Community work and exile politics: Kurdish refugee associations in London. *Journal of Refugee Studies,* 11(3), 215-230

Wahlbeck, O. (2007). Work in the kebab economy: A study of the ethnic economy of Turkish immigrants in Finland. *Ethnicities,* 7, 543-563.

Waldinger, R. (1983). *Ethnic Enterprise and Industrial Change: A Case Study of the New York Garment Industry.* Ph.D. diss., Harvard University.

Waldinger, R. (1985). Immigrant enterprise and the structure of the labour market. In B. Roberts, R. Finnegann & Duncan Gallie (Eds.), *New Approaches to Economic Life: Economic Restructuring, Unemployment and the Social Division of Labor* (pp. 213-228). Manchester: Manchester University Press.

Waldinger, R. (1989). Structural opportunity or ethnic advantage? Immigrant business development in New York. *International Migration Review*, 23, 1, 48-73

Waldinger, R. (1996). *Still the promised city? African-Americans and new immigrants in postindustrial New York*. Cambridge, Mass.: Harvard University Press.

Waldinger, R. (1997). *Social capital or social closure? Immigrant networks in the labor market.* Research Paper 26. Lewis Center for Regional Policy Studies, UCLA. Retrieved from https://works.bepress.com/roger_waldinger/4/

Waldinger, R. (1999). Network, bureaucracy, and exclusion: Recruitment and selection in an immigrant metropolis. In D. Bean Frank & S. Bell-Rose (Eds.), *Immigration and Opportunity: Race Ethnicity and Employment in the United States* (pp. 228–60). New York: Russell Sage Foundation.

Waldinger, R., H., Aldrich & R., Ward. (1990). Opportunities, group characteristics, and strategies. In R. Waldinger, H. Aldrich and R. Ward (Eds.), *Ethnic Entrepreneurs: Immigrant Business in Industrial Societies* (pp. 13-48). London: Sage Publications.

Wallerstein, I. (1974). *The Modern World System: Capitalist Agriculture and the Origins of the European World Economy in the Sixteenth Century*. New York: Academic Press.

Ward, R., & Jenkins, R. (Eds). (1984). *Ethnic communities in business*. Cambridge: Cambridge University Press.

Waters, Malcolm. (1996). *Globalization*. New York: Routledge .

Werbner, P. (1984). Business on trust: Pakistani entrepreneurship in the Manchester garment trade. In Ward, R. and Jenkins, R. (Eds.) *Ethnic Communities in Business: Strategies for Economic Survival* (pp.166-188). Cambridge: Cambridge University Press.

Werbner, P. (1990). Renewing an industrial past: British Pakistani entrepreneurship in Manchester. *Migration*, 8, 17-41.

Westwood, S. & Bhachu, P. (eds). (1988). *Enterprising Women: Ethnicity, Economy, and Gender Relations*. London: Routledge.

Wilpert, C. (1998). Migration and informal work in the new Berlin: New forms of work or new sources of labor? *Journal of Ethnic and Migration Studies*, 24, 2, 269-294.

Willis, J., Datta, K., Evans, Y., Herbert, J., May, J. and McIlwaine, C. (2009). *Global Cities at Work: New Migrant Divisions of Labour*. London: Pluto Press.

Wilson, K.L., & Portes, A. (1980). Immigrant Enclaves: An Analysis of the Labor Market Experiences of Cubans in Miami. *American Journal of Sociology*, 86, 295-319.

Yeros, P. (1999). Introduction: On the uses and implications of constructivism. In P. Yeros (ed.) *Ethnicity and Nationalism in Africa. Constructivist Reflections and Contemporary Politics* (pp. 1-15). Basingstoke: Macmillan.

Yeung, H. (2002). Entrepreneurship in International Business: An Institutional Perspective. *Asia Pacific Journal of Management*, 19 (1), 29-61.

Yuengert, A. M. (1995). Testing Hypotheses of Immigrant Self-Employment. *Journal of Human Resources*, 30, 194-204.

Zhou, M. (2004). Revisiting Ethnic Entrepreneurship: Convergencies, Controversies, and Conceptual Advancements. *International Migration Review*, 38, 1040-1074.

Index